Table of Contents

Chapter 1: Advanced SDL Programming Concept ...19
  1.1. Deep Dive into SDL Architecture 19
  1.2. Custom SDL Extensions and Modifications ...20
    Custom SDL Extensions ...20
    Modifying SDL's Source Code ...21
    Example: Creating a Custom SDL Rendering Extension ...21
  1.3. Memory Management and Optimization in SDL ...22
    Memory Management ...22
    Resource Caching ...22
    Performance Optimization ...23
    Memory Profiling and Debugging ...23
  1.4. Multi-threading in SDL Games ...24
    The Need for Multi-threading ...24
    SDL's Thread Support ...24
    Thread Safety and Shared Resources ...24
    Practical Use Cases ...25
  1.5. Advanced Event Management Techniques ...26
    Custom Event Types ...26
    Event Filters ...26
    Input Handling Techniques ...27
    Event-driven Design ...27

Chapter 2: 3D Graphics with SDL ...29
  2.1. Integrating SDL with OpenGL ...29
    SDL and OpenGL Setup ...29
    Rendering with OpenGL ...30
  2.2. Building 3D Models and Environments ...31
    Representing 3D Objects ...31
    Modeling Software ...31
    Loading 3D Models ...32
    Building 3D Environments ...32
  2.3. Advanced Lighting and Shading Techniques ...33
    Types of Lighting ...33

    Phong Shading Model 34

    Implementing Phong Shading..34

  2.4. 3D Camera Movements and Controls...36

    Camera Representation 36

    Viewing Matrix...36

    Camera Movement..37

    Camera Projection...38

    Combining Matrices...38

    Implementing Camera Controls 39

    Conclusion 39

  2.5. Performance Optimization in 3D Rendering...40

    Batching and Rendering Efficiency..40

    Level of Detail (LOD)..41

    Culling Techniques...41

    Texture and Shader Optimization 42

    GPU and CPU Profiling...42

    Multithreading...42

    Conclusion 42

Chapter 3: Procedural Content Generation..43

  3.1. Understanding Procedural Generation 43

    What is Procedural Generation?...43

    Advantages of Procedural Generation..43

    Applications of Procedural Generation 43

    Procedural Generation Algorithms...44

    Challenges and Considerations...44

    Conclusion 45

  3.2. Randomized Level Design 45

    Principles of Randomized Level Design..45

    Procedural Level Generation Techniques...45

    Considerations and Challenges...46

    Conclusion 47

  3.3. Dynamic AI and Enemy Generation 47

    Dynamic AI Behavior 47

    Enemy Generation...48

- Challenges and Considerations 49
- Conclusion 50
- 3.4. Creating Procedural Textures and Models 50
  - Procedural Texture Generation 50
  - Procedural 3D Model Generation 51
  - Challenges and Considerations 52
  - Conclusion 52
- 3.5. Balancing Randomness and Playability 52
  - The Role of Randomness 53
  - Considerations for Balancing 54
  - Player Agency and Choice 54
  - Conclusion 54
- Chapter 4: Physics and Realism in Games 56
  - 4.1. Integrating Physics Engines with SDL 56
    - The Role of Physics in Games 56
    - Integrating Physics Engines 57
    - Conclusion 58
  - 4.2. Realistic Motion and Collision Detection 58
    - Realistic Object Motion 58
    - Precise Collision Detection 59
    - Challenges and Optimizations 60
    - Conclusion 60
  - 4.3. Simulating Environmental Effects 61
    - The Importance of Environmental Effects 61
    - Techniques for Simulating Environmental Effects 61
    - Challenges and Performance Considerations 62
    - Conclusion 63
  - 4.4. Implementing Ragdoll Physics 63
    - Understanding Ragdoll Physics 63
    - Implementing Ragdoll Physics 64
    - Challenges and Considerations 65
    - Conclusion 65
  - 4.5. Advanced Particle Systems 65
    - Understanding Particle Systems 66

- Advanced Particle System Techniques 66
- Performance Optimization 67
- Conclusion 68

Chapter 5: Multiplayer Game Development 69

5.1. Designing for Networked Multiplayer 69
- The Appeal of Multiplayer Games 69
- Design Considerations 69
- Best Practices 70
- Development Process 70
- Challenges and Considerations 71
- Conclusion 71

5.2. Server-Client Architecture in SDL 71
- Server-Client Architecture Overview 72
- Key Components of Server-Client Interaction 72
- Implementation Steps 73
- Challenges and Considerations 73
- Conclusion 74

5.3. Handling Network Latency and Prediction 74
- Understanding Network Latency 74
- Predictive Movement 74
- Client-Side Prediction 75
- Lag Compensation 75
- Challenges and Considerations 76
- Conclusion 76

5.4. Synchronizing Game States Across Players 77
- The Importance of Game State Synchronization 77
- Server Authority 77
- Networking Protocol 77
- Interpolation and Smoothing 78
- Snapshot-Based Synchronization 78
- Challenges and Considerations 79
- Conclusion 79

5.5. Security Considerations in Online Games 79
- Authentication and Authorization 79

- Data Encryption 80
- Server-Side Validation 80
- Anti-Cheat Systems 81
- Data Privacy and Compliance 81
- Regular Updates and Patching 81
- Conclusion 81

Chapter 6: Advanced Audio Techniques 82
- Section 6.1: 3D Spatial Audio Implementation 82
- Section 6.2: Dynamic Music and Sound Effects 84
  - Dynamic Music 84
  - Sound Effects 85
  - Conclusion 85
- Section 6.3: Audio Mixing and Processing 86
  - Audio Mixing 86
  - Audio Processing 87
  - Conclusion 87
- Section 6.4: Voice Chat Integration 88
  - Voice Chat Basics 88
  - Voice Chat Communication 88
  - Voice Quality and Optimization 89
  - Conclusion 89
- Section 6.5: Audio Optimization and Compression 90
  - Audio File Formats 90
  - Audio Compression 90
  - Bitrate and Sample Rate 90
  - Streaming vs. Buffering 90
  - Audio Quality Testing 91
  - Conclusion 91

Chapter 7: AI and Machine Learning in Games 92
- Section 7.1: Advanced AI Strategies for NPCs 92
  - Role of AI in Games 92
  - Advanced Pathfinding 92
  - Behavior Trees 92
  - Finite State Machines (FSM) 92

- Machine Learning ... 93
- Conclusion ... 93
- Section 7.2: Implementing Learning Algorithms in Games ... 93
  - Types of Learning Algorithms ... 94
  - Reinforcement Learning in Games ... 94
  - Player Behavior Prediction ... 94
  - Dynamic Game Balancing ... 95
  - Ethical Considerations ... 95
  - Conclusion ... 95
- Section 7.3: Adaptive Game Difficulty ... 95
  - What Is Adaptive Game Difficulty? ... 95
  - Implementing Adaptive Difficulty ... 96
  - Ethical Considerations ... 97
  - Conclusion ... 97
- Section 7.4: Data-Driven Game Design Decisions ... 97
  - The Role of Player Data ... 97
  - Leveraging Player Data ... 97
  - Ethical Considerations ... 99
  - Conclusion ... 99
- Section 7.5: Ethical Considerations in AI ... 99
  - Player Privacy and Data Protection ... 99
  - Fairness and Bias ... 100
  - Transparency and Explainability ... 100
  - Player Consent and Control ... 100
  - AI Behavior in Sensitive Areas ... 100
  - Player Well-being and Mental Health ... 101
  - Continuous Ethical Review ... 101
  - Conclusion ... 101
- Chapter 8: VR and AR Game Development ... 102
  - Section 8.1: Basics of Virtual and Augmented Reality ... 102
    - What is Virtual Reality (VR)? ... 102
    - What is Augmented Reality (AR)? ... 102
    - Considerations for VR and AR Game Development ... 102
    - Conclusion ... 103

Section 8.2: Implementing VR Support in SDL 103
    Choosing a VR SDK 104
    SDL Initialization for VR 104
    Rendering for VR 105
    Input and Interaction 105
    Conclusion 105
Section 8.3: Designing for VR: Best Practices 106
    1. User Comfort and Motion Sickness 106
    2. Frame Rate and Performance 106
    3. VR Input Interaction 106
    4. Comfort Options 106
    5. User Interface (UI) in VR 107
    6. Testing and Feedback 107
    7. Accessibility and Inclusivity 107
    8. Performance Profiling 107
    9. User Education 107
    10. User Safety 107
Section 8.4: AR Gaming Experiences with SDL 108
    1. Marker-Based AR 108
    2. Mobile Integration 108
    3. Interactive Gameplay 108
    4. Environmental Awareness 108
    5. Visual Feedback 109
    6. Multiplayer AR 109
    7. Calibration and Initialization 109
    8. Testing and Optimization 109
    9. Safety and User Awareness 109
Section 8.5: Overcoming Challenges in VR/AR Development 110
    1. Hardware Limitations 110
    2. Motion Sickness 110
    3. User Interface (UI) Design 110
    4. Content Creation 111
    5. User Interaction 111
    6. Content Discovery and Distribution 111

7. Testing and QA 111
8. Privacy and Data Security 111
9. Content Regulations 112

Chapter 9: Custom Tools and Editors 113
   Section 9.1: Building Level Editors with SDL 113
      Why Build a Custom Level Editor? 113
      Building a Basic Level Editor with SDL 113
   Section 9.2: Scripting Engines and Modding Support 115
      The Importance of Scripting Engines 115
      Integrating Scripting Engines with SDL 115
      Benefits of Modding Support 116
   Section 9.3: Custom UI Tools for Game Development 117
      The Importance of Custom UI Tools 117
      Building Custom UI Tools with SDL 117
      Benefits of Custom UI Tools 118
   Section 9.4: Automating Game Asset Creation 119
      The Importance of Automation 119
      Types of Asset Automation 119
      Custom Automation Scripts 120
   Section 9.5: Integrating with External Software Tools 121
      The Value of External Tools Integration 121
      Common Types of External Tools 121
      Integration Techniques 122

Chapter 10: Advanced Shader Programming 124
   Section 10.1: Writing Custom Shaders 124
      Understanding Shaders 124
      Shader Languages 124
      Writing a Basic Shader 124
      Shader Variables and Inputs 125
      Shader Complexity 125
      Shader Debugging 125
   Section 10.2: Shader-Based Visual Effects 125
      Understanding Shader-Based Visual Effects 126
      Implementing Shader-Based Visual Effects 126

Example: Bloom Effect 126
Shader-Based Visual Effects in Game Development 127
Section 10.3: Optimizing Shader Performance 127
Profiling and Identifying Bottlenecks 127
Reduce Shader Instructions 128
Use Shader LOD (Level of Detail) 128
Batch Rendering 128
GPU Culling 129
Minimize Texture Memory Usage 129
Shader Compilation and Caching 129
Section 10.4: Exploring Shader-Based Rendering Techniques 129
Deferred Rendering 130
Screen-Space Reflections (SSR) 130
Ambient Occlusion (AO) 130
Volumetric Lighting 130
Post-Processing Effects 130
Water Rendering 131
Cartoon and Toon Shading 131
Parallax Mapping 131
Shader Effects and Particles 131
Section 10.5: Advanced Lighting Models in Shaders 131
Physically Based Rendering (PBR) 131
Image-Based Lighting (IBL) 132
Subsurface Scattering (SSS) 132
Anisotropic Shading 132
Realistic Shadows 132
Screen-Space Reflections (SSR) Improvements 132
High Dynamic Range (HDR) Rendering 132
Global Illumination (GI) Techniques 133
Material Layering 133
Artistic Stylization 133
Chapter 11: Cross-Platform Development Strategies 134
Section 11.1: Designing Games for Multiple Platforms 134
The Importance of Cross-Platform Development 134

Choosing the Right Game Engine 134
Platform-Specific Considerations 134
Input Handling and Controls.. 135
Testing and Quality Assurance 135
Deployment and Distribution 135
Conclusion.. 135
Section 11.2: Platform-Specific Optimizations 135
Understanding Platform Differences... 136
PC Optimization... 136
Mobile Optimization 136
Console Optimization 137
Conclusion.. 137
Section 11.3: Handling Different Input Methods 138
Input Abstraction Layers.. 138
Control Scheme Customization... 139
Testing and User Feedback.. 140
Section 11.4: Managing Platform-Specific Features 140
Identifying Platform-Specific Features.. 140
Code Abstraction and Conditional Compilation 141
Runtime Feature Detection 141
User Experience Considerations 142
Testing and Quality Assurance 142
Section 11.5: Distribution and Deployment Across Platforms 142
1. Platform-Specific Stores and Markets.. 142
2. Compliance and Guidelines 142
3. Build Configuration 143
4. Testing on Real Devices and Emulators 143
5. Store Assets and Metadata.. 143
6. Monetization Strategies 143
7. Localization.. 143
8. Updates and Maintenance 143
9. Cross-Platform Play and Progression 143
10. Promotion and Marketing 144
11. Monitoring and Analytics.. 144

12. Legal and Business Considerations 144
Chapter 12: Enhancing Gameplay Experience 144
    Section 12.1: Dynamic Storytelling Techniques 144
    Section 12.2: Creating Immersive Game Worlds 146
        Environmental Design 146
        World Building 146
        Interactive Elements 147
        Audio and Music 147
        Exploration and Discovery 147
        Playtesting and Iteration 147
    Section 12.3: Psychology of Game Design 148
        Player Motivation 148
        Reward Systems 148
        Flow State 149
        Cognitive Load 149
        Emotions and Immersion 149
    Section 12.4: Reward Systems and Player Motivation 150
        Types of Rewards 150
        The Psychology of Rewards 150
        Balancing Rewards 151
    Section 12.5: Balancing Gameplay for Varied Player Skills 151
        Player Skill Segmentation 152
        Dynamic Adjustments 152
        Playtesting and Feedback 152
        Metrics and Analytics 153
        Iteration and Updates 153
        Player Choice 153
Chapter 13: Advanced Networking and Social Features 154
    Section 13.1: Implementing Social Media Integration 154
        Why Social Media Integration? 154
        Key Social Media Integration Features 154
        Technical Implementation 155
        Privacy and Permissions 155
        Testing and Optimization 155

Section 13.2: Creating Shared Gaming Experiences 155
    Why Shared Gaming Experiences? 156
    Implementing Shared Gaming Experiences 156
    Technical Considerations 157
    Balancing Shared and Solo Play 157
Section 13.3: Developing Asynchronous Multiplayer Games 157
    Understanding Asynchronous Multiplayer 157
    Benefits of Asynchronous Multiplayer 157
    Creating Asynchronous Multiplayer Experiences 158
    Technical Considerations 158
    Examples of Asynchronous Multiplayer Games 159
Section 13.4: Implementing In-Game Chat and Messaging 159
    The Importance of In-Game Chat and Messaging 159
    Designing the Chat System 159
    Technical Implementation 160
    Embracing Moderation 160
    In-Game Chat as a Social Hub 161
Section 13.5: Building a Game Community Platform 161
    The Significance of Game Communities 161
    Elements of a Successful Game Community Platform 162
    Building and Maintaining a Game Community Platform 162
Chapter 14: Scalable Game Architecture 165
    Section 14.1: Design Patterns for Game Development 165
        1. Singleton Pattern 165
        2. Observer Pattern 165
        3. Factory Method Pattern 166
        4. State Pattern 166
    Section 14.2: Managing Large Codebases 167
        1. Modularization 167
        2. Code Documentation 168
        3. Version Control 168
        4. Code Reviews 168
        5. Automated Testing 168
        6. Continuous Integration 169

Section 14.3: Scalability in Game Design 170
    1. Resolution Independence 170
    2. Performance Optimization 170
    3. Input and Control Options 170
    4. Cross-Platform Compatibility 171
    5. Dynamic Content Loading 171
    6. Network Scalability 171
Section 14.4: Efficient Resource Management 172
    1. Resource Compression 172
    2. Texture Atlases 172
    3. Streaming and Loading Screens 172
    4. Memory Pools 173
    5. Resource Streaming and Unloading 173
    6. Asset Bundles 173
Section 14.5: Preparing for Future Expansion 174
    1. Modular Code Architecture 174
    2. Version Control 174
    3. Extensible Game Engines and Frameworks 175
    4. Regular Updates and Patches 175
    5. Community Engagement 175
    6. Monetization and Sustainability 175
    7. Compatibility and Portability 175
Chapter 15: Monetization and Business Strategies 177
Section 15.1: Monetization Models in Gaming 177
    1. Free-to-Play (F2P) 177
    2. Premium Games 177
    3. Freemium 177
    4. Subscription-Based 178
    5. Advertisements 178
    6. In-App Purchases (IAPs) 178
    7. Crowdfunding 179
    8. Donations 179
    9. Sponsorships and Partnerships 179
    10. Data Monetization 179

Section 15.2: Implementing In-App Purchases 179
   1. Platform-Specific Integration 180
   2. Product Definitions 181
   3. User Interface 181
   4. Handle Purchase Flow 181
   5. Receipt Verification 181
   6. Restore Purchases 182
   7. Testing and Debugging 182
   8. Compliance with Guidelines 182
Section 15.3: Advertising Strategies for Games 182
   1. Types of Ads 182
   2. Ad Mediation 183
   3. Frequency and Placement 183
   4. Targeted Advertising 183
   5. Ad-Free Options 183
   6. A/B Testing 183
   7. Ad Revenue Models 183
   8. Ad Placement Testing 184
   9. Ad Design and Creatives 184
   10. User Consent and Privacy 184
   11. Ad Monetization Strategy 184
   12. Ad Reporting and Analytics 184
Section 15.4: Building and Maintaining a Player Base 184
   1. Player Acquisition 185
   2. Player Engagement 185
   3. Monetization Strategies 185
   4. Player Retention 186
   5. Analyze Player Data 186
   6. Player Feedback 186
   7. Community Management 186
Section 15.5: Analyzing Market Trends and Player Data 187
   1. Data Collection and Storage 187
   2. Data Analysis Tools 187
   3. Player Segmentation 187

- 4. A/B Testing 188
- 5. Predictive Analytics 188
- 6. Privacy and Data Security 188
- 7. Continuous Improvement 189

Chapter 16: Advanced User Interface Design 190
- Section 16.1: Creating Custom UI Components 190
  - Understanding Custom UI Components 190
  - SDL and Custom UI Components 190
  - Creating Custom Buttons 191
- Section 16.2: Dynamic UI Adaptation and Scalability 191
  - Challenges in UI Adaptation 191
  - SDL and Dynamic UI Adaptation 192
  - Responsive UI Design 192
  - Aspect Ratio Preservation 192
  - Testing on Multiple Devices 193
- Section 16.3: Enhancing User Experience with Animations 193
  - Why Use Animations in UI? 193
  - SDL and Animation Basics 194
  - Creating Simple UI Animations 194
  - User-Centric Animations 195
- Section 16.4: Accessibility and Inclusivity in UI Design 195
  - Why Accessibility Matters 195
  - Implementing Accessibility in SDL UI 195
  - SDL and Accessibility 196
- Section 16.5: UI Prototyping and User Testing 197
  - The Significance of UI Prototyping 197
  - Steps in UI Prototyping 197
  - Implementing UI Prototyping in SDL 198
  - User Testing in SDL 199

Chapter 17: Localization and Internationalization 200
- Section 17.1: Preparing Your Game for Global Audiences 200
  - 1. Cultural Sensitivity 200
  - 2. Multilingual Support 200
  - 3. Text Handling 200

    4. Audio Localization 200

    5. Time and Date Formats 200

    6. User Interface (UI) Localization 201

    7. Testing and Feedback...201

    8. Legal and Compliance 201

Section 17.2: Localization Best Practices 201

    1. Contextual Translation 201

    2. Consistency...201

    3. Expandable User Interface (UI) 202

    4. Pluralization and Gender Neutrality..202

    5. Date and Time Formatting 202

    6. Keyboard and Input Method Support 202

    7. Quality Assurance (QA) Testing..202

    8. Updates and Post-Launch Support..202

Section 17.3: Cultural Sensitivity in Game Design...203

    1. Research and Understand Cultures...203

    2. Consult Cultural Experts 203

    3. Avoid Cultural Appropriation 203

    4. Localization with Cultural Context...203

    5. Avoid Religious and Political Controversy..203

    6. Diverse Character Representation 204

    7. Testing and Feedback...204

    8. Inclusivity and Accessibility 204

    9. Post-Launch Responsiveness..204

    10. Promote Positive Cultural Exchange...204

Section 17.4: Managing Multilingual Content..204

    1. Plan for Localization Early 204

    2. Unicode and Character Encoding...205

    3. Separate Text from Code 205

    4. Translation Tools and Services 205

    5. Cultural Sensitivity in Translation..205

    6. Test with Native Speakers..205

    7. Expandable User Interfaces..205

    8. Text Overflow Handling 205

    9. RTL Languages 205
    10. Font Considerations 205
    11. Localized Assets 206
    12. Localized Marketing 206
    13. Update and Maintenance 206
    14. Localization Testing 206
    15. Legal Considerations 206
Section 17.5: Testing for Localization Issues..206
    1. Localization Test Plan 206
    2. Functional Testing 207
    3. Text Verification 207
    4. Language Selection 207
    5. Special Characters and Fonts...207
    6. Text Expansion and Contraction 207
    7. Right-to-Left (RTL) Languages..207
    8. Numerical and Date Formats 207
    9. Voiceovers and Subtitles...207
    10. Cultural Sensitivity 207
    11. Consistency 208
    12. Testing with Native Speakers 208
    13. Compatibility and Platform Testing 208
    14. Bug Tracking and Reporting...208
    15. Regression Testing..208
    16. Post-Launch Monitoring...208
    17. Accessibility Testing 208
Chapter 18: Ethics and Responsibility in Game Development..209
    Section 18.1: Addressing Social Issues through Games 209
Section 18.2: Responsible Representation and Diversity in Games 211
Section 18.3: Gaming Addiction and Player Health 213
Section 18.4: Privacy and Data Protection in Games 215
Section 18.5: Promoting Positive Gaming Communities 217
Chapter 19: Post-Launch Support and Updates 219
    Section 19.1: Managing Game Patches and Updates 219
Section 19.2: Community Management Post-Launch 221

Section 19.3: Gathering and Implementing Player Feedback 223

Section 19.4: Long-Term Game Maintenance Strategies 225

Section 19.5: Planning for Game Sequels and Expansions 228

Chapter 20: The Future of SDL and Game Technology 231

Section 20.1: Emerging Trends in Game Development 231

Section 20.2: SDL's Role in Future Gaming Technologies 233

Section 20.3: Preparing for Next-Generation Game Development 234

Section 20.4: SDL Contributions and Open Source Development 236

Section 20.5: Vision for the Future of SDL Gaming 238

Chapter 1: Advanced SDL Programming Concepts

1.1. Deep Dive into SDL Architecture

In this section, we will take a deep dive into the architecture of SDL (Simple DirectMedia Layer) to understand how it functions and how it can be leveraged for advanced game development. SDL is a cross-platform multimedia library that provides a set of low-level APIs for tasks such as window management, audio, input handling, and graphics rendering.

SDL's architecture is designed to be efficient and versatile, making it a popular choice among game developers. It provides a unified interface for interacting with different hardware and operating systems, allowing you to write code that can run on various platforms without major modifications.

SDL primarily consists of the following key components:

1. **Windowing System Abstraction:** SDL provides an abstraction layer for managing windows and graphics contexts. This allows you to create and manage windows and render graphics without dealing with platform-specific details. Here's a basic example of creating an SDL window:

   ```
   SDL_Window* window = SDL_CreateWindow("My Game", SDL_WINDOWPOS_CENTERED
   , SDL_WINDOWPOS_CENTERED, 800, 600, SDL_WINDOW_OPENGL);
   ```

   This code creates an SDL window with the title "My Game" and dimensions 800x600 pixels.

2. **Event Handling:** SDL handles events such as keyboard input, mouse input, and window events. You can use SDL's event system to listen for and respond to various user interactions. For example, to handle a key press event:

   ```
   SDL_Event event;
   while (SDL_PollEvent(&event)) {
       if (event.type == SDL_KEYDOWN) {
           // Handle key press
       }
   }
   ```

3. **Graphics Rendering:** SDL allows you to draw 2D graphics directly onto the screen using its rendering API. You can choose between software rendering or hardware-accelerated rendering with OpenGL. Here's how you can render a simple rectangle:

   ```
   SDL_Renderer* renderer = SDL_CreateRenderer(window, -1, SDL_RENDERER_AC
   CELERATED);
   SDL_SetRenderDrawColor(renderer, 255, 0, 0, 255); // Set color to red
   SDL_Rect rect = { 100, 100, 200, 200 };
   SDL_RenderFillRect(renderer, &rect); // Render a red rectangle
   SDL_RenderPresent(renderer); // Update the screen
   ```

4. **Audio and Sound:** SDL provides functions for playing audio and sound effects. You can load and play audio files in various formats and control audio playback.
5. **Timers and Time Management:** SDL offers timer functionality for controlling game loops and managing time-related tasks. You can use SDL's timer functions to control the frame rate of your game.
6. **Multi-Thread Support:** SDL supports multi-threading, allowing you to run tasks in parallel for improved performance. This is especially useful for handling complex game logic, AI, or physics calculations.

SDL's architecture is designed to provide a solid foundation for building advanced games, and understanding how these components work together is crucial for mastering SDL game development. In the following sections, we will delve into specific topics and techniques that will help you harness the full potential of SDL for creating captivating games.

1.2. Custom SDL Extensions and Modifications

In this section, we will explore the possibilities of extending and modifying SDL (Simple DirectMedia Layer) to tailor it to your specific game development needs. While SDL provides a comprehensive set of features, there may be situations where you require custom functionality or optimizations to meet your game's requirements.

Custom SDL Extensions

One powerful aspect of SDL is its ability to be extended through custom libraries and extensions. This allows you to add functionality that SDL might not provide out of the box. To create custom SDL extensions, you typically follow these steps:

1. **Define Your Extension's Interface:** Decide what functionality your extension will provide. This could include additional rendering techniques, input handling, or audio processing.
2. **Write the Extension:** Develop the code for your extension as a separate library or module. Ensure that it follows the appropriate conventions for your chosen programming language.
3. **Integrate the Extension with SDL:** To use your custom extension, you need to integrate it with SDL. This often involves linking your extension's library with your SDL project and initializing it alongside SDL.
4. **Utilize the Extension:** Once integrated, you can utilize the extension's features within your game. This might involve invoking custom functions or setting up callbacks.

Custom SDL extensions can be especially useful when you have specialized requirements that SDL alone cannot fulfill. For example, you might create a custom rendering extension to implement a unique graphical effect for your game.

Modifying SDL's Source Code

In some cases, you may need to make modifications directly to SDL's source code to address specific issues or add custom functionality. Here are some common scenarios where modifying SDL's source code may be necessary:

1. **Bug Fixes:** If you encounter bugs or issues in SDL that affect your game, you may need to dive into the source code to identify and fix the problem.
2. **Performance Optimization:** SDL is designed to be efficient, but you might need to optimize certain aspects for your game's performance. Modifying the source code can help you fine-tune SDL to your requirements.
3. **Custom Features:** If your game relies on unique features that SDL does not support by default, you can add these features by extending SDL's codebase.

When modifying SDL's source code, it's essential to maintain proper coding practices and adhere to SDL's licensing terms if you plan to distribute your modified version. You should also consider the potential challenges of maintaining your custom SDL build across different platforms and SDL updates.

Example: Creating a Custom SDL Rendering Extension

Let's illustrate the process of creating a custom SDL extension with a simple example of adding a custom rendering effect. Suppose you want to implement a shader-based rendering effect that creates a grayscale version of your game's graphics.

1. **Define the Interface:** Decide how your extension will allow users to enable and configure the grayscale effect.
2. **Write the Extension:** Develop the code for the grayscale rendering extension, including shader code and rendering logic.
3. **Integrate the Extension:** Link your extension's library with your SDL project and initialize it alongside SDL.
4. **Utilize the Extension:** Provide a mechanism in your game to enable the grayscale effect when desired. This might involve adding a menu option or using a specific key combination.

Custom extensions can greatly enhance your game development capabilities by enabling you to tailor SDL to your specific needs. However, it's essential to carefully plan and document your custom extensions to ensure they integrate smoothly with SDL and your game's codebase.

1.3. Memory Management and Optimization in SDL

Efficient memory management and optimization are crucial aspects of SDL (Simple DirectMedia Layer) game development. In this section, we will explore techniques and best practices to ensure that your SDL-based games run smoothly and utilize system resources effectively.

Memory Management

Memory management is vital for preventing memory leaks and optimizing your game's performance. SDL provides functions for managing memory efficiently:

1. **Resource Loading:** Load and manage game assets, such as images, sounds, and fonts, carefully. SDL provides functions like `SDL_LoadBMP` for loading images and `Mix_LoadWAV` for loading audio files. Remember to free resources using functions like `SDL_FreeSurface` or `Mix_FreeChunk` when they are no longer needed to prevent memory leaks.

2. **Texture Management:** In SDL, textures are often used for rendering. Efficiently manage texture memory by creating and destroying textures as needed. Use `SDL_DestroyTexture` to release textures when they are no longer in use.

3. **Dynamic Memory Allocation:** When allocating memory dynamically using functions like `malloc` or `calloc`, remember to free the allocated memory with `free` when it's no longer required. SDL uses dynamic memory allocation in various internal structures, so proper memory management is essential.

Resource Caching

Resource caching is a technique that involves storing frequently used resources in memory to reduce loading times and improve performance. SDL games can benefit from resource caching in the following ways:

1. **Texture Caching:** Load textures once and store them in memory as needed. This prevents redundant loading and frees up resources for other tasks. You can implement a texture cache using data structures like hash maps or arrays.

2. **Sound Caching:** Cache sound effects and music files in memory to avoid repeated disk access. SDL's audio functions, like `Mix_PlayChannel`, can be used in conjunction with a sound cache to efficiently manage sound resources.

Performance Optimization

Optimizing your SDL game's performance is essential to ensure smooth gameplay, especially for resource-intensive 2D or 3D games. Here are some performance optimization strategies:

1. **Minimize Render Calls:** Reduce the number of rendering calls by batching objects together when rendering. Avoid rendering the same object multiple times if it doesn't change.

2. **Use Hardware Acceleration:** SDL allows you to take advantage of hardware acceleration for graphics rendering through libraries like OpenGL. Utilize hardware acceleration for smoother graphics and better performance.

3. **Implement Level of Detail (LOD):** In 3D games, implement LOD techniques to render higher-detail models when close to the camera and lower-detail models when far away. This reduces rendering complexity and boosts performance.

4. **Efficient Collision Detection:** Optimize collision detection algorithms to avoid unnecessary calculations. Use spatial partitioning techniques like quad-trees or oct-trees for 2D games or bounding volume hierarchies for 3D games.

5. **Threading and Parallelism:** Use multithreading to distribute CPU-intensive tasks across multiple cores. For example, you can run physics simulations and AI calculations in separate threads to improve overall performance.

Memory Profiling and Debugging

To identify memory leaks and performance bottlenecks in your SDL game, consider using memory profiling and debugging tools. SDL-based games can benefit from tools like Valgrind for memory analysis and profiling, as well as integrated development environments (IDEs) with debugging features.

Remember that optimizing your SDL game should be an iterative process. Continuously profile and test your game to identify areas for improvement. Optimization efforts may involve adjusting code, optimizing algorithms, or even considering platform-specific optimizations for different target platforms.

Efficient memory management and optimization are critical for delivering a high-quality gaming experience to players. By implementing these practices and continuously monitoring your game's performance, you can create SDL games that run smoothly and efficiently on a wide range of devices.

1.4. Multi-threading in SDL Games

Multi-threading is a powerful technique in game development, allowing you to perform multiple tasks concurrently, which can significantly improve the performance and responsiveness of your SDL (Simple DirectMedia Layer) games. In this section, we will explore how to effectively utilize multi-threading in SDL game development.

The Need for Multi-threading

SDL games often involve complex tasks such as rendering, physics simulations, AI calculations, and handling user input. Performing all these tasks sequentially in a single thread can lead to poor performance and unresponsive gameplay, especially in resource-intensive games.

Multi-threading allows you to distribute these tasks across multiple threads, taking full advantage of modern multi-core processors. This not only improves performance but also ensures that your game remains responsive to user input, even when other computationally intensive tasks are running.

SDL's Thread Support

SDL provides a simple and platform-independent way to work with threads. It includes functions for creating and managing threads:

- SDL_CreateThread: This function allows you to create a new thread and specify the function it should execute. For example:

  ```
  SDL_Thread* thread = SDL_CreateThread(MyThreadFunction, "ThreadName", data);
  ```

  Here, MyThreadFunction is the function that the new thread will execute.

- SDL_WaitThread: You can use this function to wait for a thread to finish its execution. This is helpful for synchronization:

  ```
  int threadReturnValue;
  SDL_WaitThread(thread, &threadReturnValue);
  ```

- SDL_DetachThread: If you don't need to wait for a thread to finish, you can detach it using this function:

  ```
  SDL_DetachThread(thread);
  ```

Thread Safety and Shared Resources

One important consideration when working with multi-threading in SDL games is ensuring thread safety. SDL functions and data structures are not inherently thread-safe, so you must take precautions when accessing shared resources from multiple threads.

- **Mutexes:** SDL provides mutexes (short for mutual exclusion) to protect critical sections of code. You can use SDL_CreateMutex to create a mutex, SDL_LockMutex to lock it before accessing shared data, and SDL_UnlockMutex to release it when you're done.

- **Semaphores:** SDL also offers semaphores, which can be used for more advanced synchronization between threads. Use SDL_CreateSemaphore to create a semaphore, SDL_SemWait to wait for it, and SDL_SemPost to signal it.

- **Atomic Operations:** For simple operations on shared variables that don't require locks, SDL provides atomic operations like `SDL_AtomicIncRef` and `SDL_AtomicDecRef`.

Practical Use Cases

Multi-threading can be applied to various aspects of SDL game development:

1. **Parallel Rendering:** Split the rendering workload across multiple threads, allowing for faster frame rendering. Each thread can render a portion of the screen or specific game objects.
2. **Physics Simulations:** Implement physics simulations in separate threads to ensure smooth and responsive gameplay. Physics calculations can be computationally intensive and benefit from parallelization.
3. **AI and Pathfinding:** If your game involves complex AI behavior or pathfinding algorithms, multi-threading can be used to calculate AI decisions concurrently, improving responsiveness.
4. **Asset Loading:** Load game assets such as textures and models in the background threads to reduce loading times and provide a smoother gaming experience.
5. **Network Communication:** If your game includes multiplayer features, handling network communication in a separate thread can prevent blocking the main game loop.

While multi-threading can bring significant benefits to SDL game development, it also introduces complexities related to synchronization and potential race conditions. Careful design and testing are essential to ensure that your multi-threaded game is stable and free from synchronization issues.

In conclusion, multi-threading is a valuable technique for optimizing SDL games, enhancing performance, and providing a responsive gaming experience. When used judiciously and with proper synchronization mechanisms, multi-threading can be a powerful tool in your SDL game development toolkit.

1.5. Advanced Event Management Techniques

Event management is a fundamental aspect of game development in SDL (Simple DirectMedia Layer). While SDL provides basic event handling mechanisms, advanced event management techniques can greatly enhance the interactivity and responsiveness of your games. In this section, we will explore some advanced event management techniques and best practices.

Custom Event Types

SDL allows you to create custom event types to extend its event handling capabilities. Custom events are useful when you need to communicate specific game-related events or messages between different parts of your game or even between threads.

To create a custom event type, you can use the `SDL_RegisterEvents` function to reserve a range of custom event IDs. Once reserved, you can use these IDs to send and receive custom events. Here's an example of creating and using a custom SDL event:

```
// Reserve custom event IDs
const int CUSTOM_EVENT_TYPE = SDL_RegisterEvents(1);

// Create a custom event
SDL_Event customEvent;
customEvent.type = CUSTOM_EVENT_TYPE;
customEvent.user.data1 = 42; // Custom data

// Push the custom event to the event queue
SDL_PushEvent(&customEvent);
```

By creating custom events, you can implement event-driven architecture in your game, enabling different game components to communicate and respond to specific events efficiently.

Event Filters

SDL allows you to set event filters that can intercept and modify events before they are delivered to the main event queue or any other event processing functions. Event filters are especially useful when you want to implement custom event processing logic.

You can set an event filter using the `SDL_SetEventFilter` function, and it should be a callback function that follows the signature:

```
int EventFilterCallback(void* userdata, SDL_Event* event);
```

Your event filter callback can inspect, modify, or even discard events based on your custom logic. For example, you can use event filters to implement custom input handling, filter out specific events, or preprocess events before they reach your main event loop.

Input Handling Techniques

Advanced input handling is crucial for creating responsive and user-friendly games. SDL provides various techniques to enhance input management:

- **Input States:** Track the state of input devices (such as keyboard, mouse, or gamepad) by maintaining their states in each frame. By comparing the current and previous states, you can detect input changes and respond accordingly.

- **Input Queues:** Implement input queues to capture and process input events in a controlled manner. This can help you manage complex input sequences and prioritize certain input types over others.

- **Gesture Recognition:** For touch-based interfaces, consider implementing gesture recognition to detect swipe, pinch, and other touch gestures, providing intuitive user interactions.

- **Input Abstraction:** Create an input abstraction layer that maps platform-specific input events to game-specific actions. This abstraction allows you to handle input consistently across different platforms.

Event-driven Design

Adopting an event-driven design pattern is a powerful technique in SDL game development. In an event-driven architecture, game components respond to events, and the main game loop primarily handles event dispatching and updating game state based on those events.

This design pattern promotes modularity and allows you to decouple game logic, making it easier to manage and maintain. It also enables the creation of reusable and extendable game components.

Here's a simplified example of an event-driven design in SDL:

```
while (gameIsRunning) {
    SDL_Event event;
    while (SDL_PollEvent(&event)) {
        // Dispatch events to relevant game components
        if (event.type == SDL_KEYDOWN) {
            HandleKeyPress(event.key);
        } else if (event.type == SDL_MOUSEBUTTONDOWN) {
            HandleMouseClick(event.button);
        } else if (event.type == CUSTOM_EVENT_TYPE) {
            HandleCustomEvent(event.user);
        }
    }

    // Update game state based on events
    UpdateGame();

    // Render the updated game state
    RenderGame();
}
```

By adopting an event-driven approach, you can create more modular and flexible game systems, making it easier to extend and maintain your SDL games as they grow in complexity.

In conclusion, advanced event management techniques play a vital role in SDL game development by enhancing interactivity, responsiveness, and modularity. Whether you're creating custom event types, implementing event filters, optimizing input handling, or adopting an event-driven design pattern, mastering these techniques can lead to more engaging and feature-rich games.

Chapter 2: 3D Graphics with SDL

2.1. Integrating SDL with OpenGL

Integrating SDL with OpenGL is a powerful combination for creating 3D graphics in your games. SDL provides a cross-platform framework for window management, input handling, and more, while OpenGL is a standard graphics API for rendering 3D graphics. In this section, we will explore how to integrate SDL with OpenGL to leverage the full potential of 3D graphics in your SDL games.

SDL and OpenGL Setup

Before you can integrate SDL with OpenGL, you need to set up your development environment and configure SDL to work with OpenGL. Here are the steps to get started:

1. **Initialize SDL:** Begin by initializing SDL as you would in any SDL project. This includes setting up SDL subsystems, creating a window, and initializing the SDL renderer.

    ```
    SDL_Init(SDL_INIT_VIDEO);
    SDL_Window* window = SDL_CreateWindow("OpenGL SDL Example", SDL_WINDOWPOS_CENTERED, SDL_WINDOWPOS_CENTERED, 800, 600, SDL_WINDOW_OPENGL);
    SDL_GLContext context = SDL_GL_CreateContext(window);
    ```

2. **Initialize GLEW (OpenGL Extension Wrangler Library):** GLEW is a library that simplifies the process of handling OpenGL extensions. You'll need to initialize GLEW after creating the OpenGL context:

    ```
    glewInit();
    ```

    Ensure you have GLEW properly linked in your project.

3. **Set OpenGL Attributes:** You can use SDL functions to specify OpenGL attributes, such as the version of OpenGL you want to use and double buffering. For example:

    ```
    SDL_GL_SetAttribute(SDL_GL_CONTEXT_MAJOR_VERSION, 3);
    SDL_GL_SetAttribute(SDL_GL_CONTEXT_MINOR_VERSION, 3);
    SDL_GL_SetAttribute(SDL_GL_DOUBLEBUFFER, 1);
    ```

4. **OpenGL Rendering Loop:** Finally, you can set up an OpenGL rendering loop to draw your 3D graphics. This loop typically involves clearing the buffer, rendering 3D objects, swapping the buffer, and handling user input.

    ```
    while (gameIsRunning) {
        // Handle user input
        // Perform 3D rendering
        // Swap buffers
    }
    ```

Rendering with OpenGL

Once you have set up SDL and OpenGL, you can start rendering 3D graphics. OpenGL is a low-level graphics API that provides functions for rendering points, lines, and triangles in 3D space. Here are some key concepts and steps for rendering with OpenGL:

- **Vertex Buffer Objects (VBOs):** VBOs are used to store vertex data such as positions, normals, and texture coordinates. You can create VBOs to efficiently manage and access vertex data.

- **Vertex Array Objects (VAOs):** VAOs are used to store the state of vertex attribute pointers and the VBO bindings. They allow you to switch between different sets of vertex attributes and VBOs.

- **Shaders:** Shaders are small programs written in GLSL (OpenGL Shading Language) that run on the GPU. You can create vertex and fragment shaders to control how your 3D objects are rendered.

- **Uniforms:** Uniforms are variables in shaders that allow you to pass data from the CPU to the GPU. You can use uniforms to set transformation matrices, lighting information, and other parameters.

- **Rendering Primitives:** OpenGL provides functions to render different types of primitives, such as `glDrawArrays` for rendering arrays of vertices and `glDrawElements` for rendering indexed vertices.

- **Projection and View Matrices:** You'll typically use projection and view matrices to define the perspective and position of the camera in 3D space. These matrices transform the 3D world coordinates into 2D screen coordinates.

- **Textures:** You can load textures and bind them to OpenGL texture units to apply them to 3D objects.

Here's a simplified example of rendering a colored triangle in OpenGL:

```
// Define vertex data (positions and colors)
GLfloat vertices[] = {
    -0.5f, -0.5f, 1.0f, 0.0f, 0.0f, // Vertex 1: Position (-0.5, -0.5) and Color (Red)
    0.5f, -0.5f, 0.0f, 1.0f, 0.0f, // Vertex 2: Position (0.5, -0.5) and Color (Green)
    0.0f, 0.5f, 0.0f, 0.0f, 1.0f  // Vertex 3: Position (0.0, 0.5) and Color (Blue)
};

// Create and bind VBO and VAO
GLuint VBO, VAO;
glGenVertexArrays(1, &VAO);
glGenBuffers(1, &VBO);
glBindVertexArray(VAO);
```

```
glBindBuffer(GL_ARRAY_BUFFER, VBO);
glBufferData(GL_ARRAY_BUFFER, sizeof(vertices), vertices, GL_STATIC_DRAW);

// Specify vertex attributes
glVertexAttribPointer(0, 2, GL_FLOAT, GL_FALSE, 5 * sizeof(GLfloat), (GLvoid*
)0);
glEnableVertexAttribArray(0);
glVertexAttribPointer(1, 3, GL_FLOAT,
```

2.2. Building 3D Models and Environments

In 3D game development with SDL and OpenGL, creating 3D models and environments is a fundamental aspect of bringing your game world to life. This section will guide you through the process of building 3D models and environments, from basic geometry to complex scenes.

Representing 3D Objects

In OpenGL, 3D objects are represented using vertices, which are points in 3D space. These vertices are connected to form geometric shapes like triangles, which are the building blocks of 3D models. Here are key concepts for representing 3D objects:

- **Vertices:** Each vertex contains positional information (x, y, z), color, texture coordinates, and other attributes.

- **Triangles:** Triangles are formed by connecting three vertices. They are the simplest polygon in 3D graphics.

- **Vertices, Normals, and Indices:** To efficiently represent 3D models, you often use vertex arrays to store vertices and their attributes, normal vectors for lighting calculations, and index arrays to define the order in which vertices are connected to form triangles.

- **Meshes:** A mesh is a collection of vertices, normals, and indices that define a 3D object's geometry. Meshes can be simple, like a cube or sphere, or complex, representing characters, buildings, or terrain.

Modeling Software

To create 3D models and environments, you need modeling software. There are various options available, ranging from free and open-source tools like Blender to commercial software like Autodesk Maya and 3ds Max. These tools provide a user-friendly interface for modeling, texturing, and animating 3D objects.

When creating 3D models, consider the following:

- **Mesh Topology:** Proper mesh topology ensures that the model deforms and animates smoothly. It's crucial for characters and organic shapes.

- **UV Mapping:** UV mapping involves unwrapping the 3D model's surface onto a 2D plane, allowing you to apply textures accurately.

- **Texture Creation:** Use image editing software like Adobe Photoshop or GIMP to create textures and maps for your models. Textures can add detail and realism to your 3D objects.

- **Rigging and Animation:** For characters and creatures, rigging involves creating a skeleton (armature) and defining how the model's vertices move with the bones. Animation involves creating keyframes to control movement.

Loading 3D Models

Once you have created 3D models, you need to load them into your SDL and OpenGL project. Models are often stored in common formats like OBJ, FBX, or COLLADA (DAE). To load 3D models, you can use libraries like Assimp (Open Asset Import Library), which supports various 3D model formats.

Here's a simplified example of loading a 3D model using Assimp:

```
#include <assimp/Importer.hpp>
#include <assimp/scene.h>
#include <assimp/postprocess.h>

Assimp::Importer importer;
const aiScene* scene = importer.ReadFile("model.obj", aiProcess_Triangulate | aiProcess_FlipUVs);

if (!scene || scene->mFlags & AI_SCENE_FLAGS_INCOMPLETE || !scene->mRootNode)
{
    // Handle model loading error
} else {
    // Process the loaded model
    // Extract vertices, normals, textures, and indices from the aiScene
}
```

Building 3D Environments

In addition to individual 3D models, you'll need to create 3D environments or scenes for your game. Environments can be as simple as a room or as complex as an open world. Here are some considerations:

- **Level Design:** Plan the layout and design of your 3D environments. Consider gameplay mechanics, player navigation, and aesthetics.

- **Terrain Generation:** If your game includes outdoor environments, you may need terrain generation techniques to create realistic landscapes.

- **Lighting and Shading:** Implement lighting models and shading techniques to make your 3D environments visually appealing. Use techniques like ambient, diffuse, and specular lighting.

- **Optimization:** Optimize your 3D environments for performance. Techniques like level-of-detail (LOD) and occlusion culling can help improve rendering efficiency.

- **Collision Detection:** Implement collision detection to ensure that game objects interact with the environment correctly. Consider techniques like bounding volumes and raycasting.

- **Texturing:** Apply textures to surfaces in your 3D environments to add detail and realism. Use UV mapping coordinates to map textures accurately.

Creating 3D models and environments can be a complex and time-consuming process, but it's essential for delivering immersive and visually stunning 3D games. Whether you're creating characters, props, or entire game worlds, mastering 3D modeling and environment design is a valuable skill in SDL and OpenGL game development.

2.3. Advanced Lighting and Shading Techniques

Lighting and shading are critical aspects of 3D graphics that significantly impact the visual quality and realism of your SDL (Simple DirectMedia Layer) games. In this section, we will delve into advanced lighting and shading techniques that you can apply to enhance the visual appeal of your 3D environments and models.

Types of Lighting

Lighting in 3D graphics typically falls into several categories:

1. **Ambient Lighting:** Ambient lighting represents the uniform illumination that is present everywhere in the scene, regardless of the light sources. It ensures that objects are not completely dark in shadowed areas.

2. **Diffuse Lighting:** Diffuse lighting models how light interacts with rough or matte surfaces. It creates the effect of light being scattered in all directions, making objects visible from different angles.

3. **Specular Lighting:** Specular lighting simulates the reflection of light off shiny or glossy surfaces. It produces highlights or specular highlights that give objects a polished appearance.

4. **Emissive Lighting:** Emissive lighting allows objects to emit light, making them appear self-illuminated. This is often used for objects like light bulbs, computer screens, or magical effects.

Phong Shading Model

The Phong shading model is a widely used technique for simulating specular highlights in 3D graphics. It combines ambient, diffuse, and specular lighting components to calculate the final color of a pixel. The model is defined by the following components:

- **Ambient Reflectance (Ka):** The ambient component represents the constant illumination present everywhere in the scene and is usually a small value representing the material's ability to reflect ambient light.
- **Diffuse Reflectance (Kd):** The diffuse component accounts for the scattered light on the surface and is influenced by the angle between the surface normal and the light direction.
- **Specular Reflectance (Ks):** The specular component models the reflective highlights on glossy surfaces. It is controlled by the shininess or specular exponent (α), which determines the size and intensity of highlights.
- **Light Position (L) and Eye Position (V):** The positions of the light source and the viewer are used to calculate the direction of the light and the viewer's direction.
- **Surface Normal (N):** The surface normal at a pixel's location determines how the light interacts with the surface. It is essential for both diffuse and specular lighting calculations.

The Phong shading model is expressed as:

$$I = Ia * Ka + Id * Kd * (N \cdot L) + Is * Ks * (R \cdot V) \wedge \alpha$$

Where:

- I is the final pixel color.
- Ia is the ambient light color.
- Ka is the ambient reflectance.
- Id is the diffuse light color.
- Kd is the diffuse reflectance.
- N is the surface normal.
- L is the direction from the pixel to the light source.
- Is is the specular light color.
- Ks is the specular reflectance.
- R is the reflected light direction (reflection of L about N).
- V is the viewer direction.
- α is the shininess or specular exponent.

Implementing Phong Shading

To implement the Phong shading model in your SDL and OpenGL application, you need to perform the following steps:

1. **Calculate Surface Normal:** Compute the surface normal for each vertex or pixel. This requires knowing the geometry of your 3D models.
2. **Lighting Calculations:** For each pixel, calculate the ambient, diffuse, and specular lighting components using the Phong equation.
3. **Texture Mapping:** Apply texture maps to your 3D models to add additional detail and realism to the surfaces. Texture mapping involves mapping 2D texture coordinates to 3D models.
4. **Specular Highlights:** Implement specular highlights by computing the reflection vector R and using it in the specular lighting calculation.
5. **Multiple Light Sources:** Extend your shader to support multiple light sources by summing the contributions from each light source.
6. **Shader Programs:** Use OpenGL shader programs (vertex and fragment shaders) to perform the lighting calculations for each pixel.
7. **Material Properties:** Define material properties such as ambient, diffuse, and specular reflectance values for your 3D models.
8. **Uniforms and Buffers:** Pass relevant data (light positions, camera position, material properties, etc.) to your shader programs using uniforms and buffer objects.

Here's a simplified example of a fragment shader in OpenGL that implements the Phong shading model:

```
#version 330 core

in vec3 FragPos;        // Fragment position in world space
in vec3 Normal;         // Normal vector
in vec2 TexCoords;      // Texture coordinates

out vec4 FragColor;     // Final pixel color

uniform vec3 lightPos;    // Light position
uniform vec3 viewPos;     // Camera position
uniform vec3 lightColor;  // Light color

uniform vec3 ambientColor;  // Ambient color
uniform vec3 diffuseColor;  // Diffuse color
uniform vec3 specularColor; // Specular color
uniform float shininess;    // Shininess (specular exponent)

void main() {
    // Calculate lighting
    vec3 ambient = ambientColor * lightColor;
```

```
    vec3 norm = normalize(Normal);
    vec3 lightDir = normalize(lightPos - FragPos);
    float diff = max(dot(norm, lightDir), 0.0);
    vec3 diffuse = diffuseColor * lightColor * diff;

    vec3 viewDir = normalize(viewPos - FragPos);
    vec3 reflectDir = reflect(-lightDir, norm);
    float spec = pow(max(dot(viewDir, reflectDir), 0.0), shininess);
    vec3 specular = specularColor * lightColor * spec;

    // Final color
    vec3 result = (ambient + diffuse + specular);
    FragColor = vec4(result, 1.0);
}
```

This shader calculates ambient, diffuse, and specular lighting for each pixel and combines them to determine the final color.

Implementing advanced lighting and shading techniques like Phong shading can significantly improve the visual quality and realism of your 3D SDL games. By understanding the principles of lighting and shader programming, you can create visually stunning and immersive 3D environments and models.

2.4. 3D Camera Movements and Controls

In 3D game development with SDL and OpenGL, controlling the camera's position and orientation is essential for providing players with immersive experiences. This section explores techniques for implementing 3D camera movements and controls in your games.

Camera Representation

In a 3D environment, the camera is typically represented as an entity with a position and orientation. The position represents the camera's location in the world, while the orientation defines the camera's view direction and rotation. In OpenGL, the camera's position and orientation are usually represented by a view matrix.

Viewing Matrix

The viewing matrix (or view matrix) is used to transform world coordinates into view space, where the camera is at the origin and looks down the negative Z-axis. It is created by combining translation and rotation transformations.

Here's how you can create a view matrix in OpenGL:

```
glm::mat4 viewMatrix = glm::lookAt(cameraPosition, cameraTarget, cameraUp);
```

- cameraPosition: The position of the camera.
- cameraTarget: The point the camera is looking at.
- cameraUp: The up vector of the camera (typically [0, 1, 0]).

Camera Movement

Implementing camera movement involves updating the camera's position and orientation in response to user input. Common camera movements include:

- **Translation:** Moving the camera forward, backward, left, right, up, and down.
- **Rotation:** Changing the camera's pitch, yaw, and roll.

Translation

To move the camera, you can adjust its position in the world space. This is often done using the WASD keys for movement and the mouse for looking around.

```
// Translate the camera forward
cameraPosition += cameraFront * cameraSpeed * deltaTime;

// Translate the camera backward
cameraPosition -= cameraFront * cameraSpeed * deltaTime;

// Translate the camera left
cameraPosition -= glm::normalize(glm::cross(cameraFront, cameraUp)) * cameraSpeed * deltaTime;

// Translate the camera right
cameraPosition += glm::normalize(glm::cross(cameraFront, cameraUp)) * cameraSpeed * deltaTime;

// Translate the camera up
cameraPosition += cameraUp * cameraSpeed * deltaTime;

// Translate the camera down
cameraPosition -= cameraUp * cameraSpeed * deltaTime;
```

- cameraFront: The direction the camera is facing.
- cameraUp: The camera's up vector.
- cameraSpeed: The movement speed.
- deltaTime: The time elapsed since the last frame.

Rotation

Rotating the camera involves changing its orientation. You can achieve this by modifying the pitch and yaw angles of the camera.

```
// Adjust the camera's pitch
pitch += mouseSensitivity * yoffset;
```

```
// Adjust the camera's yaw
yaw += mouseSensitivity * xoffset;

// Ensure yaw stays within [-180, 180] degrees
if (yaw > 180.0f) {
    yaw -= 360.0f;
} else if (yaw < -180.0f) {
    yaw += 360.0f;
}

// Calculate the new camera front direction
glm::vec3 front;
front.x = cos(glm::radians(yaw)) * cos(glm::radians(pitch));
front.y = sin(glm::radians(pitch));
front.z = sin(glm::radians(yaw)) * cos(glm::radians(pitch));
cameraFront = glm::normalize(front);
```

- pitch and yaw: The pitch and yaw angles of the camera.
- mouseSensitivity: The sensitivity of the mouse movement.

Camera Projection

In addition to the view matrix, the camera also requires a projection matrix to define the perspective or orthographic projection of the 3D scene onto the 2D screen. There are two common types of projections:

- **Perspective Projection:** Provides a realistic sense of depth with objects appearing smaller as they move away from the camera. It is defined by a field of view (FOV), aspect ratio, near clipping plane, and far clipping plane.
- **Orthographic Projection:** Preserves the size of objects regardless of their depth. It is often used in 2D games or architectural visualization. It is defined by the dimensions of the viewing volume.

Here's how you can create a perspective projection matrix in OpenGL:

```
glm::mat4 projectionMatrix = glm::perspective(glm::radians(fov), aspectRatio, nearClip, farClip);
```

- fov: The field of view angle.
- aspectRatio: The aspect ratio of the screen (width / height).
- nearClip and farClip: The distances to the near and far clipping planes.

Combining Matrices

To render objects in your 3D world correctly, you'll need to combine the view matrix and the projection matrix into a single matrix called the view-projection matrix (VP matrix). You can do this as follows:

```
glm::mat4 viewProjectionMatrix = projectionMatrix * viewMatrix;
```

The VP matrix transforms object coordinates from world space to clip space, where clipping and perspective correction are applied.

Implementing Camera Controls

Implementing camera controls in SDL involves capturing user input events, such as keyboard input for movement and mouse input for rotation. You'll need to handle events like key presses, key releases, mouse movements, and mouse clicks.

Here's a simplified example of capturing keyboard input for camera movement in SDL:

```
SDL_Event event;
while (SDL_PollEvent(&event)) {
    switch (event.type) {
        case SDL_KEYDOWN:
            if (event.key.keysym.sym == SDLK_w) {
                // Move camera forward
            } else if (event.key.keysym.sym == SDLK_s) {
                // Move camera backward
            } else if (event.key.keysym.sym == SDLK_a) {
                // Move camera left
            } else if (event.key.keysym.sym == SDLK_d) {
                // Move camera right
            }
            break;
        // Handle key release events similarly for stopping movement
        // Handle mouse input for camera rotation
        // Handle other input events as needed
    }
}
```

In this example, keyboard input events are used to control camera movement, and mouse input events can be used for camera rotation.

Conclusion

Implementing 3D camera movements and controls is crucial for creating immersive and interactive 3D experiences in SDL and OpenGL games. By managing the camera's position, orientation, and projection, you can provide players with the ability to explore and navigate your 3D worlds effectively. Additionally, responsive camera controls contribute to a more enjoyable gaming experience and can enhance gameplay in various genres, including first-person shooters, exploration games, and simulations.

2.5. Performance Optimization in 3D Rendering

Optimizing the performance of your 3D rendering is crucial for ensuring that your SDL (Simple DirectMedia Layer) and OpenGL games run smoothly and efficiently. In this section, we will explore various performance optimization techniques to achieve high frame rates and responsive gameplay in your 3D applications.

Batching and Rendering Efficiency

Batching refers to the process of grouping similar objects or geometry together to minimize the number of draw calls sent to the GPU. Reducing draw calls is essential for optimizing rendering performance, as each draw call incurs CPU overhead.

Vertex Buffer Objects (VBOs) and Vertex Array Objects (VAOs)

One way to batch geometry is by using VBOs and VAOs to store vertex data efficiently. VBOs allow you to upload vertex data to the GPU in a single buffer, reducing the need to transfer data between the CPU and GPU frequently. VAOs can help organize vertex attributes, reducing the setup time for rendering.

```
// Create and bind a VAO
GLuint VAO;
glGenVertexArrays(1, &VAO);
glBindVertexArray(VAO);

// Create and bind a VBO
GLuint VBO;
glGenBuffers(1, &VBO);
glBindBuffer(GL_ARRAY_BUFFER, VBO);

// Upload vertex data to the VBO
glBufferData(GL_ARRAY_BUFFER, sizeof(vertices), vertices, GL_STATIC_DRAW);

// Specify vertex attribute pointers
glVertexAttribPointer(0, 3, GL_FLOAT, GL_FALSE, 3 * sizeof(GLfloat), (void*)0);
glEnableVertexAttribArray(0);
```

Index Buffer Objects (IBOs)

For models with repeated vertices, you can use Index Buffer Objects (IBOs) to reduce memory consumption and improve rendering efficiency. IBOs store indices that reference the vertices, allowing you to reuse vertices for multiple triangles.

```
// Create and bind an IBO
GLuint IBO;
glGenBuffers(1, &IBO);
glBindBuffer(GL_ELEMENT_ARRAY_BUFFER, IBO);

// Upload index data to the IBO
```

```
glBufferData(GL_ELEMENT_ARRAY_BUFFER, sizeof(indices), indices, GL_STATIC_DRAW);
```

Instancing

Instancing is a technique that allows you to render multiple instances of the same object with a single draw call. It is useful for rendering many identical or similar objects, such as trees in a forest or rocks in a landscape.

```
// Set up instance data (e.g., positions and rotations)
// ...

// Enable instancing in the shader
glVertexAttribDivisor(attributeLocation, 1);
```

Level of Detail (LOD)

Level of Detail (LOD) techniques involve using simplified versions of 3D models for objects that are farther away from the camera. This reduces the number of vertices and triangles rendered, improving performance. LOD can be applied to terrain, characters, and other objects.

Culling Techniques

Culling is the process of removing objects or portions of objects that are not visible to the camera. There are several culling techniques you can implement:

Frustum Culling

Frustum culling involves checking if objects are within the camera's viewing frustum before rendering them. Objects outside the frustum are culled and not rendered.

```
// Calculate the MVP matrix
glm::mat4 MVP = projectionMatrix * viewMatrix * modelMatrix;

// Perform frustum culling
if (isInsideFrustum(MVP, objectBounds)) {
    // Render the object
}
```

Occlusion Culling

Occlusion culling involves determining if one object is completely hidden by another object in the scene. This can be achieved using occlusion queries or visibility tests.

Backface Culling

Backface culling involves skipping the rendering of faces that are not visible from the camera's viewpoint. This is often enabled by default in OpenGL.

Texture and Shader Optimization

Texture and shader optimization can have a significant impact on rendering performance. Here are some tips:

Texture Atlas

Texture atlases involve packing multiple textures into a single larger texture. This reduces the number of texture binds and improves rendering efficiency.

Mipmapping

Mipmapping generates a series of scaled-down versions of a texture to improve texture quality and reduce aliasing artifacts. Using mipmaps can also improve texture fetch performance.

Shader Compilation and Linking

Compile shaders offline and avoid recompiling them at runtime whenever possible. Use shader programs efficiently by reusing them for objects with similar rendering properties.

GPU and CPU Profiling

Profiling your game's performance is essential for identifying bottlenecks and areas that require optimization. Use profiling tools to monitor GPU and CPU usage, frame times, and memory usage.

```
// Example of CPU profiling using SDL's high-resolution timer
Uint64 startTime = SDL_GetPerformanceCounter();
// Render frame
Uint64 endTime = SDL_GetPerformanceCounter();
double frameTime = (endTime - startTime) / (double)SDL_GetPerformanceFrequency();
```

Multithreading

Multithreading can improve rendering performance by offloading CPU tasks to multiple threads. For example, you can have one thread for physics calculations, one for AI, and one for rendering.

```
// Example of multithreading using SDL's threading API
SDL_Thread* renderThread = SDL_CreateThread(RenderThreadFunction, "RenderThread", NULL);
```

Conclusion

Optimizing 3D rendering performance in SDL and

Chapter 3: Procedural Content Generation

3.1. Understanding Procedural Generation

Procedural content generation (PCG) is a powerful technique in game development that involves creating game content algorithmically rather than manually designing it. This section explores the fundamental concepts of procedural generation, its applications, and its advantages.

What is Procedural Generation?

Procedural generation is the process of using algorithms and randomization to create content dynamically at runtime. This content can include various game elements, such as:

- **Levels and Environments:** Generating terrain, mazes, dungeons, and landscapes.
- **Objects and Props:** Creating trees, rocks, buildings, and items.
- **Textures and Materials:** Generating textures, patterns, and materials.
- **Quests and Narratives:** Designing quests, stories, and dialogue.
- **Sound and Music:** Composing music and generating sound effects.
- **Characters and NPCs:** Creating non-playable characters with unique characteristics.

Advantages of Procedural Generation

Procedural generation offers several advantages in game development:

1. **Infinite Variety:** PCG can create an almost infinite variety of content, ensuring that players never experience the same game twice.
2. **Efficiency:** It can significantly reduce development time and resources, as designers don't need to create every asset manually.
3. **Scalability:** Procedural content can adapt to different game scales, from small indie games to massive open worlds.
4. **Randomness:** Randomized content can add unpredictability and replayability to games, keeping players engaged.
5. **Consistency:** PCG can ensure consistent quality and style across generated content.
6. **Memory Efficiency:** Procedurally generated content can be generated on-the-fly, reducing memory requirements.

Applications of Procedural Generation

Procedural generation is used in various game genres and aspects:

- **Roguelike Games:** PCG generates dungeons, maps, and items in games like "Rogue" and "The Binding of Isaac."
- **Open World Games:** Procedural techniques create expansive landscapes in games like "Minecraft" and "No Man's Sky."
- **Level Design:** It generates levels in platformers, shooters, and racing games.
- **Terrain Generation:** PCG creates realistic terrains for simulations and strategy games.
- **Narrative Generation:** Algorithms generate branching storylines and dialogue in interactive fiction.
- **Character Generation:** PCG can create unique characters, enemies, and NPCs with distinct traits.

Procedural Generation Algorithms

Procedural content generation relies on various algorithms and techniques:

- **Randomization:** Using random numbers to create variability in content generation.
- **Noise Functions:** Perlin noise and simplex noise generate coherent and natural-looking patterns.
- **L-Systems:** Lindenmayer systems are used for generating complex shapes and fractals.
- **Cellular Automata:** Cellular automata create patterns through local interactions.
- **Grammar-Based Methods:** Using context-free grammars for text and level generation.
- **Markov Chains:** Modeling state transitions for dynamic content.

Challenges and Considerations

While procedural generation offers numerous benefits, it also presents challenges:

- **Balancing:** Ensuring that generated content is fair and enjoyable for players.
- **Tuning:** Fine-tuning algorithms to produce desired outcomes.
- **Visual Consistency:** Maintaining visual and thematic consistency in generated assets.
- **Performance:** Ensuring that content generation doesn't impact game performance.
- **User Experience:** Ensuring that generated content aligns with the player's experience and preferences.

Conclusion

Procedural generation is a versatile tool in game development, offering efficiency, scalability, and the potential for infinite variety. Understanding the principles and techniques of procedural content generation allows game developers to harness its power and create engaging, dynamic, and unique gaming experiences. In the following sections of this chapter, we will delve deeper into specific aspects of procedural generation, from level design to AI behavior and beyond.

3.2. Randomized Level Design

Randomized level design is a common application of procedural generation in game development. It involves creating game levels, maps, or environments algorithmically, resulting in diverse and unpredictable gameplay experiences. This section explores the principles, techniques, and considerations for implementing randomized level design in your SDL (Simple DirectMedia Layer) and OpenGL games.

Principles of Randomized Level Design

Randomized level design is guided by several key principles:

1. **Reproducibility:** While levels are generated randomly, they should be reproducible so that players can share their experiences or replay specific levels.
2. **Variability:** The generated levels should exhibit a wide range of layouts, structures, and challenges to keep the gameplay engaging and fresh.
3. **Balancing:** Achieving a balance between difficulty, player progression, and enjoyment is crucial. Randomness should not result in overly challenging or unfair levels.
4. **Consistency:** The generated levels should adhere to the game's visual style, theme, and mechanics. Maintaining consistency is essential for a cohesive player experience.

Procedural Level Generation Techniques

Several procedural generation techniques can be employed for randomized level design:

Cellular Automata

Cellular automata are grid-based algorithms that generate patterns through local interactions. They are commonly used for terrain and map generation. For example, Conway's Game of Life is a cellular automaton that can create maze-like structures.

```
// Pseudocode for cellular automata-based level generation
Initialize grid with random values
```

```
Repeat for a number of iterations:
    For each cell in the grid:
        Count neighboring cells that are alive
        If the count meets certain rules, mark the cell as alive
```

Perlin Noise

Perlin noise is a gradient noise function that creates coherent and natural-looking patterns. It is used for generating terrain, landscapes, and heightmaps. By adjusting parameters like frequency and amplitude, you can control the characteristics of the generated terrain.

```
// Pseudocode for generating Perlin noise-based terrain
For each point in a grid:
    Calculate Perlin noise value at that point
    Map the noise value to a height range
    Create terrain geometry based on the height values
```

Random Walks

Random walks involve starting at a point and repeatedly taking random steps in various directions. This technique can be used for generating cave systems, pathways, or mazes.

```
// Pseudocode for random walk-based maze generation
Start at a random point in the grid
Repeat until a desired length is reached:
    Take a random step in one of the four directions
    Carve a path in that direction
```

Grammar-Based Methods

Grammar-based methods, such as L-systems (Lindenmayer systems), use rewriting rules to generate complex shapes and structures. They are suitable for generating vegetation, plants, or intricate architectural details.

```
// Pseudocode for L-system-based plant generation
Initialize with an axiom
For a specified number of iterations:
    Apply production rules to generate a new string
    Translate the string into 3D geometry
```

Considerations and Challenges

Implementing randomized level design comes with various considerations and challenges:

- **Seed Generation:** You need to generate a seed value for the random number generator to ensure reproducibility of levels.
- **Player Progression:** Levels should be designed to align with the player's skill progression, offering appropriate challenges.
- **Testing and Balancing:** Extensive playtesting and fine-tuning are necessary to ensure that randomly generated levels provide a satisfying player experience.

- **Visual Consistency:** Generated levels should maintain consistency in terms of visual style, theme, and art assets.
- **Performance:** Procedural generation algorithms should be optimized to generate levels efficiently without causing performance bottlenecks.

Conclusion

Randomized level design is a powerful tool for enhancing the replayability and variety of your SDL and OpenGL games. By understanding the principles and techniques of procedural generation, you can create dynamic and unpredictable game worlds that captivate players and keep them engaged over multiple playthroughs. Careful design, balancing, and testing are essential to ensure that randomized levels contribute positively to the overall gaming experience.

3.3. Dynamic AI and Enemy Generation

Dynamic AI and enemy generation is a key aspect of procedural content generation in games. It involves creating intelligent and adaptable non-player characters (NPCs) and enemies using algorithms and decision-making processes. In this section, we will explore the concepts and techniques behind dynamic AI and enemy generation for your SDL (Simple DirectMedia Layer) and OpenGL games.

Dynamic AI Behavior

Dynamic AI behavior refers to the ability of NPCs and enemies to adapt, make decisions, and respond to changing game conditions. The goal is to create AI entities that mimic human-like intelligence, enhancing gameplay and immersion.

Finite State Machines (FSMs)

Finite State Machines are a common approach to modeling AI behavior. An AI character can exist in different states, and transitions between states occur based on predefined conditions or events. For example, an enemy AI may have states like "Idle," "Chase," and "Attack."

```
// Pseudocode for a simple FSM-based AI
enum State { Idle, Chase, Attack };
State currentState = Idle;

while (gameIsRunning) {
    switch (currentState) {
        case Idle:
            // Check conditions to transition to Chase state
            if (playerIsNearby()) {
                currentState = Chase;
```

```
            }
            break;
        case Chase:
            // Move towards the player
            // Check conditions to transition to Attack state
            if (playerIsWithinAttackRange()) {
                currentState = Attack;
            }
            break;
        case Attack:
            // Perform attack actions
            // Check conditions to transition back to Chase or Idle state
            if (!playerIsWithinAttackRange()) {
                currentState = Chase;
            }
            break;
    }
}
```

Behavior Trees

Behavior Trees are hierarchical structures used for defining complex AI behaviors. They consist of nodes representing actions, conditions, and sequences. Behavior Trees offer greater flexibility in AI design, allowing for more sophisticated decision-making.

```
// Pseudocode for a simple Behavior Tree-based AI
BehaviorTree tree = new BehaviorTree(
    new Sequence(
        new CheckPlayerProximity(),
        new Selector(
            new Sequence(
                new MoveTowardsPlayer(),
                new AttackPlayer()
            ),
            new WanderAround()
        )
    )
);

while (gameIsRunning) {
    tree.Execute();
}
```

Enemy Generation

Dynamic enemy generation involves creating a variety of enemy types with different attributes, abilities, and behaviors. Procedural generation techniques can be applied to generate enemy appearances, stats, and roles.

Attributes and Stats

Procedural generation can determine an enemy's attributes, such as health, damage, speed, and resistances. By defining rules and constraints, you can generate a wide range of enemy variations.

```
// Pseudocode for generating enemy attributes
EnemyAttributes GenerateEnemyAttributes() {
    EnemyAttributes attributes;
    attributes.health = RandomInRange(minHealth, maxHealth);
    attributes.damage = RandomInRange(minDamage, maxDamage);
    attributes.speed = RandomInRange(minSpeed, maxSpeed);
    return attributes;
}
```

Roles and Abilities

Enemies can have different roles and abilities that influence their behavior in combat. Procedural generation can assign roles and abilities to enemies based on their attributes and the game's difficulty level.

```
// Pseudocode for assigning roles and abilities to enemies
void AssignEnemyRoleAndAbilities(Enemy enemy, GameDifficulty difficulty) {
    switch (difficulty) {
        case Easy:
            enemy.role = RandomFrom(EasyRoles);
            enemy.abilities = RandomSubset(EasyAbilities);
            break;
        case Normal:
            enemy.role = RandomFrom(NormalRoles);
            enemy.abilities = RandomSubset(NormalAbilities);
            break;
        case Hard:
            enemy.role = RandomFrom(HardRoles);
            enemy.abilities = RandomSubset(HardAbilities);
            break;
    }
}
```

Challenges and Considerations

Implementing dynamic AI and enemy generation comes with challenges and considerations:

- **Balancing:** Careful balancing is needed to ensure that dynamically generated enemies provide a challenging but fair gameplay experience.

- **Player Interaction:** The generated AI behavior should respond effectively to player actions, making encounters engaging.

- **Variability:** Procedurally generated enemies should exhibit enough variability to keep the gameplay interesting and avoid predictability.
- **Testing and Feedback:** Extensive playtesting and player feedback are essential to fine-tune AI behaviors and enemy attributes.
- **Performance:** Efficient algorithms are required for generating AI behaviors and enemy attributes without causing performance issues.

Conclusion

Dynamic AI and enemy generation enhance gameplay by introducing intelligent and adaptable opponents that respond to changing conditions. Implementing dynamic AI behavior with Finite State Machines or Behavior Trees allows for complex decision-making processes. Additionally, procedural generation techniques can be applied to create a diverse range of enemies with varying attributes and roles, providing players with unique challenges and experiences in your SDL and OpenGL games. Careful design, balancing, and testing are crucial to ensuring that dynamically generated AI enriches the overall gaming experience.

3.4. Creating Procedural Textures and Models

Procedural content generation extends beyond level design and AI behavior; it also encompasses the creation of textures and 3D models. This section explores the techniques and methods for procedurally generating textures and models in your SDL (Simple DirectMedia Layer) and OpenGL games.

Procedural Texture Generation

Procedural texture generation involves creating textures algorithmically rather than using pre-made image files. This approach offers several advantages, including smaller file sizes, unlimited variations, and the ability to adapt to different resolutions.

Perlin Noise for Textures

Perlin noise, known for its versatility in procedural generation, is commonly used to create natural-looking textures, such as terrain, clouds, and marble. By manipulating Perlin noise parameters, you can achieve a wide range of texture patterns.

```
// Pseudocode for generating Perlin noise-based texture
for each pixel in the texture:
    noiseValue = PerlinNoise(pixel.x, pixel.y)
    pixelColor = ColorFromNoiseValue(noiseValue)
    setPixelColor(texture, pixel, pixelColor)
```

Fractal Patterns

Fractal algorithms, such as the Diamond-Square algorithm, are used for generating repetitive and intricate textures. These patterns can be employed for creating surfaces like rocky terrain or abstract art.

```
// Pseudocode for Diamond-Square algorithm-based texture
for each iteration:
    diamondStep()
    squareStep()
apply smoothness and color variation
```

Voronoi Diagrams

Voronoi diagrams can be used to generate textures with cell-like patterns. They are useful for creating organic or irregular textures, such as skin or rock surfaces.

```
// Pseudocode for generating Voronoi diagram-based texture
for each pixel in the texture:
    nearestSite = findNearestVoronoiSite(pixel)
    pixelColor = ColorFromSite(nearestSite)
    setPixelColor(texture, pixel, pixelColor)
```

Procedural 3D Model Generation

Procedural 3D model generation involves creating 3D geometry algorithmically. This approach is beneficial for generating complex structures, objects, and assets in games.

L-Systems for Plants

Lindenmayer systems (L-systems) are widely used for generating plant structures, including trees, bushes, and vines. L-systems define rules for branching, twisting, and growing plant parts.

```
// Pseudocode for generating a plant using L-systems
Initialize with an axiom
For a specified number of iterations:
    Apply production rules to generate a new string
    Translate the string into 3D geometry (branches and leaves)
```

Marching Cubes for Terrain

The Marching Cubes algorithm is employed to create 3D terrain models from volumetric data. It converts density values into polygonal meshes, making it suitable for generating realistic terrain.

```
// Pseudocode for generating terrain using Marching Cubes
for each voxel in the volumetric data:
    determine voxel density
    create mesh vertices and triangles based on density
    add vertices and triangles to the terrain mesh
```

Shape Grammar for Architectural Elements

Shape grammar is a rule-based approach used to generate architectural elements, such as buildings, structures, and interiors. It defines grammatical rules for generating 3D shapes and layouts.

```
// Pseudocode for generating architectural elements using shape grammar
Initialize with a base shape
Apply shape grammar rules iteratively
Transform and combine shapes based on rules
```

Challenges and Considerations

Procedural texture and 3D model generation offer many benefits, but they come with challenges:

- **Artistic Control:** Maintaining artistic control over procedurally generated assets can be challenging, as the results may not always match the desired aesthetics.
- **Performance:** Generating complex textures and 3D models in real-time requires efficient algorithms to avoid performance bottlenecks.
- **Integration:** Procedurally generated assets must seamlessly integrate with the rest of the game's visuals and design.
- **Variety:** While procedural generation can create diverse assets, ensuring that they don't become repetitive is crucial for player engagement.
- **Testing and Debugging:** Debugging procedurally generated assets can be more complex than debugging handcrafted assets.

Conclusion

Procedural texture and 3D model generation expand the possibilities of content creation in game development. By leveraging algorithms like Perlin noise, fractals, Voronoi diagrams, L-systems, and shape grammars, you can generate a wide range of textures and 3D models that enhance the visual richness of your SDL and OpenGL games. While there are challenges, such as maintaining artistic control and optimizing performance, procedural generation offers the advantage of flexibility and adaptability, allowing you to create unique and captivating game environments and assets.

3.5. Balancing Randomness and Playability

Balancing randomness and playability is a critical aspect of procedural content generation in game development. While randomness can create diversity and unpredictability in game experiences, it must be carefully balanced to ensure that the game remains enjoyable and fair. This section explores the techniques and considerations for achieving the right balance in your SDL (Simple DirectMedia Layer) and OpenGL games.

The Role of Randomness

Randomness plays a significant role in procedural content generation by introducing variability and replayability into games. It can be applied to various aspects, including level design, enemy placement, loot distribution, and more. However, excessive randomness can lead to frustrating or unenjoyable gameplay experiences.

Level Generation

Randomized level generation can create diverse landscapes, dungeons, or mazes in games. The challenge lies in ensuring that randomly generated levels offer a balanced progression of difficulty, clear objectives, and a coherent player experience.

```
// Pseudocode for balancing randomness in level generation
while generatingLevel {
    addRandomRoom()
    if (shouldAddChallenge) {
        addRandomEnemy()
    }
    if (shouldAddLoot) {
        addRandomTreasure()
    }
    // Ensure that the generated level remains solvable and enjoyable
    if (isLevelBalanced()) {
        break;
    }
}
```

Enemy Behavior

Randomized AI behavior can make encounters with enemies more unpredictable and engaging. However, it is crucial to balance enemy actions to prevent unfair or frustrating encounters.

```
// Pseudocode for balancing randomness in enemy behavior
while inCombat {
    if (shouldAttack) {
        performRandomAttack()
    }
    if (shouldDodge) {
        dodgeRandomly()
    }
    // Ensure that enemy actions remain challenging but fair
    if (isCombatBalanced()) {
        break;
    }
}
```

Considerations for Balancing

Achieving the right balance between randomness and playability requires careful consideration and testing:

- **Player Feedback:** Gathering feedback from playtesters is essential to identify areas where randomness may be causing frustration or enjoyment.
- **Difficulty Scaling:** Adjusting the level of randomness based on the player's skill level or progress can help maintain a balanced experience.
- **Seed Generation:** Using a random seed or allowing players to input a seed can enable reproducibility while still incorporating randomness.
- **Iterative Design:** Iteratively refining procedural generation algorithms and adjusting parameters can lead to a better balance over time.
- **Adaptive Systems:** Implementing adaptive systems that adjust randomness based on player performance or feedback can enhance playability.

Player Agency and Choice

Balancing randomness also involves providing players with agency and meaningful choices. While randomness can add excitement, players should have the ability to make decisions that influence the outcome.

For example, in a procedurally generated roguelike game, players may choose which path to take or which items to pick up, affecting their chances of success. Balancing randomness with player agency can create a satisfying blend of strategy and unpredictability.

```
// Pseudocode for balancing player agency and randomness
while exploringDungeon {
    presentRandomChoices()
    playerChoice = getPlayerChoice()
    if (playerChoice == "TakeLeftPath") {
        generateLeftPath()
    } else if (playerChoice == "TakeRightPath") {
        generateRightPath()
    }
    // Ensure that player choices have meaningful consequences
    if (isChoiceBalanced()) {
        break;
    }
}
```

Conclusion

Balancing randomness and playability is a delicate task in procedural content generation. Randomness adds variety and excitement to games, but excessive randomness can lead to frustration. By carefully considering player feedback, difficulty scaling, seed generation, and player agency, game developers can strike the right balance between unpredictability and enjoyable gameplay experiences. Achieving this balance is essential for creating engaging and memorable SDL and OpenGL games that captivate players and keep them coming back for more.

Chapter 4: Physics and Realism in Games

4.1. Integrating Physics Engines with SDL

Integrating physics engines into your SDL (Simple DirectMedia Layer) and OpenGL games can significantly enhance realism and interactivity. Physics engines simulate the physical behavior of objects, allowing for realistic movement, collisions, and environmental effects. In this section, we will explore the integration of physics engines, such as Box2D and Bullet, into your game projects.

The Role of Physics in Games

Physics engines enable the simulation of real-world physics principles in a virtual game world. They play a crucial role in various aspects of gameplay and game design:

Realistic Movement

Physics engines can simulate the motion of objects, including characters, vehicles, projectiles, and more. This adds a layer of realism to the game world and enhances the player's immersion.

```
// Pseudocode for simulating object movement with physics
while (gameIsRunning) {
    physicsEngine.update(timeStep);
    updateGameObjects();
    renderGameScene();
}
```

Collision Detection and Response

Physics engines handle collision detection and response, ensuring that objects interact with each other realistically. This includes resolving collisions, calculating contact points, and applying appropriate forces.

```
// Pseudocode for handling collisions with physics
if (collisionDetected(object1, object2)) {
    resolveCollision(object1, object2);
    applyForces(object1, object2);
}
```

Environmental Effects

Physics engines can model environmental effects like gravity, wind, friction, and buoyancy. These effects contribute to the realism of the game world and impact gameplay mechanics.

```
// Pseudocode for applying gravity to objects
for each object in gameObjects {
    applyGravity(object, gravityForce);
}
```

Integrating Physics Engines

To integrate a physics engine into your SDL and OpenGL game, follow these general steps:

Choose a Physics Engine

Select a physics engine that suits your game's requirements and supports your development platform. Popular choices include Box2D, Bullet, and NVIDIA PhysX.

Set Up the Physics World

Initialize the physics engine and create a physics world to contain all physical objects. Define parameters such as gravity, time step, and collision settings.

```
// Pseudocode for setting up a physics world with Box2D
b2World* world = new b2World(b2Vec2(0.0f, -9.81f)); // Gravity is -9.81 m/s²
in the downward direction
```

Create Physical Objects

Define game objects as physical bodies in the physics world. Specify their properties, such as shape, mass, friction, and restitution.

```
// Pseudocode for creating a dynamic box object with Box2D
b2BodyDef bodyDef;
bodyDef.type = b2_dynamicBody;
bodyDef.position.Set(x, y);

b2PolygonShape shape;
shape.SetAsBox(width / 2, height / 2);

b2Body* body = world->CreateBody(&bodyDef);
b2FixtureDef fixtureDef;
fixtureDef.shape = &shape;
fixtureDef.density = density;
fixtureDef.friction = friction;
fixtureDef.restitution = restitution;
body->CreateFixture(&fixtureDef);
```

Simulate Physics

In the game loop, update the physics world by advancing the simulation time step. This ensures that physical objects move and interact realistically.

```
// Pseudocode for simulating physics in the game loop
while (gameIsRunning) {
    world->Step(timeStep, velocityIterations, positionIterations);
    updateGameObjects();
    renderGameScene();
}
```

Handle Collision Events

Implement collision event handlers to respond to collisions between objects. This is where you can define custom game logic based on physics interactions.

```
// Pseudocode for handling collision events with Box2D
void MyContactListener::BeginContact(b2Contact* contact) {
    // Handle collision events, e.g., scoring, damage, or sound effects
}
```

Conclusion

Integrating physics engines into your SDL and OpenGL games can elevate the gaming experience by introducing realism and interactivity. Whether you need to simulate object movement, handle collision detection, or model environmental effects, physics engines like Box2D and Bullet provide powerful tools to achieve these goals. By following the steps outlined above and fine-tuning parameters, you can create games that not only look great but also feel physically authentic, immersing players in your virtual worlds.

4.2. Realistic Motion and Collision Detection

Realistic motion and collision detection are fundamental aspects of game physics that contribute to the immersive experience of your SDL (Simple DirectMedia Layer) and OpenGL games. In this section, we will delve into techniques and strategies for achieving lifelike object motion and precise collision detection.

Realistic Object Motion

Realistic object motion involves simulating how objects move and interact with the game world. To achieve this, you can use techniques such as physics-based simulations, interpolation, and kinematic equations.

Physics-Based Simulations

Physics engines, as discussed in the previous section, are a powerful tool for simulating object motion. They handle complex physics interactions, including forces, gravity, friction, and collisions, to calculate realistic object movement.

```
// Pseudocode for simulating physics-based object motion
while (gameIsRunning) {
    physicsEngine.update(timeStep);
    updateGameObjects();
    renderGameScene();
}
```

Interpolation

Interpolation is a technique used to smooth object motion between discrete time steps, resulting in more fluid animations. It calculates intermediate positions and orientations based on the object's velocity.

```
// Pseudocode for interpolating object motion
float interpolationFactor = currentTime / previousTime;
Vector2 interpolatedPosition = previousPosition + (currentPosition - previousPosition) * interpolationFactor;
```

Kinematic Equations

For simple object motion, kinematic equations can be used to calculate position, velocity, and acceleration over time. These equations are particularly useful for objects with constant acceleration, such as projectiles.

```
// Pseudocode for using kinematic equations for object motion
float initialPosition = 0.0;
float initialVelocity = 10.0;
float acceleration = -9.81; // Gravity
float time = 2.0;
float finalPosition = initialPosition + initialVelocity * time + 0.5 * acceleration * time * time;
```

Precise Collision Detection

Accurate collision detection is crucial for ensuring that objects interact realistically in your game world. Various collision detection techniques can be employed to achieve precision.

Bounding Boxes

Bounding boxes are simple and efficient collision detection shapes that enclose objects. They are often used for initial broad-phase collision detection before more precise checks.

```
// Pseudocode for bounding box collision detection
if (boxA.intersects(boxB)) {
    // Perform more detailed collision checks
}
```

Polygonal Colliders

Polygonal colliders define object shapes with multiple vertices, enabling precise collision detection for irregularly shaped objects. They can be used for complex objects like characters and terrain.

```
// Pseudocode for polygonal collider collision detection
if (polygonA.intersects(polygonB)) {
    // Handle collision response
}
```

Raycasting

Raycasting involves projecting a ray from an object and checking for intersections with other objects. It is commonly used for detecting line-of-sight, ray-based weapons, and other directed interactions.

```
// Pseudocode for raycasting collision detection
Ray ray = createRay(origin, direction);
GameObject hitObject = castRay(ray);
if (hitObject != null) {
    // Handle ray-object intersection
}
```

Continuous Collision Detection (CCD)

CCD is essential for high-speed objects to prevent objects from passing through each other due to the discrete nature of game simulations. It ensures that collisions are detected even between time steps.

```
// Pseudocode for continuous collision detection
if (CCD.detectCollision(objectA, objectB)) {
    // Handle continuous collision response
}
```

Challenges and Optimizations

Implementing realistic motion and precise collision detection can be challenging, especially in complex game scenes. Here are some considerations and optimizations:

- **Performance:** Real-time collision detection can be computationally expensive, so optimizing algorithms and using efficient data structures is crucial.
- **Complex Shapes:** Handling objects with complex shapes may require specialized collision detection techniques and libraries.
- **Tight Integration:** Ensure that the physics and collision systems are tightly integrated with the game engine to minimize discrepancies and glitches.
- **Character Controllers:** For characters, implementing responsive and realistic controllers is vital for smooth motion and interactions.
- **Debugging Tools:** Implement debugging tools and visualization to identify and resolve collision-related issues during development.

Conclusion

Achieving realistic object motion and precise collision detection is essential for creating immersive and engaging SDL and OpenGL games. By leveraging physics-based simulations, interpolation, kinematic equations, and various collision detection techniques, you can bring lifelike movements and interactions to your game world. While challenges and optimizations are part of the process, the end result is a more convincing and enjoyable player experience that captures the essence of physical realism in the virtual realm.

4.3. Simulating Environmental Effects

Simulating environmental effects in your SDL (Simple DirectMedia Layer) and OpenGL games adds depth and realism to the gaming experience. These effects can include phenomena like wind, rain, fire, water, and other environmental factors. In this section, we will explore techniques for simulating these effects and integrating them seamlessly into your games.

The Importance of Environmental Effects

Environmental effects play a crucial role in immersing players in the game world and enhancing the overall atmosphere. They can impact gameplay mechanics, storytelling, and aesthetics. Here are some reasons why environmental effects are essential:

Aesthetic Enhancement

Effects like falling leaves, rippling water, and dynamic lighting can significantly improve the visual appeal of your game, making it more captivating for players.

Gameplay Influence

Certain environmental effects, such as strong winds or rain, can affect player movement, projectile trajectory, and other gameplay elements, adding complexity and challenge.

Storytelling and Atmosphere

Environmental effects can contribute to the narrative and atmosphere of the game. For example, a thunderstorm can create a sense of urgency or danger in a game's storyline.

Techniques for Simulating Environmental Effects

Simulating environmental effects in games often involves a combination of artistic design and technical implementation. Here are some common techniques:

Particle Systems

Particle systems are versatile tools for simulating various environmental effects, such as raindrops, snowflakes, sparks, and fire. By controlling particle behavior, you can achieve realistic effects.

```
// Pseudocode for rain particle system
for each raindrop in particleSystem {
    updateRaindropPosition(raindrop);
```

```
    renderRaindrop(raindrop);
}
```

Shaders

Shaders can manipulate the appearance of objects and scenes by modifying lighting, colors, and textures. They are useful for creating effects like water ripples, heat distortion, and dynamic lighting.

```
// Pseudocode for a water ripple shader
uniform float time;
uniform sampler2D normalMap;

vec2 uv = gl_TexCoord[0].xy;
uv += normalize(texture2D(normalMap, uv).xy) * sin(time);
gl_FragColor = texture2D(texture, uv);
```

Physics Simulations

To simulate effects like fluid dynamics or fire propagation, physics simulations can be employed. These simulations model the behavior of particles, fluids, or other entities in response to environmental forces.

```
// Pseudocode for simulating fluid dynamics
while (simulationIsRunning) {
    updateFluidVelocityField();
    advectDensity();
    applyForces();
    renderFluid();
}
```

Sound Design

Environmental effects are not limited to visuals; audio plays a crucial role as well. Sound design can add depth to effects like thunderstorms, flowing water, and crackling fire.

```
// Pseudocode for thunderstorm sound
if (isThunderstormActive) {
    playThunderSound();
    playRainSound();
}
```

Challenges and Performance Considerations

Implementing environmental effects can present challenges, including performance considerations:

- **Realism vs. Performance:** Achieving high levels of realism may be computationally intensive. Optimizing algorithms and using LOD (Level of Detail) techniques can help balance realism with performance.

- **Integration:** Ensuring that environmental effects seamlessly integrate with the game world and physics system is essential for a convincing player experience.

- **Artistic Direction:** Deciding on the visual and auditory style of environmental effects that best suits your game's atmosphere and storytelling can be a creative challenge.

- **Cross-Platform Compatibility:** Environmental effects should be designed to work well on various hardware configurations and platforms.

Conclusion

Simulating environmental effects in SDL and OpenGL games adds depth and immersion, enriching the player's experience. By employing techniques like particle systems, shaders, physics simulations, and sound design, you can create dynamic and captivating game worlds. Balancing realism with performance and ensuring integration with the game's overall design are key considerations in implementing these effects successfully. Ultimately, well-executed environmental effects can transform a good game into a memorable and immersive one.

4.4. Implementing Ragdoll Physics

Ragdoll physics is a fascinating aspect of game development that involves simulating the realistic behavior of characters or objects when they are subjected to external forces or collisions. This technique is widely used to create lifelike character animations, especially in games where characters can interact with the environment dynamically. In this section, we will explore the principles and techniques behind implementing ragdoll physics in your SDL (Simple DirectMedia Layer) and OpenGL games.

Understanding Ragdoll Physics

Ragdoll physics simulates the dynamic movement and deformation of an object or character's body in response to various forces, such as gravity, impacts, or user interactions. The term "ragdoll" reflects the way the character's limbs and joints behave, similar to a limp ragdoll.

Key components of ragdoll physics include:

Rigid Bodies

The character's body is divided into multiple rigid bodies, representing various body parts such as the head, torso, limbs, and joints. Each rigid body behaves as an independent physics object.

Joints and Constraints

Joints and constraints connect the rigid bodies, allowing them to pivot and move relative to each other. These joints mimic the articulation of real joints like shoulders, elbows, knees, and hips.

Forces and Torques

Forces like gravity and user inputs, as well as torques applied to joints, dictate the movement and behavior of the ragdoll. These forces simulate the physical world's impact on the character.

Implementing Ragdoll Physics

Implementing ragdoll physics in your game involves several steps:

1. Create the Ragdoll Model

Define the structure of the ragdoll by specifying the number of rigid bodies, joints, and constraints. Assign properties like mass, size, and initial positions to each body part.

2. Define Joints and Constraints

Set up the joints and constraints between the rigid bodies to replicate the anatomical connections and articulation of the character. Common types of joints include hinge joints for limbs and ball-and-socket joints for hips and shoulders.

3. Apply Forces and Torques

Apply external forces, such as gravity or user interactions, to the ragdoll's rigid bodies and joints. These forces drive the ragdoll's motion and reaction to the game world.

```
// Pseudocode for applying gravity to a ragdoll
for each rigidBody in ragdoll {
    applyForce(rigidBody, gravityForce);
}
```

4. Update Physics

In the game loop, update the physics simulation for the ragdoll. This includes solving constraints, calculating joint torques, and updating the positions and orientations of rigid bodies.

```
// Pseudocode for updating the ragdoll physics
while (gameIsRunning) {
    updateRagdollPhysics(ragdoll);
    updateGameObjects();
    renderGameScene();
}
```

5. Handle Collisions

Ensure that the ragdoll interacts with the game world and other objects realistically by implementing collision detection and response.

6. User Interaction

Allow user inputs or scripted events to influence the ragdoll's behavior. For example, you can implement ragdoll activation or manipulation through user actions.

Challenges and Considerations

Implementing ragdoll physics can be complex, and several challenges must be addressed:

- **Performance:** Simulating multiple rigid bodies and joints can be computationally intensive. Optimization techniques like simplified collision detection and LOD (Level of Detail) can help.
- **Stability:** Maintaining stability in the simulation, especially during complex interactions, requires careful tuning of joint constraints and damping.
- **Articulation:** Ensuring that the ragdoll's movements appear natural and physically plausible is an ongoing challenge in ragdoll physics implementation.
- **Character Animation:** Integrating ragdoll physics seamlessly with character animations and inverse kinematics (IK) systems is vital for realistic character behavior.

Conclusion

Ragdoll physics is a powerful technique for creating realistic and dynamic character animations in your SDL and OpenGL games. By modeling the character's body as a collection of rigid bodies, joints, and constraints, you can achieve lifelike reactions to forces and collisions. While the implementation may be challenging, the result is more immersive and visually engaging gameplay that enhances the player's experience. Ragdoll physics adds a layer of realism and interactivity that can be particularly beneficial in action, adventure, and simulation games.

4.5. Advanced Particle Systems

Particle systems are versatile and essential components in game development that enable the creation of a wide range of visual effects, from realistic fire and smoke to magical spells and explosions. In this section, we will delve into advanced particle systems in SDL (Simple DirectMedia Layer) and OpenGL games, exploring techniques to create stunning visual effects and optimize their performance.

Understanding Particle Systems

A particle system is a collection of individual particles that collectively create visual effects by simulating the behavior of small, discrete entities. These particles can represent various phenomena, including fire, smoke, raindrops, sparks, and more. Key aspects of particle systems include:

Particle Attributes

Each particle typically has attributes such as position, velocity, color, size, lifespan, and texture. These attributes control how particles behave and appear over time.

Emission

Emission determines when and where particles are spawned or emitted. It can be triggered by game events or follow a continuous pattern, like a fountain of water.

Motion and Behavior

Particles move based on their attributes and may follow predefined trajectories or respond to external forces, such as gravity or wind.

Rendering

Rendering involves transforming particle attributes into visible pixels on the screen. Techniques like billboarding (always facing the camera) are commonly used to create 2D particle effects in 3D environments.

Advanced Particle System Techniques

To create captivating visual effects, consider implementing the following advanced techniques:

Particle Interactions

Allow particles to interact with each other, influencing their behavior. For example, particles could collide, merge, or create secondary effects when they come into contact.

```
// Pseudocode for particle collision and interaction
for each particleA in particles {
    for each particleB in particles {
        if (particleA.intersects(particleB)) {
            handleParticleCollision(particleA, particleB);
        }
    }
}
```

Texture Animation

Animate particle textures by cycling through a sequence of images over a particle's lifespan. This technique is useful for effects like animated fire or explosions.

```
// Pseudocode for texture animation in particles
float animationTime = currentTime - particle.spawnTime;
int currentFrame = animationTime / frameDuration;
particle.texture = particleAnimationFrames[currentFrame];
```

GPU Acceleration

Offload particle simulation and rendering to the GPU (Graphics Processing Unit) for improved performance. Techniques like compute shaders can efficiently handle large numbers of particles.

Volumetric Effects

Create volumetric effects, such as smoke or fog, by using particles to fill a 3D space. Volumetric particle systems can interact with lighting and occlusion, enhancing realism.

```
// Pseudocode for 3D volumetric particle system
for each particle in volumeParticles {
    updateParticlePosition(particle);
    renderVolumetricParticle(particle);
}
```

Performance Optimization

Optimizing particle systems is crucial for maintaining a smooth gaming experience. Here are some optimization strategies:

Level of Detail (LOD)

Use LOD techniques to reduce the number of particles or simplify their behavior when they are distant from the camera.

Culling

Implement frustum and occlusion culling to skip rendering particles that are not visible to the camera.

Particle Pooling

Reuse particle objects instead of creating and destroying them frequently. Maintain a pool of particles and recycle them to reduce memory allocation overhead.

SIMD (Single Instruction, Multiple Data)

Leverage SIMD instructions for parallel processing of particle attributes, improving the efficiency of particle updates.

Asynchronous Updates

Consider updating particles on a separate thread or asynchronously to prevent blocking the main game loop.

Conclusion

Advanced particle systems in SDL and OpenGL games open up a world of possibilities for creating stunning visual effects. By mastering techniques like particle interactions, texture animation, GPU acceleration, and volumetric effects, you can design mesmerizing scenes that immerse players in your game world. Performance optimization is equally essential to ensure that particle systems run smoothly on various hardware configurations. With careful planning and creative implementation, advanced particle systems can elevate your game's visuals and captivate players with dazzling and immersive effects.

Chapter 5: Multiplayer Game Development

5.1. Designing for Networked Multiplayer

Designing and implementing multiplayer functionality in games is a complex and exciting endeavor. Multiplayer games offer players the opportunity to connect and interact with each other in virtual worlds, creating dynamic and engaging experiences. In this section, we will explore the design considerations and best practices for creating networked multiplayer games using SDL (Simple DirectMedia Layer) and OpenGL.

The Appeal of Multiplayer Games

Multiplayer games have gained immense popularity due to several factors:

Social Interaction

They enable players to connect and compete with friends and strangers worldwide, fostering social interactions and a sense of community.

Competitive Challenge

Multiplayer modes often provide a higher level of challenge and competition than single-player experiences, driving player engagement.

Cooperative Play

Cooperative multiplayer games allow players to collaborate and work together towards common goals, promoting teamwork and camaraderie.

Design Considerations

When designing networked multiplayer games, consider the following key factors:

Game Genre

The choice of game genre influences the multiplayer experience. Some genres, like first-person shooters (FPS) or massively multiplayer online role-playing games (MMORPGs), are inherently suited to multiplayer gameplay, while others may require creative adaptation.

Game Mechanics

Adapt game mechanics to accommodate multiplayer interactions. Balance gameplay to ensure a fair and enjoyable experience for all players.

Network Architecture

Select an appropriate network architecture, such as peer-to-peer (P2P) or client-server, based on your game's requirements. Consider factors like latency, scalability, and security.

Synchronization

Implement synchronization mechanisms to ensure that all players experience the game world consistently. Techniques like lockstep synchronization or server-authoritative models may be necessary.

Best Practices

Here are some best practices for designing networked multiplayer games:

Latency Mitigation

Address latency by optimizing network communication, predicting player actions, and implementing lag compensation techniques.

Cheat Prevention

Implement security measures to prevent cheating and ensure fair play. This may involve server-side validation and anti-cheat systems.

Scalability

Design your game to handle varying numbers of players and server loads. Use load balancing and cloud hosting services for scalability.

Matchmaking

Implement effective matchmaking algorithms to pair players with others of similar skill levels and preferences.

Development Process

The development process for multiplayer games involves several stages:

Prototyping

Create a prototype to test and refine core multiplayer mechanics and interactions. Gather feedback from playtesting.

Backend Development

Develop the server infrastructure, including player authentication, game state management, and communication protocols.

Client Implementation

Implement multiplayer functionality in the game client, including networking code, synchronization, and player interactions.

Testing

Thoroughly test the multiplayer experience to identify and resolve bugs, latency issues, and other network-related problems.

Deployment

Deploy the game server and client to hosting environments and prepare for public release.

Challenges and Considerations

Developing multiplayer games presents unique challenges:

- **Latency:** Dealing with network latency requires careful design and synchronization techniques.
- **Security:** Protecting against cheating and unauthorized access is an ongoing concern.
- **Player Management:** Managing player accounts, profiles, and interactions can be complex.
- **Scalability:** Ensuring that the game can handle a growing player base without performance degradation is crucial.

Conclusion

Designing networked multiplayer games is an exciting journey that offers players opportunities for social interaction, competitive challenges, and cooperative play. By considering the game genre, mechanics, network architecture, and synchronization, and following best practices in latency mitigation, cheat prevention, scalability, and matchmaking, you can create engaging and immersive multiplayer experiences using SDL and OpenGL. Despite the challenges, the rewards of developing successful multiplayer games are well worth the effort, as they bring players together in virtual worlds and communities, fostering lasting connections and enjoyment.

5.2. Server-Client Architecture in SDL

Implementing a server-client architecture is a fundamental aspect of developing networked multiplayer games using SDL (Simple DirectMedia Layer) and OpenGL. This architecture allows players to connect to a central server, which manages game state, interactions, and communication between clients. In this section, we will explore the design and implementation of a server-client model for multiplayer games.

Server-Client Architecture Overview

The server-client architecture consists of two main components: the game server and multiple game clients.

Game Server

- **Game State Management:** The server is responsible for maintaining the authoritative game state, including player positions, scores, and world state.
- **Client Synchronization:** It synchronizes the state with all connected clients, ensuring that all players have a consistent view of the game world.
- **Game Logic:** The server executes game logic, validates player actions, and enforces the rules of the game to prevent cheating.
- **Networking:** It handles incoming and outgoing network communication, managing player connections and data transmission.

Game Clients

- **Rendering:** Clients render the game world and provide the player with a visual representation of the game.
- **User Input:** They capture player input and send it to the server for processing.
- **Network Communication:** Clients communicate with the server to exchange game state updates, player actions, and receive responses.

Key Components of Server-Client Interaction

When implementing the server-client architecture, several components play crucial roles in the communication and synchronization between the server and clients:

Networking Library

Choose a networking library compatible with SDL to handle communication between the server and clients. Libraries like SDL_net, ENet, or dedicated networking frameworks can simplify network communication.

Serialization

To transmit game state and player actions over the network, use serialization to convert complex data structures into a format that can be transmitted efficiently. Common formats include JSON, Protocol Buffers, or custom binary formats.

Protocol Design

Design a communication protocol that defines how data is structured and transmitted between the server and clients. This protocol should encompass messages for game state synchronization, player actions, and other relevant information.

Server Tick Rate

Determine the server tick rate, which represents the frequency at which the server updates the game state and sends updates to clients. A higher tick rate results in smoother gameplay but requires more network bandwidth.

Lag Compensation

Implement lag compensation techniques to ensure that player actions are processed fairly, considering network latency. Techniques like client-side prediction and server reconciliation can mitigate the impact of lag.

Implementation Steps

Here's a simplified overview of the implementation steps for a server-client architecture in SDL:

Server Implementation
1. Set up the game server, including network socket initialization, game state management, and game logic execution.
2. Accept incoming client connections and create a dedicated thread or process to handle each client.
3. Define the communication protocol for exchanging game state updates, player actions, and chat messages.
4. Implement server-side prediction and reconciliation to handle lag compensation.
5. Continuously update the game state based on player actions and send updates to all connected clients at the server tick rate.

Client Implementation
1. Initialize the client application, including network socket setup, rendering, and user input capture.
2. Connect to the game server and establish a reliable communication channel.
3. Implement client-side prediction to provide immediate feedback to players while waiting for server responses.
4. Send player input to the server, such as movement commands, ability activations, or chat messages.
5. Receive and apply game state updates from the server, adjusting the client's local state to match the authoritative server state.

Challenges and Considerations

Developing a server-client architecture for multiplayer games presents several challenges:

- **Security:** Implement robust security measures to prevent cheating, unauthorized access, and data tampering.
- **Scalability:** Design the server to handle a growing number of players while maintaining performance.
- **Bandwidth Management:** Optimize network bandwidth usage to reduce latency and accommodate players with varying connection speeds.
- **Error Handling:** Implement error handling and recovery mechanisms to address network disruptions and unexpected issues gracefully.
- **Server Hosting:** Choose appropriate server hosting solutions, whether cloud-based or dedicated hardware, to ensure reliable game server availability.

Conclusion

Implementing a server-client architecture is a vital step in creating networked multiplayer games using SDL and OpenGL. This architecture allows for synchronized gameplay, fair competition, and social interaction among players. By carefully designing the communication protocol, handling serialization, addressing lag compensation, and considering security and scalability, you can build engaging and robust multiplayer experiences. While challenges exist, the rewards of creating immersive multiplayer games that connect players worldwide are well worth the effort.

5.3. Handling Network Latency and Prediction

In networked multiplayer games, handling network latency is a critical aspect of providing a smooth and responsive gaming experience. Network latency refers to the delay or lag in data transmission between the game server and clients. This delay can lead to players experiencing delayed responses to their actions, which can negatively impact gameplay. In this section, we will explore techniques for managing network latency and implementing prediction mechanisms to improve the perceived responsiveness of multiplayer games developed using SDL (Simple DirectMedia Layer) and OpenGL.

Understanding Network Latency

Network latency is influenced by various factors, including the physical distance between the server and clients, the quality of network connections, and the processing time required for data to travel between devices. High latency can result in delayed player input, slow game updates, and visual discrepancies between players.

Predictive Movement

One way to mitigate the effects of network latency is by implementing predictive movement for player characters and objects. Predictive movement involves extrapolating the future positions of game objects based on their current state and recent actions. This allows clients to display objects in their expected positions, reducing the perception of lag.

Example: Predictive Character Movement

```
// Pseudocode for predictive character movement
while (gameIsRunning) {
    // Predict the character's next position based on current state and input
    predictedPosition = predictNextPosition(character);

    // Render the character at the predicted position
    renderCharacter(predictedPosition);

    // Send player input to the server
    sendPlayerInputToServer(input);

    // Receive updates from the server and adjust the character's state
    serverUpdate = receiveServerUpdate();
    character.update(serverUpdate);
}
```

Client-Side Prediction

Client-side prediction is a technique where the client predicts the outcome of player actions before receiving confirmation from the server. This allows the client to provide immediate feedback to the player, reducing perceived lag. Once the server's response arrives, the client reconciles its predictions with the authoritative server state.

Example: Client-Side Prediction

```
// Pseudocode for client-side prediction
while (gameIsRunning) {
    // Capture player input and predict its effect on the character
    predictedState = predictClientState(input);

    // Render the character at the predicted state
    renderCharacter(predictedState);

    // Send player input and predicted state to the server
    sendInputAndStateToServer(input, predictedState);

    // Receive updates from the server and reconcile client and server states
    serverUpdate = receiveServerUpdate();
    reconcileStates(predictedState, serverUpdate);
}
```

Lag Compensation

Lag compensation techniques aim to compensate for network latency by adjusting the outcome of actions based on the time when they were initiated by the player. This ensures that players' actions are still effective even if they experience latency.

Example: Lag Compensation for Projectile Weapons

```
// Pseudocode for lag compensation with projectile weapons
while (gameIsRunning) {
    // Capture player input and predict the weapon's firing time
    predictedFiringTime = predictFiringTime(input);

    // Render the weapon firing at the predicted time
    renderProjectileFiring(predictedFiringTime);

    // Send player input and predicted firing time to the server
    sendInputAndFiringTimeToServer(input, predictedFiringTime);

    // Receive updates from the server and apply lag compensation
    serverUpdate = receiveServerUpdate();
    applyLagCompensation(predictedFiringTime, serverUpdate);
}
```

Challenges and Considerations

Implementing network latency management and prediction mechanisms can be complex and introduces several challenges:

- **Synchronization:** Ensuring that client predictions align with the server's authoritative state is crucial to prevent cheating.
- **Interpolation:** Smoothing out the transition between predicted and corrected states can improve visual quality.
- **Server Authority:** The server should have the final say in determining game outcomes to prevent cheating and inconsistencies.
- **Prediction Errors:** Prediction errors can occur due to variations in latency and packet loss, which require careful handling.

Conclusion

Handling network latency and implementing prediction mechanisms are essential for creating responsive and enjoyable multiplayer games. By incorporating predictive movement, client-side prediction, and lag compensation, developers can reduce the perception of lag and improve the overall gaming experience. However, it is vital to strike a balance between responsiveness and accuracy while maintaining server authority to ensure fair and competitive gameplay in SDL and OpenGL-based multiplayer games.

5.4. Synchronizing Game States Across Players

Synchronizing game states across players is a fundamental aspect of multiplayer game development using SDL (Simple DirectMedia Layer) and OpenGL. In a multiplayer game, it is crucial to ensure that all players have a consistent view of the game world, including player positions, game objects, and events. In this section, we will explore the challenges and techniques involved in synchronizing game states to create a cohesive and fair multiplayer experience.

The Importance of Game State Synchronization

Game state synchronization ensures that all players perceive the same game world, allowing them to interact with each other and respond to changes in a shared environment. Without proper synchronization, players may experience discrepancies, leading to unfair advantages or confusion.

Server Authority

In most multiplayer games, a central game server acts as the authoritative source of truth for the game world. The server maintains the master copy of the game state and enforces the rules of the game. Clients communicate with the server to exchange information and receive updates.

Example: Player Movement

```
// Pseudocode for player movement synchronization
while (gameIsRunning) {
    // Capture player input and update the local player's position
    localPlayer.update(input);

    // Send the updated player position to the server
    sendPlayerPositionToServer(localPlayer.position);

    // Receive updates from the server to adjust the local game state
    serverUpdate = receiveServerUpdate();
    localGameWorld.applyServerUpdate(serverUpdate);
}
```

Networking Protocol

A well-defined networking protocol is essential for transmitting game state updates between the server and clients. The protocol outlines the structure of messages, the order of data transmission, and the rules for handling communication.

Example: Networking Protocol

```
// Pseudocode for a simple networking protocol
message PlayerPosition {
    int playerId;
    float x, y, z;
}
```

```
message ServerUpdate {
    PlayerPosition[] playerPositions;
    // Other game state updates...
}
```

Interpolation and Smoothing

To create smooth and visually pleasing multiplayer experiences, interpolation and smoothing techniques are often employed. These techniques help mitigate the effects of network latency and packet loss by interpolating between received state updates.

Example: Interpolation
```
// Pseudocode for position interpolation
while (gameIsRunning) {
    // Capture player input and update the local player's position
    localPlayer.update(input);

    // Send the updated player position to the server
    sendPlayerPositionToServer(localPlayer.position);

    // Receive updates from the server with timestamps
    serverUpdate = receiveServerUpdate();

    // Interpolate positions between updates for smooth movement
    interpolatePlayerPositions(serverUpdate);
}
```

Snapshot-Based Synchronization

Snapshot-based synchronization involves periodically sending snapshots of the game state to clients. Clients then use these snapshots to update their local game world. This approach reduces the amount of data transmitted, improving efficiency.

Example: Snapshot-Based Synchronization
```
// Pseudocode for snapshot-based synchronization
while (gameIsRunning) {
    // Capture player input and update the local player's position
    localPlayer.update(input);

    // Send the updated player position to the server
    sendPlayerPositionToServer(localPlayer.position);

    // Periodically request snapshots from the server
    if (timeSinceLastSnapshotRequest >= snapshotInterval) {
        requestGameSnapshotFromServer();
        timeSinceLastSnapshotRequest = 0;
    }

    // Receive and apply snapshots from the server
```

```
    serverSnapshot = receiveServerSnapshot();
    localGameWorld.applySnapshot(serverSnapshot);
}
```

Challenges and Considerations

Synchronizing game states across players introduces several challenges:

- **Latency:** Network latency can lead to delays in receiving updates, affecting real-time responsiveness.

- **Consistency:** Ensuring that all players have an identical view of the game world requires careful synchronization.

- **Optimization:** Minimizing network bandwidth usage and optimizing the synchronization process is essential for performance.

- **Cheating Prevention:** Preventing cheating through unauthorized state manipulation is a continuous concern.

Conclusion

Synchronizing game states across players is a critical aspect of multiplayer game development using SDL and OpenGL. By establishing server authority, defining a robust networking protocol, implementing interpolation and smoothing techniques, and considering snapshot-based synchronization, developers can create seamless and immersive multiplayer experiences. Overcoming the challenges of latency, consistency, optimization, and cheating prevention is essential for delivering fair and engaging multiplayer gameplay in SDL and OpenGL-based games.

5.5. Security Considerations in Online Games

Ensuring the security of online multiplayer games is of paramount importance to provide fair and enjoyable experiences for players. In multiplayer games developed using SDL (Simple DirectMedia Layer) and OpenGL, various security considerations must be addressed to prevent cheating, unauthorized access, and data manipulation. This section delves into the security aspects of online games and explores strategies to safeguard the integrity of gameplay.

Authentication and Authorization

Authentication and authorization are the initial lines of defense against unauthorized access to online games. These mechanisms verify the identity of players and determine their level of access to game resources.

Authentication

Authentication involves validating the identity of players during the login process. Common authentication methods include:

- **Username and Password:** Players provide a unique username and a corresponding password. The server verifies the entered credentials against a secure database.
- **OAuth:** OAuth allows players to log in using their existing social media or third-party accounts. This method can simplify the registration process.

Authorization

Authorization determines what actions and resources each player is permitted to access within the game. Role-based access control (RBAC) and permissions systems are commonly used for authorization. For example, administrators may have elevated privileges, while regular players have limited access.

Data Encryption

Encrypting data transmitted between clients and the server is crucial to protect against eavesdropping and data tampering. Secure socket layer (SSL) or transport layer security (TLS) protocols can be employed to establish encrypted connections.

Example: Encrypting Network Communication

```
// Pseudocode for setting up encrypted communication
SSLContext sslContext = createSSLContext();
SSLServerSocket serverSocket = sslContext.createServerSocket(port);
SSLSocket clientSocket = sslContext.createSocket(host, port);

// Encrypted communication is established
```

Server-Side Validation

Server-side validation is essential to prevent client-side cheating and data manipulation. Critical game actions and decisions should be validated on the server to ensure fairness.

Example: Server-Side Validation

```
// Pseudocode for server-side validation of player movement
function validatePlayerMovement(player, newPosition) {
    // Calculate the expected position based on the player's current state
    expectedPosition = calculateExpectedPosition(player);

    // Compare the expected position with the client-provided newPosition
    if (expectedPosition != newPosition) {
        // Reject the movement as it doesn't match the server's expectation
        log("Invalid player movement detected");
        return false;
    }
```

```
    // Apply the valid movement to the game state
    player.setPosition(newPosition);
    return true;
}
```

Anti-Cheat Systems

Implementing anti-cheat systems is crucial to detect and prevent cheating in online games. Anti-cheat measures may include:

- **Client Integrity Checks:** Regularly verify the integrity of the client application to detect modifications or hacks.

- **Behavior Analysis:** Analyze player behavior to identify suspicious patterns or abnormal actions.

- **Reporting Systems:** Allow players to report suspected cheaters, leading to investigations and actions.

Data Privacy and Compliance

Compliance with data privacy regulations, such as the General Data Protection Regulation (GDPR) and Children's Online Privacy Protection Act (COPPA), is essential when handling player data. Developers must ensure that player information is collected, stored, and processed in a secure and compliant manner.

Regular Updates and Patching

Regularly updating and patching the game is crucial to address security vulnerabilities and exploit attempts. Developers should have a system in place to quickly respond to emerging threats and release updates as needed.

Conclusion

Security considerations are integral to the development and maintenance of online multiplayer games using SDL and OpenGL. Authentication, authorization, data encryption, server-side validation, anti-cheat systems, data privacy compliance, and regular updates are essential components of a comprehensive security strategy. By prioritizing security, developers can create a fair and enjoyable gaming environment that protects players from cheating and ensures the integrity of online gameplay.

Chapter 6: Advanced Audio Techniques

Section 6.1: 3D Spatial Audio Implementation

Spatial audio is a crucial aspect of game development that enhances the immersion of players by providing sound that appears to come from specific directions in 3D space. In this section, we will delve into the implementation of 3D spatial audio using SDL, discussing the fundamental concepts, techniques, and SDL features required to create an immersive audio experience in your games.

Understanding 3D Spatial Audio

3D spatial audio simulates sound sources and their positions within the virtual game world, making it seem as if the sounds are coming from specific locations relative to the player's perspective. This adds depth and realism to the audio experience, contributing significantly to the overall gameplay immersion.

In 3D spatial audio, each sound source has attributes like position, direction, and velocity. These attributes determine how the sound is perceived by the player. For example, a sound source behind the player will be heard differently than one in front, creating a realistic sense of space.

SDL's Audio Capabilities

SDL provides a comprehensive set of audio functionalities that allow developers to create 3D spatial audio effects. SDL's audio features enable you to load and play audio samples, control volume, and apply various audio effects. To implement 3D spatial audio, you'll use SDL's audio features in conjunction with 3D positional audio techniques.

Positional Audio in SDL

SDL's positional audio features allow you to specify the position and direction of audio sources in 3D space. When implementing 3D audio, you typically have a listener (representing the player's position and orientation) and multiple sound sources. SDL calculates how each sound source should be heard based on its attributes and the listener's position.

To use positional audio in SDL, you'll need to set up the listener's position and orientation and configure each sound source's attributes. SDL will then calculate the audio properties, such as volume and panning, to create a 3D audio effect.

```
// Set the Listener's position and orientation
SDL_SetListenerPosition(listenerPosX, listenerPosY, listenerPosZ);
SDL_SetListenerOrientation(listenerForwardX, listenerForwardY, listenerForwardZ, listenerUpX, listenerUpY, listenerUpZ);

// Configure a sound source's position
SDL_SetSourcePosition(soundSource, sourcePosX, sourcePosY, sourcePosZ);
```

Attenuation and Doppler Effect

In 3D spatial audio, sound should attenuate as it moves away from the listener. SDL provides control over the attenuation factors, allowing you to simulate the natural decrease in volume as sound sources move farther away.

Additionally, the Doppler effect is an essential aspect of 3D audio, which alters the pitch of a sound source as it moves towards or away from the listener. SDL allows you to control the Doppler effect parameters, providing a more realistic audio experience when objects in the game world produce sound while in motion.

```
// Set the attenuation factors
SDL_SetSourceDistanceAttenuation(soundSource, constantFactor, linearFactor, quadraticFactor);

// Configure Doppler effect
SDL_SetDopplerFactors(speedOfSound, listenerSpeedX, listenerSpeedY, listenerSpeedZ);
```

Sound Occlusion and Obstruction

To make 3D audio more realistic, SDL allows you to simulate sound occlusion and obstruction. Occlusion occurs when an object obstructs the direct path of sound from the source to the listener, reducing the sound's volume. Obstruction occurs when the object partially obstructs the sound path, causing a muffled effect.

SDL provides functions to calculate and apply occlusion and obstruction effects, enhancing the immersive quality of your game's audio.

Environmental Audio Effects

SDL also supports environmental audio effects that simulate different acoustic environments, such as caves, open fields, or closed rooms. These effects modify the sound characteristics to match the selected environment, adding depth to the audio experience.

To implement environmental audio effects, you can use SDL's reverb and filtering functionalities.

```
// Apply environmental reverb
SDL_SetReverbEnvironment(soundSource, reverbEnvironment);

// Apply audio filtering
SDL_SetAudioFilter(soundSource, filterType, filterParameters);
```

Conclusion

In this section, we've explored the implementation of 3D spatial audio using SDL. Understanding the concepts of 3D audio, SDL's audio capabilities, positional audio, attenuation, Doppler effect, sound occlusion, obstruction, and environmental audio effects are essential steps toward creating an immersive audio experience in your games. By effectively utilizing these features, you can enhance gameplay and immerse players in your game world through realistic and dynamic audio experiences.

Section 6.2: Dynamic Music and Sound Effects

Dynamic music and sound effects are crucial components of game audio that can greatly enhance the player's experience. In this section, we will explore how to implement dynamic music and sound effects using SDL, allowing you to create immersive and responsive audio experiences in your games.

Dynamic Music

Dynamic music systems adapt the game's music to match the current gameplay situation or mood. This can involve smoothly transitioning between different tracks, altering the tempo, or adding or removing layers of music. Implementing dynamic music requires careful planning and the use of SDL's audio capabilities.

Music Tracks and Themes

To create dynamic music, you need to compose and organize your music into separate tracks or themes. Each track or theme should represent a specific emotional or gameplay state. For example, you might have tracks for exploration, combat, and suspense. These tracks can be seamlessly combined or transitioned between based on the in-game events and player actions.

Crossfading and Transitions

SDL provides functions for smoothly crossfading between music tracks. Crossfading allows you to blend the audio from one track into another, ensuring a seamless transition. You can use these functions to create transitions between different gameplay states, ensuring that the music always matches the player's experience.

```
// Crossfade between two music tracks
Mix_FadeOutMusic(fadeOutMilliseconds); // Fade out the current track
Mix_FadeInMusic(newTrack, fadeInMilliseconds); // Fade in the new track
```

Interactive Music

Interactive music systems respond to in-game events and player actions. For example, the music might become more intense during a boss battle or quieter during a dialogue scene. SDL's audio capabilities allow you to trigger specific music events based on in-game conditions.

```
// Trigger music event based on gameplay conditions
if (playerIsInCombat) {
    PlayCombatMusic();
```

```
} else if (playerIsExploring) {
    PlayExplorationMusic();
}
```

Sound Effects

Sound effects play a crucial role in enhancing the realism and immersion of games. Implementing dynamic sound effects involves responding to in-game events and actions with appropriate audio feedback.

Event-Driven Sound Effects

SDL provides mechanisms for triggering sound effects in response to game events. For example, when a player fires a weapon, collides with an object, or opens a door, you can play corresponding sound effects. By associating sound effects with events, you can create a more responsive and engaging game world.

```
// Play sound effect when player fires a weapon
if (playerFiresWeapon) {
    PlayWeaponFireSound();
}
```

Sound Variations and Randomization

To prevent sound effects from becoming repetitive, it's a good practice to include variations of each sound effect. SDL allows you to load multiple variations of a sound and randomly select one to play. This randomization adds diversity to the audio experience.

```
// Randomly select and play a footstep sound variation
int randomFootstep = rand() % numFootstepVariations;
PlayFootstepSound(footstepVariations[randomFootstep]);
```

Real-Time Audio Filters

SDL also supports real-time audio filters that can modify the sound of individual sound effects on the fly. You can use filters to add effects like reverb, echo, or pitch shifting to sound effects based on in-game conditions or environmental factors.

```
// Apply real-time audio filter to a sound effect
SDL_SetAudioFilter(soundEffect, filterType, filterParameters);
```

Conclusion

Dynamic music and sound effects are powerful tools for creating immersive and engaging gameplay experiences. By implementing dynamic music transitions, interactive music systems, event-driven sound effects, sound variations, and real-time audio filters using SDL, you can elevate your game's audio to a new level of quality and responsiveness. Careful audio design and integration can significantly enhance the player's immersion and enjoyment of your game.

Section 6.3: Audio Mixing and Processing

Audio mixing and processing play a crucial role in shaping the overall audio experience of a game. In this section, we will explore the concepts and techniques of audio mixing and processing using SDL, allowing you to create rich and immersive soundscapes for your games.

Audio Mixing

Audio mixing involves combining multiple audio sources, such as music, sound effects, and voiceovers, into a single audio output. SDL provides tools for mixing audio streams, enabling you to control the volume, panning, and positioning of each source within the audio mix.

Audio Channels and Groups

SDL allows you to organize audio sources into channels and groups. Channels are individual audio tracks that can be adjusted independently. Groups provide a way to manage and control multiple channels collectively. For example, you can group all sound effects channels to apply global effects or volume adjustments.

```
// Create an audio channel for background music
int musicChannel = Mix_PlayMusic(music, -1);

// Group sound effects channels for volume control
Mix_GroupChannels(0, numSoundEffectChannels - 1, soundEffectsGroup);
```

Volume Control

SDL provides functions to control the volume of audio channels and groups. This allows you to dynamically adjust the volume of different audio elements in response to in-game events or player preferences. For example, you can lower the background music volume during a dialogue scene.

```
// Adjust the volume of a music channel
Mix_Volume(musicChannel, newVolume);

// Adjust the volume of a sound effects group
Mix_VolumeGroup(soundEffectsGroup, newVolume);
```

Panning and Spatial Positioning

Panning is the process of distributing audio between the left and right speakers to create a sense of direction or position in the audio mix. SDL allows you to control the panning of individual channels, which is especially useful for implementing 3D audio effects.

```
// Set the panning of a sound effect channel
Mix_SetPanning(channel, leftPanning, rightPanning);
```

Real-Time Effects and Filters

SDL supports real-time audio effects and filters that can be applied to individual channels or groups. You can use these effects to add depth and character to your audio mix. Common effects include reverb, echo, equalization, and pitch shifting.

```
// Apply a real-time reverb effect to a channel
Mix_SetReverb(channel, reverbType, reverbParameters);
```

Audio Processing

Audio processing involves modifying audio data in real-time to achieve specific effects or enhancements. SDL provides facilities for audio processing, enabling you to create custom audio effects or manipulate audio in response to gameplay events.

Custom Audio Effects

SDL allows you to create custom audio effects by manipulating audio samples directly. You can modify the audio data to create effects like distortion, filtering, or pitch modulation. This level of control is valuable for creating unique soundscapes or character-specific audio effects.

```
// Apply a custom audio effect to an audio sample
CustomAudioEffect(audioSample, effectParameters);
```

Real-Time Audio Synthesis

In some cases, you may want to synthesize audio in real-time, such as generating procedural sound effects or dynamic music elements. SDL provides tools for real-time audio synthesis, allowing you to generate audio data on the fly and play it through audio channels.

```
// Generate and play a procedural sound effect in real-time
GenerateProceduralSoundEffect(audioBuffer, bufferSize);
Mix_PlayChannel(channel, audioBuffer, numLoops);
```

Conclusion

Audio mixing and processing are fundamental aspects of game audio design that can greatly enhance the player's immersion and engagement. By mastering the techniques of audio mixing, volume control, panning, spatial positioning, and real-time effects using SDL, you can create rich and dynamic audio experiences in your games. Additionally, the ability to apply custom audio effects and real-time synthesis opens up endless possibilities for crafting unique and memorable audio elements that complement your game's narrative and gameplay.

Section 6.4: Voice Chat Integration

Voice chat integration is a valuable feature in multiplayer games that allows players to communicate with each other using voice instead of text. In this section, we will explore how to implement voice chat functionality in your games using SDL, enhancing the collaborative and social aspects of multiplayer gaming.

Voice Chat Basics

Voice chat functionality enables players to speak to each other in real-time during gameplay. It is commonly used in cooperative multiplayer games, team-based shooters, and online role-playing games (RPGs). Implementing voice chat requires both audio capture (microphone input) and audio playback (speaker output) capabilities.

Audio Capture

SDL provides mechanisms to capture audio from a microphone or other audio input devices. You can use these mechanisms to record the player's voice and transmit it to other players in the game.

```
// Initialize audio capture
SDL_AudioSpec captureSpec;
SDL_AudioDeviceID captureDevice = SDL_OpenAudioDevice(NULL, 1, &captureSpec, NULL, SDL_AUDIO_ALLOW_FORMAT_CHANGE);

// Start audio capture
SDL_PauseAudioDevice(captureDevice, 0);
```

Audio Playback

To enable players to hear each other's voices, SDL allows you to manage audio playback. You can receive audio data from other players and play it through the player's speakers or headphones.

```
// Initialize audio playback
SDL_AudioSpec playbackSpec;
SDL_AudioDeviceID playbackDevice = SDL_OpenAudioDevice(NULL, 0, &playbackSpec, NULL, 0);

// Start audio playback
SDL_PauseAudioDevice(playbackDevice, 0);
```

Voice Chat Communication

Voice chat communication involves transmitting audio data between players in a networked multiplayer game. SDL provides the necessary functionality to send and receive audio data over the network.

Network Integration

To implement voice chat over a network, you need a network communication system. SDL supports network communication, allowing you to establish connections between players and exchange audio data.

```
// Set up network communication for voice chat
SDLNet_Init();
TCPsocket serverSocket = SDLNet_TCP_Open(&serverIP);
TCPsocket clientSocket = SDLNet_TCP_Open(&clientIP);

// Send and receive audio data over the network
SDLNet_TCP_Send(clientSocket, audioData, audioDataSize);
SDLNet_TCP_Recv(serverSocket, receivedData, maxDataSize);
```

Voice Activation and Push-to-Talk

Voice chat systems often incorporate features like voice activation and push-to-talk (PTT). Voice activation automatically transmits audio when the player speaks, while PTT requires the player to press a designated key to transmit their voice. You can implement these features using SDL's input handling and audio capture capabilities.

```
// Implement voice activation or push-to-talk
if (isVoiceActivated) {
    if (voiceIsDetected()) {
        // Transmit audio data
    }
} else if (isPushToTalkEnabled) {
    if (pushToTalkKeyIsPressed()) {
        // Transmit audio data
    }
}
```

Voice Quality and Optimization

Voice chat quality is essential for a positive player experience. SDL provides tools for optimizing voice chat, such as audio compression and quality settings. You can fine-tune these settings to balance voice quality with network bandwidth and latency considerations.

```
// Set audio compression and quality settings
SDL_AudioSpec desiredSpec;
desiredSpec.format = AUDIO_S16LSB; // Set desired audio format
desiredSpec.freq = 44100; // Set audio frequency
desiredSpec.channels = 1; // Set mono or stereo
desiredSpec.samples = 1024; // Set audio buffer size
```

Conclusion

Voice chat integration can greatly enhance the social and cooperative aspects of multiplayer games. By implementing audio capture, playback, network communication, and voice activation or PTT using SDL, you can create a seamless voice chat experience for players, promoting teamwork and communication in your online multiplayer games. Additionally, optimizing voice quality ensures that players can communicate effectively while considering network performance and bandwidth constraints.

Section 6.5: Audio Optimization and Compression

Audio optimization and compression are critical aspects of game development that help reduce the storage space and memory usage of audio assets while maintaining acceptable audio quality. In this section, we'll explore techniques and tools for optimizing and compressing audio in SDL-based games.

Audio File Formats

SDL supports various audio file formats, including WAV, MP3, OGG, and more. Choosing the right format is the first step in audio optimization. Different formats have varying levels of compression and quality, so it's essential to strike a balance between file size and audio fidelity.

```
// Load an audio file in a specific format (e.g., WAV)
Mix_Chunk* audioChunk = Mix_LoadWAV("audio.wav");
```

Audio Compression

Audio compression reduces the size of audio files by encoding them more efficiently. SDL provides support for compressed audio formats like OGG, which offer good compression ratios without significant loss of quality.

```
// Load an OGG audio file
Mix_Music* music = Mix_LoadMUS("music.ogg");
```

Bitrate and Sample Rate

Adjusting the audio bitrate and sample rate can impact the quality and size of audio files. Lower bitrates and sample rates reduce file size but may result in lower audio quality. Experiment with different settings to find the right balance.

```
// Set the audio quality for encoding
Mix_QuerySpec(&frequency, &format, &channels);
Mix_HookMusic(SampleRateConversion, NULL);
```

Streaming vs. Buffering

SDL allows you to stream audio data from a file or buffer it entirely in memory. Streaming is useful for long audio tracks, while buffering is preferable for short sound effects. Choose the appropriate method to minimize memory usage and optimize performance.

```
// Stream audio from a file
Mix_Music* music = Mix_LoadMUS("music.ogg");

// Buffer audio in memory
Mix_Chunk* soundEffect = Mix_LoadWAV("effect.wav");
```

Audio Quality Testing

Quality testing is crucial to ensure that audio optimization doesn't degrade the player's experience. Conduct thorough testing to evaluate the audio quality at different compression levels and settings, and gather player feedback to make informed decisions.

```
// Test audio quality and gather player feedback
if (audioQualityIsAcceptable()) {
    // Continue with the chosen audio settings
} else {
    // Adjust settings or consider alternative formats
}
```

Conclusion

Audio optimization and compression are vital for managing the storage and memory requirements of your game's audio assets. By selecting the right file formats, adjusting bitrates and sample rates, and optimizing audio streaming or buffering, you can strike a balance between audio quality and file size. Regular testing and player feedback are essential to ensure that the audio remains enjoyable and immersive throughout the game. Remember that optimization is an iterative process, and fine-tuning audio settings may be necessary to achieve the best results for your SDL-based game.

Chapter 7: AI and Machine Learning in Games

Section 7.1: Advanced AI Strategies for NPCs

Artificial Intelligence (AI) is a crucial component of modern game development, enhancing the gameplay experience by creating intelligent Non-Player Characters (NPCs). In this section, we will explore advanced AI strategies and techniques that can be implemented in SDL-based games to make NPCs more engaging, challenging, and lifelike.

Role of AI in Games

AI in games is responsible for controlling NPC behavior, decision-making, and responses to player actions. Well-designed AI can create immersive and dynamic game worlds, where NPCs interact with the environment and adapt to changing circumstances.

Advanced Pathfinding

Pathfinding is a fundamental AI technique that allows NPCs to find the optimal path from one point to another in the game world. Advanced pathfinding algorithms, such as A* (A-star) or Dijkstra's algorithm, can be employed to calculate paths efficiently and avoid obstacles.

```
// Implement A* pathfinding algorithm
Path path = AStarPathfinding(startPosition, targetPosition, obstacleMap);
```

Behavior Trees

Behavior Trees are hierarchical structures that define the decision-making process of NPCs. They consist of nodes representing actions, conditions, and composite nodes for organizing behavior. Designing complex behavior trees can make NPCs respond to various in-game situations intelligently.

```
// Define a behavior tree for an NPC
BehaviorTree tree = new BehaviorTree(
    new SequenceNode(
        new HasTargetCondition(),
        new AttackAction(),
        new ChaseAction()
    )
);
```

Finite State Machines (FSM)

FSMs are another AI technique used to model NPC behavior. NPCs transition between different states based on specific conditions or events. Implementing FSMs can make NPCs exhibit diverse behaviors, such as patrolling, attacking, or fleeing.

```
// Implement an NPC's finite state machine
NPCState currentState = NPCState.Patrol;
```

```
while (true) {
    switch (currentState) {
        case NPCState.Patrol:
            // Perform patrolling behavior
            break;
        case NPCState.Attack:
            // Perform attacking behavior
            break;
        // Handle other states
    }
}
```

Machine Learning

Machine Learning (ML) techniques, such as neural networks or reinforcement learning, can be used to create adaptive NPCs that learn and improve their behavior over time. This advanced approach can lead to more realistic and challenging opponents in your game.

```
// Implement reinforcement learning for NPC behavior
NeuralNetwork neuralNetwork = new NeuralNetwork();
ReinforcementLearningAgent agent = new ReinforcementLearningAgent(neuralNetwork);

while (true) {
    agent.takeAction();
    agent.updateRewards();
    agent.learn();
}
```

Conclusion

Advanced AI strategies and techniques play a pivotal role in enhancing the gaming experience. By implementing advanced pathfinding, behavior trees, finite state machines, or even machine learning, you can create NPCs that react intelligently to player actions, exhibit diverse behaviors, and provide challenging gameplay. Careful design and implementation of AI in your SDL-based games can significantly contribute to the overall quality and enjoyment of the gaming experience.

Section 7.2: Implementing Learning Algorithms in Games

In modern game development, the integration of learning algorithms has become increasingly prevalent, allowing NPCs and in-game systems to adapt and improve based on player interactions and data. In this section, we will delve into the implementation of learning algorithms within SDL-based games, exploring how they can enhance gameplay and create dynamic, evolving experiences.

Types of Learning Algorithms

There are several types of learning algorithms commonly used in game development, including:

1. **Reinforcement Learning:** Reinforcement learning agents learn by interacting with their environment, receiving rewards or penalties based on their actions. Over time, they develop strategies that maximize their cumulative rewards.
2. **Supervised Learning:** Supervised learning involves training a model using labeled data, making it capable of recognizing patterns and making decisions. This is often used for character behavior and object recognition.
3. **Unsupervised Learning:** Unsupervised learning techniques, such as clustering and dimensionality reduction, can be used for generating procedural content or analyzing player data for insights.
4. **Neural Networks:** Neural networks, especially deep neural networks, can be employed for various tasks, such as natural language processing, image recognition, or predicting player behavior.

Reinforcement Learning in Games

Reinforcement learning is particularly popular in game AI due to its ability to create adaptive NPCs and agents. Here's a simplified example of how reinforcement learning can be implemented:

```
// Reinforcement Learning loop
while (gameIsRunning) {
    State currentState = observeGameState();
    Action chosenAction = agent.selectAction(currentState);
    executeAction(chosenAction);
    float reward = calculateReward();
    State nextState = observeGameState();
    agent.learn(currentState, chosenAction, reward, nextState);
}
```

In this loop, the agent observes the game state, selects actions, receives rewards, and updates its strategy over time.

Player Behavior Prediction

Machine learning models can be trained to predict player behavior, allowing for more responsive and engaging gameplay. For instance, a game could predict a player's next move or adapt the game's difficulty level based on their skill level.

```
// Predicting player behavior using a trained model
PlayerBehavior predictedBehavior = playerModel.predictNextMove(currentGameSta
te);
```

Dynamic Game Balancing

Learning algorithms can be used to dynamically balance the game based on player performance and preferences. If certain levels or challenges are consistently too easy or too hard, the game can adjust itself to maintain an optimal level of challenge.

```
// Dynamic game balancing based on player performance
if (playerPerformanceIsBelowAverage()) {
    increase enemy difficulty();
} else if (playerPerformanceIsAboveAverage()) {
    decrease enemy difficulty();
}
```

Ethical Considerations

While learning algorithms can enhance gameplay, they also raise ethical considerations, such as player privacy, fairness, and transparency. Game developers should be mindful of these issues when implementing learning algorithms in games.

Conclusion

Implementing learning algorithms in SDL-based games opens up exciting possibilities for creating adaptive and immersive gaming experiences. Whether it's using reinforcement learning for NPC behavior, predicting player actions, dynamically balancing the game, or addressing ethical concerns, the integration of learning algorithms can significantly enhance the depth and engagement of your games. Careful design and consideration of the specific goals and challenges of your game will determine the most suitable learning algorithm to implement for a rewarding player experience.

Section 7.3: Adaptive Game Difficulty

Adaptive game difficulty is a crucial aspect of modern game design that aims to provide players with a challenging yet enjoyable experience. In this section, we will explore the concept of adaptive game difficulty within SDL-based games and how it can enhance player engagement.

What Is Adaptive Game Difficulty?

Adaptive game difficulty refers to the dynamic adjustment of a game's challenge level based on the player's skill and performance. It ensures that players of varying skill levels can enjoy the game, from beginners to experts, without feeling overwhelmed or bored. Adaptive difficulty systems aim to strike a balance by making the game progressively more challenging or easier as needed.

Implementing Adaptive Difficulty

Implementing adaptive difficulty involves monitoring the player's performance and skill level and making real-time adjustments to various game elements. Here are some strategies for implementing adaptive difficulty:

1. Dynamic Enemy Behavior

Adjust the behavior and abilities of enemies based on the player's skill level. Beginners may face less aggressive or weaker foes, while skilled players encounter more challenging adversaries.

```
// Dynamic enemy behavior based on player skill
if (playerSkillLevel == SkillLevel.Beginner) {
    enemyBehavior = EnemyBehavior.Easy;
} else if (playerSkillLevel == SkillLevel.Expert) {
    enemyBehavior = EnemyBehavior.Challenging;
}
```

2. Variable Enemy Spawning

Control the frequency and number of enemy spawns. Beginners can have fewer enemies to deal with, while experts face larger waves or more frequent spawns.

```
// Variable enemy spawning based on player performance
if (playerPerformance == Performance.Good) {
    spawnEnemiesAtRegularIntervals();
} else if (playerPerformance == Performance.Poor) {
    reduce enemy spawns();
}
```

3. Adaptive Puzzles and Challenges

In puzzle or level-based games, adapt the complexity of puzzles or challenges. Provide hints or simpler versions of puzzles for less experienced players, while offering more complex versions for skilled players.

```
// Adaptive puzzles and challenges
if (playerSkillLevel == SkillLevel.Beginner) {
    display puzzle hints();
} else if (playerSkillLevel == SkillLevel.Expert) {
    present complex puzzles();
}
```

4. Scaling Rewards and Penalties

Adjust the rewards and penalties in the game. Skilled players might earn more points or in-game currency, while beginners receive additional lives or assistance.

```
// Scaling rewards and penalties based on player performance
if (playerPerformance == Performance.Excellent) {
    increase point rewards();
```

```
} else if (playerPerformance == Performance.Poor) {
    provide additional lives();
}
```

5. *Data-Driven Approach*

Collect and analyze player data to inform adaptive difficulty decisions. Use player behavior and performance data to fine-tune the game's difficulty over time.

```
// Data-driven adaptive difficulty adjustments
analyzePlayerData();
adjustDifficultyBasedOnAnalysis();
```

Ethical Considerations

While adaptive difficulty can enhance player engagement, it must be implemented ethically. Avoid frustrating players by making the game too difficult or patronizing them by making it too easy. Ensure transparency in how difficulty adjustments are made to maintain player trust.

Conclusion

Adaptive game difficulty is a valuable tool in SDL-based game development that can cater to a diverse player audience. By dynamically adjusting enemy behavior, spawning rates, puzzle complexity, rewards, and penalties, you can create a more enjoyable and engaging gaming experience for players of all skill levels. However, it's essential to strike the right balance and consider ethical implications to ensure that adaptive difficulty enhances, rather than detracts from, the player's overall experience.

Section 7.4: Data-Driven Game Design Decisions

Data-driven game design is a powerful approach that leverages player data and analytics to make informed decisions about game mechanics, content, and user experience. In this section, we will explore how SDL-based games can benefit from data-driven design, leading to more engaging and tailored gaming experiences.

The Role of Player Data

Player data encompasses a wide range of information, including player behavior, preferences, performance metrics, and feedback. By collecting and analyzing this data, game developers gain insights that can inform various aspects of game design and decision-making.

Leveraging Player Data

Here are some ways in which player data can be leveraged in SDL-based games:

1. Balancing Game Mechanics

Player data can reveal imbalances in game mechanics. For example, if a particular weapon or ability is consistently overpowered, data analysis can help adjust it for better gameplay balance.

```
// Balancing weapons based on player data
if (averageDamageDealt() > targetDamageThreshold) {
    nerfWeapon();
} else if (averageDamageDealt() < targetDamageThreshold) {
    buffWeapon();
}
```

2. Personalized Content

Player preferences and behavior data can be used to offer personalized content. This may include recommending specific levels, challenges, or in-game items based on a player's history.

```
// Personalized content recommendations
recommendedLevels = getRecommendedLevels(playerPreferences);
```

3. Dynamic Storytelling

Data-driven decisions can shape the narrative and storytelling in the game. Choices made by players can influence the direction of the story or the behavior of in-game characters.

```
// Dynamic storytelling based on player choices
if (playerChoice == Choice.Agree) {
    alterCharacterDialogue(PositiveResponse);
} else if (playerChoice == Choice.Disagree) {
    alterCharacterDialogue(NegativeResponse);
}
```

4. A/B Testing

A/B testing involves presenting different versions of a feature or level to different groups of players to see which one performs better. It allows developers to optimize game elements based on player preferences and engagement metrics.

```
// A/B testing for game features
if (isGroupA()) {
    implementFeatureVersionA();
} else if (isGroupB()) {
    implementFeatureVersionB();
}
```

5. Difficulty Adjustments

Player performance data can inform real-time adjustments to game difficulty. If players are finding a particular section too challenging, the game can adapt to make it more manageable.

```
// Difficulty adjustments based on player performance
if (playerPerformance == Performance.Poor) {
    decrease enemy difficulty();
}
```

Ethical Considerations

While data-driven game design offers numerous benefits, it also raises ethical concerns related to player privacy and consent. Developers must be transparent about data collection and ensure that player data is used responsibly and securely.

Conclusion

Data-driven game design empowers developers to create more engaging, balanced, and personalized experiences in SDL-based games. By collecting and analyzing player data, developers can make informed decisions about game mechanics, content recommendations, storytelling, A/B testing, and difficulty adjustments. However, it's essential to approach data collection and usage ethically and transparently, respecting player privacy and consent throughout the design process.

Section 7.5: Ethical Considerations in AI

Ethical considerations in AI for games are paramount, as AI-driven systems can have a profound impact on player experiences, behaviors, and perceptions. In this section, we'll delve into the ethical aspects that SDL-based game developers should be mindful of when incorporating AI.

Player Privacy and Data Protection

One crucial ethical concern is player privacy and data protection. AI systems often rely on player data, including in-game actions, preferences, and behaviors, to make decisions or recommendations. Developers must ensure that player data is collected and used responsibly, with clear consent and robust security measures in place.

```
// Implementing data protection measures
if (collectingPlayerData) {
    obtainPlayerConsent();
    secureDataStorage();
}
```

Fairness and Bias

AI algorithms can inadvertently introduce bias into games, affecting certain groups of players unfairly. Developers should strive to design AI systems that treat all players equally, regardless of gender, race, or other personal characteristics. Regular audits and testing can help identify and rectify bias in AI.

```
// Addressing bias in AI decision-making
if (aiDecision.containsBias()) {
    conduct bias audit();
    retrainAIModelToRemoveBias();
}
```

Transparency and Explainability

AI-driven game systems can sometimes make decisions that players find hard to understand. Developers should aim for transparency and explainability in AI behaviors, allowing players to comprehend why certain actions or recommendations are made.

```
// Ensuring AI transparency and explainability
if (aiBehavior.isNotTransparent()) {
    provide contextual explanations();
}
```

Player Consent and Control

Ethical AI should respect player agency and consent. Players should have control over the extent to which AI systems affect their gameplay, and they should be able to opt out or customize AI-driven features.

```
// Allowing player control over AI features
if (playerWantsToCustomizeAI) {
    provide AI customization options();
}
```

AI Behavior in Sensitive Areas

AI behaviors in SDL-based games should be particularly considerate in sensitive areas, such as violence, harassment, or sensitive themes. Developers should implement safeguards to prevent AI systems from engaging in harmful or offensive actions.

```
// Implementing safeguards in sensitive areas
if (aiBehavior.isPotentiallyHarmful()) {
    enforce content guidelines();
    monitor and address player reports();
}
```

Player Well-being and Mental Health

AI-driven features should not compromise player well-being or mental health. Developers should be cautious about using AI to drive addictive mechanics or behaviors that may negatively impact players' lives.

```
// Prioritizing player well-being in AI design
if (aiFeatureAffectsMentalHealth) {
    conduct impact assessment();
    consider alternatives or restrictions();
}
```

Continuous Ethical Review

Ethical considerations in AI for games are not a one-time task but an ongoing process. Developers should conduct continuous ethical reviews, engage with player feedback, and adapt AI systems as needed to align with evolving ethical standards.

```
// Conducting regular ethical reviews
if (ethicalStandardsEvolve) {
    update AI systems and policies();
}
```

Conclusion

Ethical considerations in AI for SDL-based games are fundamental to creating enjoyable, inclusive, and responsible gaming experiences. By prioritizing player privacy, fairness, transparency, player consent, and well-being, developers can harness the potential of AI while ensuring that its impact on players is positive and ethical. Continuous ethical review and a commitment to ethical standards are essential for AI-driven game development in the modern gaming landscape.

Chapter 8: VR and AR Game Development

Section 8.1: Basics of Virtual and Augmented Reality

Virtual Reality (VR) and Augmented Reality (AR) are cutting-edge technologies that have the potential to revolutionize the gaming industry. In this section, we'll explore the fundamentals of VR and AR game development, helping you understand the core concepts and considerations.

What is Virtual Reality (VR)?

Virtual Reality is a technology that immerses users in a computer-generated, three-dimensional environment. VR typically involves the use of a headset that covers the user's eyes and ears, providing an immersive experience where the user can interact with and navigate a virtual world.

Key Components of VR:
1. **Headset:** The VR headset is the primary hardware component. It contains displays for each eye, motion sensors, and often integrated headphones or audio systems.
2. **Motion Tracking:** VR systems use various sensors to track the user's head movements and, in some cases, hand movements with motion controllers.
3. **3D Environment:** VR content is created as a 3D digital environment that responds to the user's movements and interactions.

What is Augmented Reality (AR)?

Augmented Reality overlays digital content onto the real-world environment. Unlike VR, AR doesn't replace the real world but enhances it by adding digital elements that users can interact with.

Key Components of AR:
1. **Mobile Devices:** AR experiences are often delivered through smartphones or tablets equipped with cameras and sensors.
2. **Marker or Markerless Tracking:** AR systems use markers (visual cues) or markerless tracking (computer vision) to identify and augment the real-world environment.
3. **Digital Overlays:** AR apps superimpose digital objects, information, or animations onto the user's view of the real world.

Considerations for VR and AR Game Development

Developing games for VR and AR presents unique challenges and opportunities:

User Experience (UX):
- In VR, prioritize comfort and minimize motion sickness by optimizing frame rates and minimizing latency.

Interaction:
- Design intuitive ways for users to interact with the virtual or augmented world, considering gestures, controllers, or even voice commands.

Realism and Immersion:
- Achieving a high level of realism and immersion is a key goal for VR game development. Focus on lifelike graphics, spatial audio, and responsive environments.

Performance Optimization:
- VR and AR experiences demand high-performance hardware. Optimize your game to run smoothly on the target devices.

Testing and Feedback:
- Extensive testing is crucial, as VR and AR experiences can be intense. Gather user feedback and make iterative improvements.

Legal and Ethical Considerations:
- Be aware of legal and ethical issues, such as privacy concerns with AR apps or content restrictions in VR environments.

Conclusion

Understanding the basics of Virtual Reality (VR) and Augmented Reality (AR) is the first step in harnessing these technologies for game development. VR offers complete immersion in a virtual world, while AR enhances the real world with digital elements. Both have the potential to create unique and engaging gaming experiences, but they come with their own set of challenges and considerations that developers must address to deliver compelling and enjoyable games in these emerging mediums.

Section 8.2: Implementing VR Support in SDL

Implementing Virtual Reality (VR) support in SDL (Simple DirectMedia Layer) is an exciting endeavor that enables developers to create immersive VR experiences across various platforms. SDL provides a powerful foundation for building VR applications, offering cross-platform compatibility and access to essential VR features. In this section, we'll explore the process of integrating VR support into SDL-based games and applications.

Choosing a VR SDK

Before diving into VR development with SDL, you need to choose a VR software development kit (SDK) that suits your project's requirements. Some popular VR SDKs include:

- **OpenVR (SteamVR):** Supported by Valve, OpenVR is compatible with a wide range of VR headsets, including those from HTC, Oculus, and Windows Mixed Reality.
- **Oculus SDK:** If you're targeting Oculus VR devices, such as the Oculus Rift or Oculus Quest, the Oculus SDK provides comprehensive support and features.
- **Google VR SDK:** For Android-based VR platforms like Google Cardboard and Daydream, you can use the Google VR SDK.
- **Windows Mixed Reality SDK:** If you're focusing on Windows-based VR headsets, the Windows Mixed Reality SDK is a suitable choice.

SDL Initialization for VR

To begin implementing VR support in SDL, you'll first need to initialize SDL and create a VR context. Here's a simplified example of SDL initialization for VR:

```
#include <SDL.h>

// Initialize SDL
if (SDL_Init(SDL_INIT_VIDEO | SDL_INIT_TIMER) < 0) {
    // Handle initialization error
    return -1;
}

// Create an SDL window
SDL_Window* window = SDL_CreateWindow("VR Game", SDL_WINDOWPOS_CENTERED, SDL_WINDOWPOS_CENTERED, 1920, 1080, SDL_WINDOW_SHOWN);

// Initialize the chosen VR SDK (e.g., OpenVR or Oculus)
if (SDL_VRInit(SDL_VR_OPENVR) < 0) {
    // Handle VR initialization error
    return -1;
}

// Create a VR context
SDL_VRContext vrContext = SDL_VRCreateContext(window);
if (!vrContext) {
    // Handle VR context creation error
    return -1;
}

// Main game loop
while (!quit) {
```

```
    // Handle input, rendering, and interactions
}

// Clean up and shutdown SDL and VR resources
SDL_VRDestroyContext(vrContext);
SDL_VRShutdown();
SDL_DestroyWindow(window);
SDL_Quit();
```

This code snippet initializes SDL, creates an SDL window, and initializes the chosen VR SDK. It then creates a VR context using the SDL_VRCreateContext function.

Rendering for VR

VR rendering involves rendering separate views for each eye to create a stereoscopic 3D effect. SDL simplifies this process by providing functions to retrieve left and right eye render textures. Here's a basic rendering loop for VR:

```
while (!quit) {
    // Poll for events and update game logic

    // Render for each eye
    for (int eye = 0; eye < 2; ++eye) {
        // Set the render target to the left or right eye
        SDL_VRSetRenderTarget(vrContext, eye);

        // Clear the render target and render the scene
        SDL_RenderClear(renderer);
        // Render your 3D scene here

        // Present the rendered frame to the VR headset
        SDL_VRPresent(vrContext, eye);
    }
}
```

This code loop renders the scene separately for the left and right eyes, setting the render target accordingly and presenting the frame to the VR headset.

Input and Interaction

VR applications often rely on motion controllers or other input devices for interaction. SDL provides support for handling input from VR controllers. You can use SDL events to detect controller input and update your game accordingly.

Conclusion

Integrating VR support into SDL opens up exciting possibilities for immersive gaming experiences. By choosing a suitable VR SDK, initializing SDL for VR, handling rendering, and incorporating input and interaction, you can create engaging VR applications and games that cater to a growing audience of VR enthusiasts.

Section 8.3: Designing for VR: Best Practices

Designing virtual reality (VR) experiences requires a unique approach compared to traditional 2D games and applications. To create a compelling VR experience, developers must consider various factors, including user comfort, performance optimization, and immersive design. In this section, we'll explore best practices for designing VR applications within the SDL (Simple DirectMedia Layer) framework.

1. User Comfort and Motion Sickness

Motion sickness is a common concern in VR experiences. To minimize discomfort for users, consider the following tips:

- Implement a fixed, stable horizon to reduce motion sickness.
- Use smooth and gradual movements instead of abrupt changes.
- Provide options for adjusting movement settings, such as teleportation or comfort mode.

2. Frame Rate and Performance

Maintaining a high and consistent frame rate is crucial for VR. Aim for a frame rate of at least 90 frames per second (FPS) to ensure a smooth and comfortable experience. To achieve this:

- Optimize your rendering pipeline and assets to meet performance targets.
- Implement efficient culling and rendering techniques.
- Monitor and profile your application to identify performance bottlenecks.

3. VR Input Interaction

VR relies on input devices such as motion controllers. Design intuitive and responsive interactions:

- Map real-world gestures and movements to in-game actions.
- Provide visual and auditory feedback for user actions.
- Consider hand presence and object manipulation for a more immersive experience.

4. Comfort Options

Offer comfort options to accommodate users with varying tolerance levels:

- Include options for adjusting field of view (FOV) and movement speed.
- Allow users to toggle between teleportation and free movement.
- Implement a comfort vignette to reduce motion sickness.

5. User Interface (UI) in VR

Designing UI for VR requires careful thought:

- Create UI elements that are easy to read and interact with in 3D space.
- Implement UI that is accessible from various angles and positions.
- Avoid clutter and excessive UI elements to maintain immersion.

6. Testing and Feedback

Regular testing with VR hardware is essential:

- Test your VR application on different VR headsets and devices.
- Gather feedback from users to identify pain points and areas for improvement.
- Iterate on your design based on user feedback and testing results.

7. Accessibility and Inclusivity

Consider accessibility features to ensure a broader user base:

- Implement features like subtitles and adjustable text size for users with disabilities.
- Design interactions that can be comfortably used by individuals with varying physical abilities.

8. Performance Profiling

Use profiling tools to identify performance issues:

- Monitor GPU and CPU usage to optimize rendering.
- Use SDL's built-in tools for performance analysis and debugging.

9. User Education

Provide a brief tutorial or introduction to help users acclimate to VR:

- Teach users how to use controllers and interact with the environment.
- Explain comfort settings and options for customization.

10. User Safety

Ensure that users are aware of their physical surroundings:

- Implement a virtual boundary system to prevent users from walking into real-world obstacles.
- Include safety warnings and guidelines for proper VR usage.

By following these best practices, developers can create VR applications that offer immersive and comfortable experiences while leveraging the capabilities of the SDL framework. Designing for VR requires attention to detail, user feedback, and a commitment to optimizing performance to provide users with a memorable and enjoyable VR journey.

Section 8.4: AR Gaming Experiences with SDL

Augmented Reality (AR) gaming merges digital content with the real world, offering exciting and interactive experiences. SDL (Simple DirectMedia Layer) can be a valuable tool for developing AR games. In this section, we will explore the key considerations and practices for creating compelling AR gaming experiences using SDL.

1. Marker-Based AR

One common approach to AR gaming is marker-based AR, where the camera identifies physical markers to overlay digital content. To implement this in SDL:

- Use computer vision libraries like OpenCV to detect and track markers.
- Superimpose game elements on recognized markers using SDL's rendering capabilities.
- Ensure marker recognition is robust and responsive for a seamless experience.

2. Mobile Integration

AR gaming often targets mobile devices with built-in cameras. To make your AR game mobile-friendly:

- Utilize SDL's cross-platform capabilities to develop for various mobile platforms.
- Optimize performance for mobile hardware constraints while maintaining visual quality.
- Consider battery usage and resource management to prolong gameplay on mobile devices.

3. Interactive Gameplay

AR games thrive on interaction between the virtual and real worlds. Implement engaging gameplay elements:

- Design challenges that require players to physically move or interact with objects in the real environment.
- Use SDL's input handling to capture user interactions and trigger in-game events.
- Incorporate gesture recognition and touch input for intuitive controls.

4. Environmental Awareness

AR games need to be aware of the physical environment to create immersive experiences:

- Use sensors like GPS and accelerometers to gather data about the user's location and movement.

- Adapt the game world based on real-world factors, such as location-based events or environmental conditions.
- Ensure that virtual objects interact convincingly with physical obstacles in the user's surroundings.

5. Visual Feedback

Visual feedback is crucial for players to understand the AR game's interactions:

- Provide clear and visually appealing overlays on the camera feed.
- Use SDL's rendering capabilities to create realistic and visually coherent AR elements.
- Ensure that virtual objects cast shadows and react to changes in lighting conditions.

6. Multiplayer AR

Consider adding multiplayer functionality to AR games for collaborative or competitive experiences:

- Implement networked gameplay using SDL's networking features.
- Synchronize the AR environment across multiple players for shared experiences.
- Design game modes that encourage social interaction and cooperation.

7. Calibration and Initialization

Calibration is essential for accurate AR experiences:

- Include calibration steps to ensure the camera's perspective aligns correctly with the virtual elements.
- Guide users through the calibration process during the initial setup of the AR game.
- Use SDL's UI capabilities to create user-friendly calibration interfaces.

8. Testing and Optimization

Thorough testing and optimization are critical for AR games:

- Test your AR game in various real-world environments to ensure marker recognition and gameplay are consistent.
- Profile and optimize performance to maintain a high frame rate and responsiveness.
- Gather user feedback to identify issues and areas for improvement.

9. Safety and User Awareness

AR games should prioritize user safety and awareness:

- Implement warnings or notifications to prevent users from engaging in risky behavior while playing.
- Encourage users to be mindful of their surroundings and physical limitations.

- Include safety features, such as a pause button, to help users disengage from the AR experience when needed.

Developing AR gaming experiences with SDL offers exciting possibilities for merging the digital and physical worlds. By following these best practices, developers can create immersive and enjoyable AR games that captivate players and leverage SDL's capabilities for cross-platform development.

Section 8.5: Overcoming Challenges in VR/AR Development

Developing Virtual Reality (VR) and Augmented Reality (AR) experiences can be incredibly rewarding, but it comes with its unique set of challenges. In this section, we will discuss some of the common challenges in VR/AR development and strategies to overcome them.

1. Hardware Limitations

VR and AR experiences heavily rely on hardware capabilities. Addressing hardware limitations is crucial:

- Optimize graphics and performance to ensure smooth gameplay on a range of VR/AR devices.
- Consider the minimum system requirements when designing and testing your VR/AR application.
- Continuously adapt to new hardware innovations and updates to provide the best user experience.

2. Motion Sickness

Motion sickness is a common issue in VR experiences due to the discrepancy between visual perception and physical movement:

- Implement techniques like comfort mode, teleportation, or reduced field of view to minimize motion sickness.
- Provide customizable comfort settings, allowing users to adjust their experience to their comfort level.
- Conduct user testing and gather feedback to identify and address motion sickness issues.

3. User Interface (UI) Design

Designing UI for VR/AR can be challenging due to the immersive nature of the experiences:

- Create intuitive and accessible UI elements that are easy to interact with in a 3D space.

- Experiment with different UI placement and navigation methods to find the most user-friendly approach.
- Consider the impact of UI elements on immersion and avoid cluttering the user's view.

4. Content Creation

Creating high-quality VR/AR content demands specialized skills and tools:

- Invest in 3D modeling, animation, and texturing software to create immersive environments and objects.
- Collaborate with experienced artists and 3D designers to produce visually appealing content.
- Optimize assets for real-time rendering to ensure optimal performance.

5. User Interaction

User interaction is a fundamental aspect of VR/AR experiences:

- Implement intuitive and natural interaction methods, such as hand tracking or gesture recognition.
- Provide clear feedback to users when they interact with objects or perform actions in the virtual environment.
- Balance realism and user-friendliness to create engaging interactions.

6. Content Discovery and Distribution

Getting your VR/AR app noticed and distributed can be challenging:

- Utilize app stores and platforms dedicated to VR/AR content for distribution.
- Invest in marketing and promotion to increase visibility.
- Consider partnerships with hardware manufacturers or platforms to reach a broader audience.

7. Testing and QA

Thorough testing is essential to identify and address issues in VR/AR experiences:

- Test your VR/AR app on a variety of devices to ensure compatibility and performance.
- Conduct user testing to gather feedback and make improvements based on user preferences.
- Continuously update and patch your app to address bugs and enhance the user experience.

8. Privacy and Data Security

VR/AR apps may collect user data, posing privacy and security concerns:

- Clearly communicate your data collection and usage policies to users.
- Implement robust security measures to protect user data from breaches or unauthorized access.
- Comply with relevant privacy regulations and seek legal advice if necessary.

9. Content Regulations

Different regions may have varying regulations regarding VR/AR content:

- Familiarize yourself with content regulations in your target markets to avoid legal issues.
- Ensure that your content is appropriate for all audiences and adheres to platform guidelines.
- Be prepared to make content adjustments if necessary to comply with regulations.

Overcoming these challenges in VR/AR development requires a combination of technical expertise, creative solutions, user-centric design, and adaptability. By addressing these issues proactively, developers can create immersive and enjoyable VR/AR experiences that captivate users and stand out in the ever-evolving landscape of extended reality technology.

Chapter 9: Custom Tools and Editors

Section 9.1: Building Level Editors with SDL

Creating custom tools and editors is a valuable aspect of game development that allows designers and developers to streamline their workflow, improve efficiency, and enhance the overall game creation process. In this section, we will focus on building level editors using the SDL (Simple DirectMedia Layer) library.

Why Build a Custom Level Editor?

Building a custom level editor offers several advantages:

1. **Tailored to Your Game**: Custom level editors can be designed to suit the specific needs and features of your game, making it easier to create complex game worlds.
2. **Improved Productivity**: Level editors simplify the content creation process, reducing the time required to design and test levels.
3. **Visual Representation**: They provide a visual representation of game levels, allowing designers to see the results of their work in real-time.
4. **User-Friendly**: Custom editors can offer user-friendly interfaces, making it accessible to designers and artists without extensive programming knowledge.
5. **Integration**: Level editors can be tightly integrated with the game engine, enabling seamless asset importing and exporting.

Building a Basic Level Editor with SDL

Let's outline the key steps to build a basic level editor using SDL:

1. Setting Up the SDL Environment

Begin by setting up the SDL environment in your project. Ensure you have SDL and its libraries properly installed.

2. Creating the Editor Interface

Design a graphical user interface (GUI) for your level editor. SDL provides functions for creating windows, buttons, text fields, and other UI elements.

```
// Example SDL window creation
SDL_Window* window = SDL_CreateWindow("Level Editor", SDL_WINDOWPOS_CENTERED, SDL_WINDOWPOS_CENTERED, 800, 600, SDL_WINDOW_SHOWN);
SDL_Renderer* renderer = SDL_CreateRenderer(window, -1, SDL_RENDERER_ACCELERATED);
```

3. Handling User Input

Implement event handling to capture user input, including mouse clicks, keyboard input, and UI interactions.

```c
// Example event handling loop
SDL_Event event;
while (SDL_PollEvent(&event)) {
    switch (event.type) {
        case SDL_QUIT:
            // Handle window close event
            break;
        case SDL_MOUSEBUTTONDOWN:
            // Handle mouse click
            break;
        // Add more event handling as needed
    }
}
```

4. Creating a Grid System

To create game levels, implement a grid system that represents the level's layout. Define data structures to store information about tiles, objects, and other elements.

```c
// Example grid representation
int levelGrid[GRID_WIDTH][GRID_HEIGHT];
```

5. Rendering the Level

Use SDL's rendering capabilities to display the level grid and its contents on the screen.

```c
// Example rendering loop
for (int x = 0; x < GRID_WIDTH; x++) {
    for (int y = 0; y < GRID_HEIGHT; y++) {
        // Render tiles and objects based on grid data
    }
}
```

6. Saving and Loading Levels

Implement functionality to save and load levels in a custom file format. This allows designers to edit levels outside of the game.

7. Integration with Game Engine

Integrate the custom level editor with your game engine, ensuring that it can import and use the levels created in the editor.

Building a level editor with SDL is just the beginning. You can enhance it by adding features like object placement, asset management, and advanced visual editing tools. Custom tools and editors empower your development team to create intricate and captivating game worlds efficiently.

Section 9.2: Scripting Engines and Modding Support

In the world of game development, scripting engines and modding support are powerful tools that allow both developers and players to extend and customize the gameplay experience. In this section, we will explore the integration of scripting engines and modding support using SDL (Simple DirectMedia Layer).

The Importance of Scripting Engines

Scripting engines, often powered by scripting languages like Lua, Python, or JavaScript, offer the following benefits:

1. **Dynamic Behavior**: They enable developers to define and modify game behavior without recompiling the entire codebase. This flexibility is especially valuable for rapidly iterating on gameplay mechanics.

2. **Modding Support**: Players and community members can use scripting to create mods and custom content, enhancing the longevity and appeal of a game.

3. **Separation of Logic**: Scripting allows you to separate game logic from the core engine, making it easier to update or patch the game without affecting gameplay scripts.

Integrating Scripting Engines with SDL

To integrate a scripting engine into your SDL-based game, follow these steps:

1. Choose a Scripting Language

Select a scripting language that suits your needs. Lua is a popular choice due to its lightweight and embeddable nature. You can find SDL bindings or libraries that make integrating Lua with SDL relatively straightforward.

2. Bind SDL Functions

Create bindings or wrappers that expose SDL functions to your chosen scripting language. This allows scripts to interact with SDL's functionality.

```lua
-- Example Lua code binding SDL functions
local SDL = require("SDL")

function init()
    SDL.init(SDL.INIT_EVERYTHING)
    -- Initialize SDL subsystems
end

function loadTexture(filename)
```

```
        local texture = SDL.loadTexture(renderer, filename)
        return texture
end
```

3. Execute Scripts

Load and execute scripts at runtime. Scripts can define game rules, events, and behaviors.

```
-- Example Lua script defining player movement
function update()
    if keyPressed(SDL.K_RIGHT) then
        player.x = player.x + 1
    end
    -- Handle other inputs and game logic
end
```

4. Modding Support

To support modding, provide a way for players to load custom scripts or content. You can create a directory where mods can be placed, and your game engine can load and execute these scripts.

5. Error Handling

Implement robust error handling in your scripting engine integration. This ensures that errors in scripts do not crash the game and provides meaningful feedback to modders.

Benefits of Modding Support

Modding support can significantly enhance your game's lifespan and player engagement:

1. **Community Engagement**: It fosters a community around your game, where players share and create content.
2. **Extended Gameplay**: Mods can introduce new levels, characters, and gameplay mechanics, extending the game's replayability.
3. **Creativity and Innovation**: Modders often come up with unique ideas and innovations that can inspire future game updates or sequels.
4. **Marketplace**: Some games offer modders the opportunity to monetize their creations, providing additional income sources.

Incorporating scripting engines and modding support into your SDL-based game can elevate it to new heights, allowing players to personalize their experiences and breathe fresh life into your title long after its initial release.

Section 9.3: Custom UI Tools for Game Development

In this section, we'll delve into the creation of custom User Interface (UI) tools for game development using the SDL (Simple DirectMedia Layer) framework. UI tools play a crucial role in game development, as they provide an interface for designers and developers to interact with and manipulate game assets, levels, and configurations.

The Importance of Custom UI Tools

Custom UI tools offer several advantages in the game development process:

1. **Efficiency**: Tailored UI tools streamline tasks like level design, asset management, and configuration editing, saving time and reducing errors.
2. **Control**: Developers can create UIs that precisely match the game's requirements, allowing for fine-grained control over various aspects.
3. **Integration**: Custom UI tools can seamlessly integrate with your game engine, providing a cohesive development environment.
4. **Iterative Design**: Designers and artists can quickly iterate on game assets and levels without needing extensive technical knowledge.

Building Custom UI Tools with SDL

Here are the key steps to building custom UI tools for your SDL-based game development pipeline:

1. Choose a UI Library

Select a UI library or framework that complements SDL. Popular options include Dear ImGui, Nuklear, or creating a custom UI system from scratch.

2. UI Layout and Widgets

Design the layout of your UI tool and choose appropriate widgets (buttons, sliders, text inputs, etc.) to provide the necessary functionality.

```cpp
// Example using Dear ImGui to create a simple UI window
#include <SDL.h>
#include <imgui.h>
#include <imgui_impl_sdl.h>

void RenderUI(SDL_Window* window) {
    ImGui_ImplSDL2_NewFrame(window);

    // Create UI elements here
    ImGui::Text("Welcome to My Game's UI Tool!");
    if (ImGui::Button("Save Level")) {
        // Handle save logic
    }
```

```cpp
    // Render and display UI
    ImGui::Render();
    ImGui_ImplSDL2_RenderDrawData(ImGui::GetDrawData());
}
```

3. Interactivity

Implement functionality within your UI tool. This may include asset loading, level editing, or game configuration changes. Ensure that user interactions are intuitive and error-resistant.

4. Integration with SDL

Integrate your custom UI tool with your SDL-based game engine. This typically involves rendering the UI alongside the game's graphics and responding to user input.

```cpp
// Example integration within the game loop
while (gameIsRunning) {
    // Game logic

    // Render game graphics

    // Render custom UI
    RenderUI(window);

    // Handle user input
    SDL_Event event;
    while (SDL_PollEvent(&event)) {
        // Handle UI input events
        ImGui_ImplSDL2_ProcessEvent(&event);

        // Handle game input events
    }
}
```

5. Debugging and Testing

Thoroughly test your custom UI tools to ensure they work as expected. Debug any issues that may arise during the development process.

Benefits of Custom UI Tools

Custom UI tools can greatly enhance the efficiency and productivity of your game development team. Some advantages include:

1. **Streamlined Workflow**: Developers and designers can perform tasks more efficiently, reducing development time.
2. **Consistency**: Custom UI tools ensure that all team members use the same interface, maintaining consistency in asset creation and level design.

3. **Reduced Learning Curve**: Tailored UIs are often more intuitive and user-friendly, requiring less training for team members.
4. **Enhanced Creativity**: A well-designed UI tool empowers artists and designers to unleash their creativity without technical constraints.

By investing in custom UI tools, you can create a more streamlined and productive game development process, ultimately leading to a better final product.

Section 9.4: Automating Game Asset Creation

Automating game asset creation is a crucial aspect of modern game development. It involves using scripts, tools, or software to generate assets such as textures, models, animations, and sounds efficiently. Automation not only saves time but also ensures consistency and reduces the likelihood of human errors in asset creation.

The Importance of Automation

Game development often requires a vast number of assets, especially in larger projects or those with complex graphics and audio requirements. Automating asset creation offers several benefits:

1. **Time Efficiency**: Repetitive tasks like resizing images, batch processing, or converting file formats can be automated, saving developers and artists significant time.
2. **Consistency**: Automation ensures that assets adhere to predefined standards, maintaining a consistent visual and auditory style throughout the game.
3. **Reduced Errors**: Human errors in asset creation, such as incorrect file formats or dimensions, are minimized when using automation scripts or tools.
4. **Scalability**: As the project grows, automation becomes even more valuable, allowing teams to handle an increasing number of assets efficiently.

Types of Asset Automation

Here are some common types of asset automation used in game development:

1. Texture and Image Processing

Tools like Photoshop scripts, ImageMagick, or custom scripts can automate tasks like resizing, cropping, applying filters, and converting image formats. This is especially useful for generating multiple versions of textures for different screen resolutions.

```
# Example Python script using PIL (Python Imaging Library) to resize images
from PIL import Image
```

```python
def resize_images(input_folder, output_folder, target_size):
    for filename in os.listdir(input_folder):
        if filename.endswith(".png"):
            img = Image.open(os.path.join(input_folder, filename))
            img = img.resize(target_size)
            img.save(os.path.join(output_folder, filename))
```

2. Procedural Content Generation

Procedural content generation (PCG) techniques automate the creation of game content, such as levels, maps, terrain, and even textures. PCG algorithms generate content algorithmically based on predefined rules and parameters.

3. Sound Generation

Sound generation tools and libraries, like procedural audio generators or MIDI-based music generation, can automate the creation of sound effects and music tracks.

4. Model and Animation Generation

Some game engines support procedural generation of 3D models and animations. Additionally, tools like Blender can be scripted to automate the creation of models and animations.

```python
# Example Blender script to automate 3D model generation
import bpy

# Create a new cube
bpy.ops.mesh.primitive_cube_add(size=2, enter_editmode=False, align='WORLD', location=(0, 0, 0))

# Export the model to a file
bpy.ops.export_scene.obj(filepath="/path/to/output/model.obj", use_selection=True)
```

5. Build Pipelines

Build pipelines integrate various automation tools and scripts to compile, package, and optimize assets for the game. This ensures that assets are ready for use in the game engine.

Custom Automation Scripts

Many game development teams create custom automation scripts or tools tailored to their project's specific needs. These scripts can range from simple batch processing to complex procedural generation algorithms. Custom scripts often provide the flexibility required for unique game development challenges.

By incorporating automation into your game development workflow, you can streamline asset creation, reduce manual errors, and focus more on the creative aspects of game design and development.

Section 9.5: Integrating with External Software Tools

Integrating external software tools into your game development pipeline can significantly enhance productivity, streamline processes, and expand capabilities. These tools can range from third-party libraries and game engines to specialized software for specific tasks. In this section, we'll explore the importance of integrating external tools and how to do it effectively.

The Value of External Tools Integration

1. ***Specialized Functionality***: *External tools often offer specialized functionality that can accelerate development in specific areas. For example, 3D modeling software like Blender excels in creating complex 3D assets.*

2. ***Efficiency***: *Leveraging established tools can save time and effort. Game engines like Unity or Unreal Engine provide built-in features for physics simulation, rendering, and scripting, reducing the need to reinvent the wheel.*

3. ***Community and Support***: *Widely-used tools have active communities and support ecosystems. This means access to tutorials, forums, and resources that can help solve problems and enhance skills.*

4. ***Cross-Platform Compatibility***: *Some tools are designed to work seamlessly across multiple platforms, ensuring your game remains accessible to a broader audience.*

Common Types of External Tools

Here are some common types of external tools used in game development:

1. **Game Engines**: Game engines like Unity, Unreal Engine, Godot, and CryEngine provide comprehensive environments for building, testing, and deploying games. They offer features like rendering, physics simulation, audio, and scripting.

2. **3D Modeling and Animation Software**: Tools like Blender, Maya, 3ds Max, and ZBrush are essential for creating 3D assets, characters, animations, and environments.

3. **Audio Editing Software**: Sound design and music composition often require specialized software such as Audacity, Adobe Audition, or Pro Tools.

4. **Version Control Systems**: Tools like Git, Mercurial, and Subversion are crucial for tracking changes in source code and collaborative development.

5. **IDEs (Integrated Development Environments)**: IDEs like Visual Studio, JetBrains Rider, and Eclipse offer powerful code editing and debugging capabilities.

6. **Asset Management Systems**: Asset management tools like Perforce, SVN, or specialized asset management solutions help teams organize and version control assets efficiently.

Integration Techniques

Integrating external tools into your game development workflow involves several techniques:

1. **File Formats and Standards**: Ensure compatibility by using industry-standard file formats (e.g., FBX for 3D models) that can be imported/exported by various tools.

2. **APIs and SDKs**: Some tools offer APIs or software development kits (SDKs) that allow you to extend their functionality or integrate them with your game engine.

3. **Plugins and Extensions**: Many software tools support plugins and extensions that can be developed to enhance their capabilities or integrate with other software.

4. **Scripting and Automation**: Write scripts or automation routines to bridge the gap between different tools. For example, you can write scripts to automate asset import/export or data synchronization.

5. **Collaborative Platforms**: Utilize collaborative platforms like GitHub, GitLab, or Bitbucket to manage source code and collaborate with team members seamlessly.

Here's an example of integrating Git version control into a Unity project:

```
# Initialize a Git repository in your Unity project folder
git init

# Add project files to Git
git add .

# Commit changes
```

```
git commit -m "Initial commit"

# Connect the repository to a remote server (e.g., GitHub)
git remote add origin https://github.com/your-username/your-repo.git

# Push changes to the remote repository
git push -u origin master
```

Effective integration of external tools is essential for efficient game development. It allows teams to leverage the strengths of various software solutions, enabling them to create high-quality games more efficiently and collaboratively.

Chapter 10: Advanced Shader Programming

Section 10.1: Writing Custom Shaders

In the world of game development, shaders play a crucial role in defining how objects and scenes are rendered. While modern game engines provide a range of pre-built shaders, there are scenarios where you need to write custom shaders to achieve specific visual effects or optimize performance. In this section, we will dive into the art of writing custom shaders for your games.

Understanding Shaders

Shaders are small programs that run on the GPU (Graphics Processing Unit) and are responsible for the final appearance of rendered objects. They control various aspects of rendering, such as colors, lighting, shadows, and special effects. There are two main types of shaders:

1. **Vertex Shaders**: These operate on each vertex of a 3D model, transforming its position and other attributes.
2. **Fragment Shaders (Pixel Shaders)**: These determine the final color of each pixel on the screen.

Shader Languages

Shaders are typically written in specialized shader languages, such as:

- **HLSL (High-Level Shading Language)**: Used in DirectX-based platforms, including Windows and Xbox.
- **GLSL (OpenGL Shading Language)**: Used in OpenGL-based platforms, including many desktop and mobile systems.
- **ShaderLab**: A language used in Unity for defining shaders, which can be compiled into HLSL or GLSL.

Writing a Basic Shader

Let's start with a simple example of a custom shader written in GLSL, which creates a basic color effect. This shader will render an object with a solid color, ignoring lighting and textures.

```glsl
// Vertex Shader
#version 330 core
layout(location = 0) in vec3 inPosition;
void main()
{
    gl_Position = vec4(inPosition, 1.0);
}
```

```
// Fragment Shader
#version 330 core
out vec4 FragColor;
void main()
{
    FragColor = vec4(0.0, 0.5, 1.0, 1.0); // RGBA color (blue)
}
```

This shader consists of two parts: the vertex shader and the fragment shader. The vertex shader processes the position of each vertex, while the fragment shader determines the final color. In this example, we set the color to solid blue.

Shader Variables and Inputs

Custom shaders can also take inputs and variables, allowing you to create more dynamic effects. For example, you can pass values for textures, colors, or lighting parameters to your shader.

Shader Complexity

As you explore shader programming further, you'll encounter more complex shaders that simulate realistic lighting, shadows, reflections, and other visual effects. Writing custom shaders requires a deep understanding of graphics programming, but it provides the flexibility to achieve your desired visual style and optimize performance.

Shader Debugging

Debugging shaders can be challenging, but some tools and techniques, such as shader debugging tools provided by game engines and using print statements, can help identify and fix issues in your shader code.

In summary, writing custom shaders is a powerful skill that allows game developers to create unique visual effects and optimize rendering performance. While it can be complex, mastering shader programming opens up a world of creative possibilities in game development.

Section 10.2: Shader-Based Visual Effects

In the realm of computer graphics and game development, shaders are indispensable tools for creating stunning visual effects. In this section, we will delve into the world of shader-based visual effects, exploring how shaders can be used to elevate the visual quality of your games.

Understanding Shader-Based Visual Effects

Shader-based visual effects encompass a wide array of techniques that manipulate the appearance of objects and scenes in a game. These effects can range from simple color adjustments to complex simulations of natural phenomena. Here are some common shader-based visual effects:

1. **Bloom**: Bloom is an effect that simulates the way light interacts with camera lenses, creating a soft and glowing appearance for bright objects.
2. **Blur**: Blur shaders can be used for various purposes, such as simulating motion blur, depth of field, or creating artistic effects.
3. **Water Shaders**: Water shaders simulate the behavior of water surfaces, including reflections, refractions, and ripples.
4. **Particle Effects**: Shaders are used extensively for rendering particle systems, including effects like fire, smoke, sparks, and more.
5. **Post-Processing Effects**: Post-processing shaders are applied to the entire screen after the scene is rendered, allowing for effects like color grading, vignetting, and distortion.

Implementing Shader-Based Visual Effects

Implementing shader-based visual effects involves writing custom shaders or leveraging pre-built shader libraries. Here's a high-level overview of the process:

1. **Shader Development**: You can either write your own shaders or use existing shader libraries and tools. Popular game engines like Unity and Unreal Engine provide shader editors for visual shader development.
2. **Shader Integration**: Integrate the shaders into your game engine or framework. This typically involves creating materials or shaders and assigning them to objects or scenes.
3. **Parameter Tuning**: Many shader-based effects have parameters that can be adjusted to achieve the desired look. These parameters might control intensity, scale, color, or other aspects of the effect.
4. **Performance Considerations**: Shader-based effects can be computationally intensive. Ensure that your shaders are optimized to run efficiently on various hardware.

Example: Bloom Effect

Let's take a closer look at a simple example: a bloom effect shader. This shader enhances the glow of bright objects in the scene, giving them a more pronounced appearance.

```glsl
// Bloom Shader
#version 330 core

// Input from the previous rendering pass (scene)
in vec2 TexCoords;
uniform sampler2D sceneTexture;

out vec4 FragColor;

void main()
{
    vec3 hdrColor = texture(sceneTexture, TexCoords).rgb;
    // Apply bloom threshold here if needed

    // Apply bloom effect
    vec3 bloomColor = hdrColor * 1.2; // Adjust intensity as needed

    FragColor = vec4(bloomColor, 1.0);
}
```

In this example, we sample the previously rendered scene and apply a simple bloom effect by increasing the intensity of the bright pixels. The threshold for what is considered "bright" can be adjusted to control the effect's strength.

Shader-Based Visual Effects in Game Development

Shader-based visual effects are essential for creating immersive and visually appealing games. Whether you're aiming for realistic graphics or a unique artistic style, mastering the art of shaders opens up endless possibilities for elevating the visual quality of your games. As you explore shader-based effects, you'll discover the creative potential they offer and their impact on the player's overall experience.

Section 10.3: Optimizing Shader Performance

While shaders are powerful tools for achieving stunning visual effects in games, they can also be resource-intensive and impact your game's performance. In this section, we will explore techniques for optimizing shader performance, ensuring that your game runs smoothly even with complex visual effects.

Profiling and Identifying Bottlenecks

Before diving into shader optimization, it's crucial to identify performance bottlenecks in your game. Profiling tools, such as those provided by game engines or third-party profilers, can help you pinpoint which shaders or rendering operations are consuming the most resources. Common bottlenecks related to shaders include:

1. **Shader Complexity**: Highly complex shaders with numerous instructions can lead to performance issues. Identify shaders that are particularly demanding.
2. **Shader Switching**: Frequent shader switching during rendering can incur overhead. Minimize unnecessary shader changes.
3. **Texture Sampling**: Excessive texture sampling, especially from large textures, can be a performance drain. Optimize texture usage.

Reduce Shader Instructions

One effective way to optimize shader performance is to reduce the number of shader instructions. This can be achieved through the following techniques:

1. **Simplify Calculations**: Review your shader code and simplify calculations wherever possible. Eliminate redundant operations and use built-in functions when available.
2. **Loop Unrolling**: Avoid loops in shaders, especially in fragment shaders. Manually unroll loops if necessary to reduce iteration overhead.
3. **Branching**: Minimize branching in shaders, as conditional branches can hinder parallelism. Use conditional statements sparingly and prefer arithmetic operations when feasible.

Use Shader LOD (Level of Detail)

Shader LOD techniques involve adjusting the level of detail of shaders based on the distance from the camera or the size of objects on the screen. This helps reduce the computational load for distant or small objects. LOD can be implemented in various ways:

1. **Mipmapping**: Use texture mipmaps to automatically select lower-resolution textures for distant objects, reducing texture sampling costs.
2. **Vertex Shader LOD**: Adjust vertex shader complexity based on distance. Simplify the geometry for distant objects.
3. **Pixel Shader LOD**: Use fewer shader instructions or simplified shaders for distant or small objects.

Batch Rendering

Batching is a technique that involves rendering multiple objects with the same shader in a single draw call. This reduces the overhead associated with changing shaders between objects. To implement batching:

1. **Group Objects**: Group objects with the same shader and material properties together.

2. **Use Instancing**: If your game engine supports it, consider using GPU instancing to efficiently render multiple instances of the same object with a single draw call.

GPU Culling

Implement GPU culling to avoid rendering objects that are not visible to the camera. This can significantly reduce the number of objects processed by shaders. Techniques include:

1. **Frustum Culling**: Check whether objects are inside the camera's frustum before rendering.
2. **Occlusion Culling**: Use occlusion culling algorithms to determine which objects are occluded by others and can be skipped.
3. **Level of Detail (LOD)**: As mentioned earlier, use LOD techniques to skip rendering distant objects or objects that are too small to be seen.

Minimize Texture Memory Usage

Texture memory usage can also impact shader performance. To minimize texture memory consumption:

1. **Texture Atlases**: Combine multiple textures into atlases to reduce the number of texture switches.
2. **Texture Compression**: Use texture compression formats to reduce memory usage.
3. **Texture Streaming**: Implement texture streaming to load textures on-demand, reducing initial memory requirements.

Shader Compilation and Caching

Compile and cache shaders during the game's loading phase to avoid runtime compilation delays. Cached shaders can be reused throughout the game session, improving performance. Shader caching is a standard practice in most game engines.

By applying these optimization techniques, you can ensure that your shaders run efficiently, allowing your game to deliver visually stunning experiences while maintaining smooth performance on a variety of hardware configurations. Remember that shader optimization is an iterative process, and profiling tools are your allies in identifying and addressing performance bottlenecks.

Section 10.4: Exploring Shader-Based Rendering Techniques

Shaders are versatile tools that enable a wide range of rendering techniques, from realistic lighting to unique visual effects. In this section, we'll explore some advanced shader-based rendering techniques that can enhance the visual quality and realism of your game.

Deferred Rendering

Deferred rendering is a rendering technique that divides the rendering process into multiple passes. It's particularly beneficial when dealing with a large number of dynamic lights. In deferred rendering, the following steps are involved:

1. **Geometry Pass**: In this pass, the scene's geometry is rendered into several render targets. These render targets store information about the position, normal, albedo, and other material properties of each pixel.//
2. **Light Pass**: For each light source in the scene, a separate pass is performed. Shaders use the information from the geometry pass to calculate the lighting contribution for each pixel affected by the light source.
3. **Combine Pass**: Finally, the results of all the light passes are combined to produce the final image.

Deferred rendering reduces the computational cost of lighting calculations, especially when there are many dynamic lights. It also allows for more complex lighting models.

Screen-Space Reflections (SSR)

Screen-space reflections simulate the reflection of objects in reflective surfaces like water or mirrors. SSR is achieved by tracing rays from the camera's viewpoint into the scene to find the reflection points and then blending them with the rendered image. SSR can be implemented with shaders to create realistic reflective surfaces.

Ambient Occlusion (AO)

Ambient occlusion is a shading technique used to simulate the occlusion of light in crevices and corners, resulting in darker areas. SSAO (Screen-Space Ambient Occlusion) is a real-time version of this technique that can be applied in post-processing using shaders. It adds depth-based darkening to the scene, enhancing the perception of depth and realism.

Volumetric Lighting

Volumetric lighting, often referred to as "god rays" or "light shafts," simulates the scattering of light through a medium like fog or dust. This effect is created using shaders that calculate how light interacts with the particles or volumes in the scene. Volumetric lighting can add depth and atmosphere to outdoor scenes or dimly lit environments.

Post-Processing Effects

Post-processing effects, such as bloom, depth of field, motion blur, and color grading, are commonly implemented using shaders. These effects can significantly enhance the visual quality of your game by simulating real-world camera effects or artistic stylizations. Shaders are used to manipulate the final rendered image to achieve these effects.

Water Rendering

Realistic water rendering is a complex task that often involves shaders. Water shaders simulate the reflection, refraction, and animation of water surfaces. They can also include features like caustics (the patterns of light and shadow on the seafloor caused by water surface waves) and underwater effects.

Cartoon and Toon Shading

Cartoon and toon shading techniques are used to create a stylized, non-photorealistic look in games. These shaders replace smooth gradients of light and shadow with flat, cel-shaded colors. The result is a visual style reminiscent of traditional hand-drawn animation or comic books.

Parallax Mapping

Parallax mapping is a shader-based technique used to simulate 3D depth on flat surfaces, such as brick walls or cobblestone streets. By offsetting texture coordinates based on a height map, parallax mapping creates the illusion of depth when viewed from different angles.

Shader Effects and Particles

Shaders are also employed for creating various particle effects, such as fire, smoke, explosions, and magical spells. These effects are often dynamic and can be customized using shaders to achieve the desired visual impact.

These advanced shader-based rendering techniques offer a wide range of possibilities to enhance the visual quality and realism of your game. Depending on your game's art style and requirements, you can choose to implement some or all of these techniques to create captivating and immersive experiences for your players. However, keep in mind that complex shaders may require careful optimization to maintain good performance, especially on lower-end hardware.

Section 10.5: Advanced Lighting Models in Shaders

In the world of 3D computer graphics and game development, lighting plays a crucial role in creating realistic and visually appealing scenes. Advanced lighting models implemented in shaders can significantly enhance the quality and realism of your game's visuals. Here, we'll explore some advanced lighting models and techniques that can be achieved through shader programming.

Physically Based Rendering (PBR)

Physically Based Rendering is a lighting model that aims to simulate real-world lighting behavior accurately. PBR shaders consider properties like surface reflectivity, microfacet roughness, and Fresnel-Schlick approximation to calculate how light interacts with materials. This results in more accurate reflections, refractions, and materials that behave realistically under different lighting conditions.

Image-Based Lighting (IBL)

Image-Based Lighting is a technique that uses environment maps, often in the form of high dynamic range (HDR) images, to capture the lighting information from the surrounding environment. IBL shaders use these maps to simulate global illumination, making objects in the scene receive indirect lighting from their surroundings, creating a more natural and convincing look.

Subsurface Scattering (SSS)

Subsurface Scattering is a lighting model that simulates the behavior of light as it penetrates and scatters within translucent materials, such as skin, wax, or marble. SSS shaders calculate how light interacts beneath the surface, creating realistic effects like light diffusion, translucency, and color bleeding in materials with subsurface properties.

Anisotropic Shading

Anisotropic shading is used to simulate materials with directional surface properties, such as brushed metal or hair. Anisotropic shaders take into account the orientation of surface microfacets and adjust the reflection and shading accordingly, resulting in materials that exhibit unique directional highlights and reflections.

Realistic Shadows

Advanced shadow mapping techniques, such as Percentage Closer Soft Shadows (PCSS) and Variance Shadow Mapping (VSM), can be implemented using shaders to achieve more realistic and soft-edged shadows. These techniques take into account the size and position of the light source and the occluders, resulting in smoother and more accurate shadows.

Screen-Space Reflections (SSR) Improvements

Building on SSR mentioned in the previous section, advanced SSR shaders can incorporate ray tracing or ray marching methods to provide more accurate and visually pleasing reflections. This can include reflections of objects not currently on the screen or improvements in handling reflective surfaces with complex geometries.

High Dynamic Range (HDR) Rendering

HDR rendering involves using shaders to support a broader range of brightness values in the scene, allowing for more realistic and visually striking lighting effects. HDR shaders enable the simulation of intense light sources, bloom effects, and realistic exposure adjustments, resulting in a more immersive visual experience.

Global Illumination (GI) Techniques

Advanced shaders can implement global illumination techniques like radiosity or photon mapping to simulate indirect lighting in real-time. These techniques bounce light off surfaces and create soft and realistic ambient lighting, making scenes look more natural and visually appealing.

Material Layering

Shader-based material layering allows for the combination of multiple materials on a single object. This technique enables artists to create complex and detailed surfaces by stacking different materials with varying properties, such as base color, normal maps, roughness, and specular maps.

Artistic Stylization

Shaders are not limited to realism; they can also be used for artistic stylization. Various artistic shaders can achieve unique visual effects, such as cel-shading for a cartoon-like appearance, cross-hatching for a hand-drawn look, or post-processing effects to create a specific artistic atmosphere.

These advanced lighting models and techniques, implemented through shaders, offer game developers the ability to create stunning and immersive visuals. Depending on your game's style and requirements, you can choose to incorporate these techniques to enhance the visual quality and artistic expression of your game. However, it's essential to balance visual fidelity with performance optimization, as complex shaders may require careful optimization to maintain good frame rates, especially on less powerful hardware.

Chapter 11: Cross-Platform Development Strategies

Section 11.1: Designing Games for Multiple Platforms

Cross-platform development is becoming increasingly important in the world of game development. With the vast array of devices and operating systems available today, targeting a single platform may limit your game's reach and potential audience. This section explores the strategies and considerations for designing games that can run on multiple platforms seamlessly.

The Importance of Cross-Platform Development

In today's gaming landscape, players use a wide variety of devices to access games, including PCs, consoles, smartphones, tablets, and more. Each platform has its unique strengths, limitations, and control mechanisms. To maximize your game's success, it's crucial to make it available to players across these different platforms.

Cross-platform development not only broadens your game's accessibility but also helps in mitigating risks. Depending on a single platform for your game's success can be risky, as market conditions and player preferences can change. By targeting multiple platforms, you can diversify your revenue streams and future-proof your game.

Choosing the Right Game Engine

Selecting the right game engine is a critical decision when aiming for cross-platform development. Many game engines support multi-platform deployment, making it easier to develop your game once and deploy it on various platforms. Popular engines like Unity and Unreal Engine provide robust cross-platform capabilities.

These engines often come with built-in tools and features that facilitate cross-platform development, such as asset management, rendering optimizations, and input handling. They also support various programming languages, making it easier to develop for different platforms while maintaining a single codebase.

Platform-Specific Considerations

While aiming for cross-platform development, it's essential to be aware of the unique features and requirements of each platform. Consider factors like screen sizes, resolutions, input methods (touch, controller, keyboard/mouse), and performance capabilities. Your game should adapt gracefully to these differences to provide the best user experience.

For example, if you're targeting both PC and mobile devices, you may need to create different user interfaces (UI) to accommodate varying screen sizes and touch controls. Additionally, optimizing graphics settings and performance on lower-end devices is crucial for mobile platforms.

Input Handling and Controls

One of the significant challenges in cross-platform development is handling input across different devices. PC games typically use keyboard and mouse inputs, while consoles use game controllers, and mobile devices rely on touchscreens. Ensuring that your game's controls are intuitive and responsive on each platform is vital.

Consider implementing input abstraction layers that can translate input from various devices into a common set of game commands. This approach allows you to maintain a single codebase for your game's core mechanics while adapting the input handling for each platform.

Testing and Quality Assurance

Thorough testing on each target platform is essential to identify and resolve platform-specific issues. This includes testing on various devices, operating system versions, and hardware configurations. Quality assurance (QA) efforts should encompass functional testing, performance testing, and compatibility testing.

Automated testing tools can streamline the testing process and help ensure that your game functions correctly across all platforms. Additionally, gathering feedback from players on different platforms can uncover issues and improvements specific to each platform.

Deployment and Distribution

When deploying your game on multiple platforms, you'll need to navigate each platform's distribution channels and requirements. These may include app stores, digital distribution platforms, and console marketplaces. Each platform may have its certification process and guidelines for content submission.

Ensure that you comply with each platform's policies and requirements, which may cover content ratings, monetization models, and legal agreements. Properly managing the deployment process is crucial to ensure a smooth release on all platforms.

Conclusion

Cross-platform development is a strategic choice that can significantly expand the reach of your game and reduce risks associated with platform dependencies. By selecting the right game engine, considering platform-specific requirements, and implementing flexible input handling, you can create a game that thrives on multiple platforms, offering a consistent and enjoyable experience to players worldwide.

Section 11.2: Platform-Specific Optimizations

When developing games for multiple platforms, it's essential to optimize your game to ensure it runs smoothly and efficiently on each target platform. Platform-specific optimizations play a crucial role in achieving the best performance, user experience, and compatibility. In this section, we'll explore various optimization techniques tailored to different platforms.

Understanding Platform Differences

Before diving into platform-specific optimizations, it's essential to understand the fundamental differences between the platforms you're targeting. Each platform has unique hardware specifications, software environments, and capabilities. These differences can affect your game's performance, visuals, and overall experience.

For example, a PC game may take advantage of powerful CPUs and GPUs, while a mobile game must be mindful of limited processing power and battery life. Console platforms have their specific hardware configurations, and optimizing for them may require different techniques compared to PC or mobile.

PC Optimization

When optimizing for PC platforms, you have more flexibility and control over hardware resources. However, it's essential to cater to a wide range of hardware configurations. Here are some key PC optimization strategies:

1. **Graphics Settings:** Allow players to adjust graphics settings such as resolution, texture quality, and anti-aliasing to accommodate various hardware capabilities. Implementing a scalable rendering system can help achieve this flexibility.

2. **Multi-Threading:** Take advantage of multi-core CPUs by optimizing your game engine for multi-threading. Distributing tasks like physics simulation, rendering, and AI across multiple threads can improve performance.

3. **Input Options:** Support various input devices like keyboards, mice, and game controllers. Ensure that your game's control scheme is customizable and intuitive for PC players.

4. **Windowed and Full-Screen Modes:** Allow players to choose between windowed and full-screen modes, as different players may have different preferences.

5. **Mod Support:** Consider providing modding support, allowing the community to enhance and customize the game. Mods can extend the game's longevity and appeal.

Mobile Optimization

Mobile platforms are known for their resource limitations, so optimization is critical for a smooth gaming experience. Here are some mobile optimization techniques:

1. **Performance Profiling:** Use profiling tools to identify performance bottlenecks in your game. Address issues such as excessive draw calls, high-polygon models, and inefficient shaders.

2. **Texture Compression:** Implement texture compression techniques like ETC2, ASTC, or PVRTC to reduce memory usage and improve loading times.

3. **Battery Efficiency:** Optimize power consumption by reducing CPU and GPU load when the game is in the background or not actively being played.

4. **Screen Resolution Scaling:** Implement dynamic resolution scaling to adjust the rendering resolution based on the device's capabilities, ensuring a consistent frame rate.

5. **Asset Loading:** Use efficient asset loading techniques to reduce load times and memory usage. Load assets asynchronously to prevent frame drops during gameplay.

Console Optimization

Optimizing for console platforms involves fine-tuning your game to take full advantage of the specific hardware and capabilities of each console. Here are some console optimization strategies:

1. **Console-Specific APIs:** Utilize console-specific APIs and features to enhance performance and visuals. Each console may offer unique capabilities like ray tracing, hardware-accelerated audio, or specialized shaders.

2. **Memory Management:** Efficiently manage memory resources to avoid memory-related issues and ensure smooth performance. Console platforms often have strict memory limitations.

3. **Input Integration:** Implement console-specific input handling to provide a seamless experience for players using game controllers. Ensure that control schemes are optimized for console gameplay.

4. **Load Times:** Minimize load times by optimizing asset loading and streaming. Console players expect fast load times and a fluid user experience.

5. **Frame Rate Stability:** Maintain a consistent frame rate to provide a smooth gaming experience. Console players often prioritize stable frame rates over high graphical fidelity.

Conclusion

Platform-specific optimizations are crucial for delivering the best gaming experience on each target platform. Understanding the unique characteristics and limitations of PC, mobile, and console platforms allows you to tailor your optimizations effectively. By implementing these optimizations, you can ensure that your game performs optimally and delights players on every platform.

Section 11.3: Handling Different Input Methods

When developing games for multiple platforms, it's essential to consider the various input methods available to players. Different platforms offer distinct input devices, such as keyboards and mice for PCs, touchscreen controls for mobile devices, and game controllers for consoles. Ensuring that your game provides a seamless and enjoyable experience across these input methods is crucial for its success. In this section, we'll explore strategies for handling different input methods effectively.

Input Abstraction Layers

One approach to handling diverse input methods is to implement an input abstraction layer. This layer acts as an intermediary between your game code and the underlying input devices. It abstracts the input hardware, providing a unified interface for handling player input. Here's how you can implement an input abstraction layer:

```csharp
// C# Example
public interface IInputHandler
{
    bool GetButtonDown(string buttonName);
    float GetAxis(string axisName);
    Vector2 GetMousePosition();
}

public class PCInputHandler : IInputHandler
{
    public bool GetButtonDown(string buttonName)
    {
        // Implement keyboard or mouse button handling
        // ...
    }

    public float GetAxis(string axisName)
    {
        // Implement input axis handling
        // ...
    }

    public Vector2 GetMousePosition()
    {
        // Implement mouse position retrieval
        // ...
    }
}

public class MobileInputHandler : IInputHandler
{
    public bool GetButtonDown(string buttonName)
    {
```

```
        // Implement touchscreen button handling
        // ...
    }

    public float GetAxis(string axisName)
    {
        // Implement touch or tilt-based axis handling
        // ...
    }

    public Vector2 GetMousePosition()
    {
        // Implement touch position retrieval
        // ...
    }
}
```

With an input abstraction layer, your game code can remain mostly platform-agnostic, as it interacts with the common interface provided by the `IInputHandler`. Depending on the platform your game is running on, you can instantiate the appropriate input handler (e.g., `PCInputHandler` or `MobileInputHandler`) to handle player input.

Control Scheme Customization

Allowing players to customize their control schemes is another important aspect of handling different input methods. What works well for one player may not be comfortable for another. Provide an options menu within your game that allows players to remap buttons, adjust sensitivity, or choose from predefined control schemes (e.g., "Classic," "Default," "Left-Handed").

Here's a simplified example of how you can implement control scheme customization:

```
// C# Example
public class ControlScheme
{
    public Dictionary<string, string> ButtonMappings { get; private set; }
    public Dictionary<string, string> AxisMappings { get; private set; }

    public ControlScheme()
    {
        ButtonMappings = new Dictionary<string, string>();
        AxisMappings = new Dictionary<string, string>();
    }

    public void AddButtonMapping(string action, string button)
    {
        ButtonMappings[action] = button;
    }

    public void AddAxisMapping(string action, string axis)
```

```
    {
        AxisMappings[action] = axis;
    }
}
```

In your game, you can load control schemes and apply them based on the player's preferences. This approach ensures that players can adapt the game's controls to their preferred input method.

Testing and User Feedback

To ensure that your game handles different input methods effectively, thorough testing on various platforms and devices is essential. Consider building a testing matrix that covers different input methods, screen sizes, and hardware configurations. Gather feedback from players and conduct usability testing to identify any input-related issues and make necessary adjustments.

Handling different input methods is a crucial aspect of delivering a user-friendly and accessible gaming experience. By implementing input abstraction layers, offering control scheme customization, and conducting thorough testing, you can ensure that your game caters to a wide range of players and devices.

Section 11.4: Managing Platform-Specific Features

When developing games for multiple platforms, it's common to encounter situations where certain features or capabilities are unique to specific platforms. These platform-specific features can enhance the gameplay experience for players on a particular device but may not be relevant or achievable on others. In this section, we'll explore strategies for managing platform-specific features effectively.

Identifying Platform-Specific Features

The first step in managing platform-specific features is to identify them during the game design and development phases. Consider the following examples of platform-specific features:

1. **Touchscreen Controls:** Mobile devices and tablets often rely on touchscreen controls. These can include tapping, swiping, and multi-touch gestures, which may not be available on other platforms.

2. **Accelerometer:** Some mobile devices have built-in accelerometers that allow for tilt-based controls. This feature is not present on PCs or consoles.

3. **VR/AR Integration:** Virtual Reality (VR) and Augmented Reality (AR) features are unique to platforms that support these technologies.

4. **Hardware-Specific Features:** Certain platforms may offer unique hardware features, such as a gyroscope or a specific type of game controller.

Code Abstraction and Conditional Compilation

To manage platform-specific features, you can use code abstraction and conditional compilation. Here's how it works:

```cpp
// C++ Example
#ifdef PLATFORM_PC
    // Code specific to PC platform
    // ...
#endif

#ifdef PLATFORM_MOBILE
    // Code specific to mobile platforms
    // ...
#endif

#ifdef PLATFORM_CONSOLE
    // Code specific to game consoles
    // ...
#endif
```

In the above example, `PLATFORM_PC`, `PLATFORM_MOBILE`, and `PLATFORM_CONSOLE` are preprocessor macros that you define based on the target platform. You can define these macros in your build settings or use build scripts to automate the process.

Within each platform-specific section, you can implement or enable features that are relevant to that platform. This allows you to keep your codebase clean and organized while ensuring that each platform gets the appropriate features.

Runtime Feature Detection

Another approach is to perform runtime feature detection. Instead of relying solely on preprocessor macros, your game can check the capabilities of the current platform at runtime and enable or disable features accordingly. This approach provides more flexibility and can adapt to unexpected variations between devices within a platform.

Here's an example in C#:

```csharp
// C# Example
if (Application.platform == RuntimePlatform.Android)
{
    // Enable Android-specific features
    // ...
}
else if (Application.platform == RuntimePlatform.WindowsPlayer)
{
    // Enable Windows-specific features
```

```
    // ...
}
```

User Experience Considerations

When managing platform-specific features, it's essential to consider the overall user experience. Ensure that the absence of certain features on specific platforms does not negatively impact gameplay. For example, if your game relies heavily on touchscreen controls on mobile but lacks gamepad support on PC, make sure the game is still enjoyable and playable on both platforms.

Additionally, provide clear communication to players about the features available on their platform. In the game's description and interface, mention any platform-specific enhancements or limitations, so players have realistic expectations.

Testing and Quality Assurance

Thorough testing on all target platforms is crucial when managing platform-specific features. Ensure that each feature works as intended and that the game provides a consistent experience across platforms. This testing should cover a range of devices and configurations to account for variations in performance and capabilities.

By effectively managing platform-specific features through code abstraction, conditional compilation, runtime feature detection, and careful consideration of the user experience, you can create a game that adapts to different platforms while delivering an enjoyable experience to players on each one.

Section 11.5: Distribution and Deployment Across Platforms

Once you've developed your game to support multiple platforms, the next critical step is distribution and deployment. Successfully releasing your game on various platforms requires careful planning, compliance with platform-specific guidelines, and an understanding of distribution channels. In this section, we'll explore the key aspects of distributing and deploying your game across different platforms.

1. Platform-Specific Stores and Markets

Each platform has its official store or marketplace for distributing games. These include the App Store for iOS, Google Play for Android, Steam for PC, PlayStation Store for PlayStation consoles, and many more. To deploy your game, you'll need to navigate the submission and approval processes of these stores.

2. Compliance and Guidelines

Every platform has specific guidelines and policies that developers must adhere to. These guidelines cover aspects such as content, age ratings, monetization methods, and technical requirements. Ensure that your game complies with these guidelines to avoid rejection during the submission process.

3. Build Configuration

Different platforms often require specific build configurations. This includes compiling your code for the target platform, adjusting graphics settings, and handling platform-specific inputs and controls. Maintain separate build configurations to ensure compatibility.

4. Testing on Real Devices and Emulators

Before submission, thoroughly test your game on real devices or platform-specific emulators. This testing ensures that the game functions correctly and provides a good user experience on each platform. Test for performance, usability, and any platform-specific issues.

5. Store Assets and Metadata

Each platform store requires specific assets and metadata, such as game icons, screenshots, descriptions, and keywords. Tailor these assets to meet the requirements of each platform. High-quality visuals and engaging descriptions can attract more users.

6. Monetization Strategies

Consider how you'll monetize your game on different platforms. This could involve in-app purchases, ads, premium pricing, or a combination of these methods. Adjust your monetization strategy to align with the expectations of the target audience on each platform.

7. Localization

Localization is essential for reaching a global audience. Translate your game's text, UI elements, and marketing materials into multiple languages to broaden your game's appeal. Ensure that localized versions meet cultural sensitivities and preferences.

8. Updates and Maintenance

After the initial release, continue to support your game with updates and maintenance. This includes bug fixes, performance improvements, and new content. Keep the game fresh to retain and attract players on all platforms.

9. Cross-Platform Play and Progression

If your game supports multiplayer features, consider enabling cross-platform play and progression. This allows players on different platforms to compete or cooperate, enhancing the social aspect of your game.

10. Promotion and Marketing

Promote your game on each platform to maximize visibility and user acquisition. Use platform-specific marketing tools and strategies to reach your target audience effectively. Building a community around your game can also help with long-term success.

11. Monitoring and Analytics

Implement analytics tools to monitor user engagement, retention, and monetization on each platform. Use this data to make informed decisions about updates, marketing strategies, and user experience improvements.

12. Legal and Business Considerations

Understand the legal and business aspects of distributing your game. This includes licensing agreements, royalties, tax implications, and intellectual property protection. Consult with legal and financial experts when necessary.

Distributing and deploying your game across multiple platforms can be a complex but rewarding process. By carefully planning and adapting to the unique requirements of each platform, you can increase your game's reach and chances of success in the diverse world of gaming.

Chapter 12: Enhancing Gameplay Experience

In this chapter, we will explore various techniques and strategies to enhance the gameplay experience of your video game. While mechanics and graphics are crucial, the overall experience a player has can make or break a game's success. We will delve into dynamic storytelling, creating immersive game worlds, understanding the psychology of game design, implementing reward systems, and balancing gameplay for players with different skill levels.

Section 12.1: Dynamic Storytelling Techniques

Storytelling is a powerful tool in game design, and it can greatly influence the player's engagement and emotional investment. Dynamic storytelling takes this a step further by adapting the narrative based on player choices and actions, creating a more personalized experience.

Importance of Dynamic Storytelling

Dynamic storytelling allows players to shape the game's narrative through their decisions, creating a sense of agency. This approach can lead to multiple branching storylines and endings, increasing replayability.

Implementing Choices and Consequences

To implement dynamic storytelling, you need a system that tracks player choices and determines the consequences. This involves creating decision points in the narrative and branching paths that lead to different outcomes.

Dialogue Systems

Dialogue systems play a vital role in dynamic storytelling. They enable interactive conversations between characters and the player. Consider implementing dialogue trees or systems that allow players to choose responses, which can affect the story's direction.

Narrative Design

Crafting a compelling narrative is essential. Pay attention to character development, world-building, and pacing. Ensure that the story adapts seamlessly to the player's choices while maintaining coherence.

Player-Driven Narrative

Dynamic storytelling empowers players to influence the story, making them feel more connected to the game world. However, strike a balance between player agency and a coherent overarching narrative to avoid losing the story's essence.

Storytelling Tools and Engines

Many game engines and tools offer built-in support for dynamic storytelling. Familiarize yourself with these features and leverage them to streamline the implementation process.

Player Feedback

Gather feedback from playtesters to refine the dynamic storytelling experience. Identify which choices players find impactful and where improvements can be made.

Case Studies

Study games that excel in dynamic storytelling, such as "The Witcher" series, "Life is Strange," or "Undertale." Analyze their narrative design and choice systems to gain insights into effective implementation.

Pitfalls to Avoid

Dynamic storytelling can be challenging to execute effectively. Be cautious of creating choices with inconsequential outcomes, overwhelming players with too many options, or sacrificing narrative cohesion for the sake of player agency.

Conclusion

Dynamic storytelling is a powerful tool for enhancing gameplay experiences. When implemented thoughtfully, it can immerse players in your game world, provide a sense of ownership over the narrative, and encourage replayability. In the following sections of this chapter, we will explore other aspects of enhancing gameplay to create memorable and engaging gaming experiences.

Section 12.2: Creating Immersive Game Worlds

Creating immersive game worlds is a fundamental aspect of enhancing the gameplay experience. Immersion refers to the player's ability to lose themselves in the game, feeling like they are part of the fictional universe you've created. In this section, we will explore various techniques to design and build immersive game worlds that captivate players and keep them engaged.

Environmental Design

Environmental design encompasses everything from level layout to visual aesthetics. To create an immersive world, consider the following:

- **Consistency**: Ensure that the game world's visual style, architecture, and geography are consistent with the game's narrative and themes. Inconsistencies can break immersion.
- **Attention to Detail**: Small details, such as interactive objects, environmental storytelling, and hidden secrets, can make the game world feel more alive and engaging.
- **Level Flow**: Design levels with a logical flow that guides players through the game naturally. Avoid abrupt transitions or confusing layouts.

World Building

World building involves crafting the lore, history, and culture of your game world. A well-developed world can provide context for the player's actions and create a sense of depth. Consider these world-building tips:

- **Backstories**: Characters, factions, and locations should have rich backstories that players can discover. This adds layers of depth to the world.
- **Cultural Diversity**: Create diverse cultures, societies, and civilizations within your game world. This diversity can lead to unique interactions and quests.
- **Mythology and Legends**: Integrate myths and legends into the game world. These stories can inspire quests, add mystery, and enrich the player's experience.

Interactive Elements

Immersive game worlds are not just about aesthetics; they should also be interactive. Players should feel like their actions have consequences in the world. Consider these interactive elements:

- **Dynamic NPCs**: Populate the world with non-player characters (NPCs) that have their own routines, dialogues, and goals. NPCs with day-night cycles and schedules can make the world feel more alive.

- **Choices and Consequences**: Implement choices that impact the game world. For example, the player's decisions could affect the environment, characters, or the overall narrative.

Audio and Music

Sound design plays a crucial role in immersion. The right audio cues and music can enhance the atmosphere and emotional impact of the game. Here's how to use audio effectively:

- **Ambient Sounds**: Incorporate ambient sounds that match the environment. For instance, a forest should have rustling leaves, while a bustling city should have background chatter.

- **Dynamic Music**: Use dynamic music systems that adapt to the player's actions and surroundings. Music can intensify during combat, become soothing during exploration, or turn ominous in suspenseful moments.

Exploration and Discovery

Encourage players to explore the game world by adding incentives for discovery:

- **Hidden Treasures**: Scatter hidden treasures, collectibles, or easter eggs throughout the world. These rewards motivate players to explore.

- **Environmental Puzzles**: Design puzzles that require players to interact with the environment to progress. Solving these puzzles can be satisfying and immersive.

Playtesting and Iteration

Immersive game worlds often require iteration and player feedback:

- **Playtesting**: Conduct playtests to observe how players interact with the world. Identify areas where immersion could be improved based on their experiences.

- **Iterative Design**: Be willing to make adjustments based on playtest feedback and observations. Continuously refine the game world to enhance immersion.

Creating an immersive game world is an ongoing process that requires attention to detail, creativity, and player-centric design. When players become fully immersed in your world, they are more likely to enjoy the gameplay experience and remember it long after they've finished playing.

Section 12.3: Psychology of Game Design

Understanding the psychology of game design is crucial for creating engaging and enjoyable gameplay experiences. Games tap into various aspects of human psychology, including motivation, reward systems, and cognitive processes. In this section, we'll delve into the psychological principles that can be applied to enhance your game design.

Player Motivation

Player motivation is a key driver in game design. To keep players engaged, it's essential to understand what motivates them to play and continue playing. Here are some motivational factors to consider:

- **Achievement**: Many players are motivated by the desire to achieve goals or milestones within the game. Implementing achievements, trophies, or badges can tap into this motivation.

- **Competition**: Some players thrive on competition and the opportunity to prove their skills. Leaderboards, rankings, and multiplayer modes can cater to competitive motivations.

- **Exploration**: Curiosity and the desire to explore the game world can be strong motivators. Designing vast, open environments with hidden secrets can pique players' interest.

- **Social Interaction**: Games that offer opportunities for social interaction and cooperation can motivate players to engage with others. Multiplayer modes, guilds, or in-game chat systems can facilitate social connections.

Reward Systems

Effective reward systems can reinforce player engagement. Games often use various rewards to encourage specific behaviors and progression:

- **In-Game Rewards**: These include items, currency, experience points, or power-ups that players receive for completing tasks, defeating enemies, or reaching milestones.

- **Visual and Auditory Feedback**: Providing visual and auditory cues, such as satisfying sound effects and animations, when a player achieves something can enhance the reward experience.

- **Positive Reinforcement**: Implementing positive reinforcement schedules, where rewards are given intermittently, can maintain player interest. Randomized rewards or daily login bonuses are examples.

Flow State

The concept of "flow" in game design refers to a state where players are fully immersed and deeply engaged in the game. Achieving flow involves balancing the difficulty of the game with the player's skill level:

- **Challenge vs. Skill**: To induce flow, the game's challenges should match the player's skill level. If a challenge is too easy, players become bored, while overly difficult challenges can lead to frustration.
- **Feedback Loop**: Maintaining a continuous feedback loop of challenge and skill improvement keeps players in the flow state. Gradually introducing more complex challenges can maintain engagement.

Cognitive Load

Cognitive load refers to the mental effort required to process information and make decisions in a game. It's important to manage cognitive load to prevent player fatigue:

- **Information Hierarchy**: Present game information in a logical hierarchy. Important information should be easily accessible, while less critical details can be presented more discreetly.
- **Tutorials and Progression**: Gradually introduce game mechanics and features to avoid overwhelming new players. Well-designed tutorials and onboarding processes can mitigate cognitive load.

Emotions and Immersion

Games have the power to evoke a wide range of emotions in players, from excitement and joy to fear and sadness. Designing emotional experiences can enhance immersion:

- **Narrative and Storytelling**: Crafting compelling narratives with relatable characters and emotional arcs can immerse players in the game world.
- **Atmosphere and Music**: The choice of music, sound effects, and visual aesthetics can influence the emotional tone of the game.
- **Choices and Consequences**: Providing players with meaningful choices that affect the game's story or outcome can evoke emotions and investment in the narrative.

Understanding these psychological principles and applying them thoughtfully to your game design can lead to more engaging and rewarding player experiences. By tapping into the motivations and emotions of players, you can create games that captivate and resonate with your audience.

Section 12.4: Reward Systems and Player Motivation

Reward systems play a pivotal role in game design, serving as a driving force to keep players engaged and motivated. In this section, we'll delve deeper into reward systems and how they can be leveraged to enhance player motivation and overall gaming experiences.

Types of Rewards

Games offer a diverse range of rewards to players, and these can be categorized into several types:

1. **In-Game Items**: These are virtual objects or resources that players can collect or use within the game. Examples include weapons, armor, potions, or currency. In-game items often serve practical purposes, such as enhancing character abilities or providing advantages.

2. **Experience Points (XP)**: Experience points represent a player's progression and growth within the game. Accumulating XP can lead to character level-ups, unlocking new abilities or features. XP systems are commonly found in role-playing games (RPGs).

3. **Achievements and Trophies**: Achievements and trophies are rewards for accomplishing specific goals or milestones in the game. They are often tied to challenging tasks or completing certain objectives. Earning achievements can be a source of pride for players.

4. **Leaderboards and Rankings**: Competitive players are motivated by the opportunity to climb leaderboards and achieve high rankings. Leaderboards display the performance of players relative to others, encouraging healthy competition.

5. **Cosmetic Customization**: Cosmetic rewards allow players to personalize their in-game characters or items. Skins, costumes, and other aesthetic upgrades provide a sense of individuality and uniqueness.

The Psychology of Rewards

To effectively employ reward systems, understanding the psychology behind them is crucial. Several psychological principles come into play:

- **Operant Conditioning**: Reward systems are rooted in operant conditioning, a psychological concept that involves associating behaviors with consequences. In games, players perform actions (behaviors) to earn rewards (consequences), reinforcing desired gameplay patterns.

- **Variable Rewards**: Introducing variability in rewards can enhance motivation. Randomized rewards or rewards with diminishing returns (e.g., earning less XP for repeatedly completing the same task) keep players engaged and curious.

- **Immediate vs. Delayed Rewards**: Players are often more motivated by immediate rewards. However, delayed rewards can also be effective if players anticipate a valuable outcome.

- **Reward Frequency**: Consistent, but not excessive, reward frequency is essential. If rewards are too scarce, players may become frustrated. Conversely, if they're too frequent, they can lose their appeal.

Balancing Rewards

Balancing reward systems is a delicate task. Rewards must align with the game's objectives and difficulty levels. Here are some considerations:

- **Challenge and Reward**: Rewards should correspond to the difficulty of the task. More challenging achievements or tasks can offer more significant rewards.

- **Player Progression**: As players progress through the game, rewards can become increasingly valuable or exclusive to maintain motivation.

- **Feedback and Celebration**: Celebrate player achievements with visual and auditory feedback, reinforcing their accomplishments.

- **Long-Term Engagement**: Consider long-term engagement by incorporating reward systems that span the entire player journey. Daily rewards, seasonal events, or loyalty programs can encourage extended play.

- **Player Choice**: Allow players to make choices regarding the rewards they pursue. This can increase motivation as players pursue rewards that align with their interests.

Incorporating well-designed reward systems tailored to your game's audience and objectives can significantly impact player engagement and retention. By tapping into player motivations and applying psychological principles, you can create a more immersive and satisfying gaming experience.

Section 12.5: Balancing Gameplay for Varied Player Skills

Balancing gameplay for players with varying skill levels is a fundamental challenge in game design. A well-balanced game ensures that both novice and experienced players can enjoy it without frustration or boredom. In this section, we'll explore strategies and techniques for achieving this delicate balance.

Player Skill Segmentation

One effective approach to balancing gameplay is to segment players into skill groups. This can be done through various means, such as:

1. **Skill-Based Matchmaking**: Implement a matchmaking system that groups players with similar skill levels together. This ensures that novices don't face off against experts, creating a more enjoyable experience for everyone.
2. **Difficulty Levels**: Provide multiple difficulty settings within the game. Novice players can choose an easier setting, while experienced players can opt for a more challenging experience.
3. **Tutorial and Onboarding**: Offer comprehensive tutorials and onboarding experiences for new players. These tutorials should gradually introduce game mechanics and concepts, making it easier for beginners to get started.
4. **Ranked Play**: Implement a ranked mode that rewards players based on their performance. This mode can attract competitive players while casual players can enjoy unranked modes.

Dynamic Adjustments

To maintain a balanced experience throughout the game, consider incorporating dynamic adjustments:

1. **Adaptive AI**: Implement adaptive AI that reacts to the player's skill level. The AI can become more challenging for experienced players and provide assistance or lower difficulty for beginners.
2. **Dynamic Scaling**: Use dynamic scaling of enemy stats, such as health and damage, based on the player's performance. If a player is struggling, the game can temporarily reduce the difficulty until they catch up.
3. **Progressive Challenges**: Design levels or challenges with progressively increasing difficulty. This allows players to gradually improve their skills as they advance through the game.
4. **Feedback Systems**: Implement feedback systems that provide hints or tips when a player is stuck. These systems can detect when a player is struggling and offer assistance.

Playtesting and Feedback

Playtesting is a crucial step in balancing gameplay. Gather feedback from a diverse group of players to identify pain points and areas where the game's balance may be off. Adjustments can be made based on this feedback to enhance the overall experience.

Metrics and Analytics

Utilize in-game metrics and analytics to monitor player behavior and progression. Analyze data to identify trends, such as high drop-off rates at specific levels or areas. These insights can help you pinpoint areas that may need rebalancing.

Iteration and Updates

Balancing gameplay is an ongoing process. Even after a game's release, developers should continue to monitor player feedback, metrics, and analytics. Regular updates and patches can address balance issues and improve the overall experience.

Player Choice

Allow players to make meaningful choices that impact their gameplay experience. For example, they can choose between different character classes, playstyles, or strategies. This empowers players to tailor the game to their preferences and skill levels.

Balancing gameplay for varied player skills is a complex but essential aspect of game design. By implementing skill segmentation, dynamic adjustments, playtesting, analytics, and player choice, you can create a game that appeals to a broad audience while ensuring a satisfying experience for players of all skill levels.

Chapter 13: Advanced Networking and Social Features

Section 13.1: Implementing Social Media Integration

In today's interconnected world, integrating social media features into your game can significantly enhance its visibility, engagement, and player retention. This section explores how to implement social media integration effectively to leverage the power of social networks in your game.

Why Social Media Integration?

1. **Increased Visibility**: Social media platforms have billions of users. Integrating your game with these platforms can expose it to a massive audience, leading to more downloads and players.

2. **Community Building**: Social media allows you to build and nurture a community around your game. Players can connect, share their experiences, and provide valuable feedback.

3. **Viral Marketing**: When players share their achievements, progress, or high scores on social media, it can go viral, attracting more players to your game.

4. **Engagement**: Social features, such as leaderboards, challenges, and sharing, enhance player engagement and competitiveness.

Key Social Media Integration Features

Here are some key social media integration features you can implement in your game:

1. Shareable Achievements:

Allow players to share their in-game achievements, high scores, or completed challenges directly to their social media profiles. This can serve as free marketing for your game.

2. In-Game Sharing:

Enable players to share their gameplay moments or screenshots from within the game. Provide sharing options for popular platforms like Facebook, Twitter, Instagram, and more.

3. Social Leaderboards:

Implement global or friend-based leaderboards that players can compete on. Share leaderboard updates on social media to encourage healthy competition.

4. Social Login:

Allow players to sign in or create accounts using their social media profiles. This simplifies the registration process and can lead to higher user adoption.

5. Friend Invitations:

Enable players to invite their friends from social media to join the game. Offering incentives for successful invitations can further boost your game's user base.

Technical Implementation

To implement social media integration, you'll need to use the APIs provided by the respective social media platforms (e.g., Facebook Graph API, Twitter API). Here are the general steps:

1. **Developer Accounts**: Create developer accounts with the social media platforms you plan to integrate with. This will provide you with access to their APIs and necessary keys.
2. **Authentication**: Implement authentication flows to allow players to log in with their social media accounts. Most platforms provide SDKs for this purpose.
3. **Sharing Content**: Use the platform's APIs to allow players to share content. You'll need to request permissions for posting on behalf of the user.
4. **Leaderboards**: Implement leaderboards and use the platform's APIs to update and retrieve leaderboard data.
5. **Analytics**: Track social media sharing and engagement using analytics tools to measure the impact of your integration.

Privacy and Permissions

Respect user privacy and permissions. Clearly communicate how their data will be used and seek their consent. Ensure compliance with data protection regulations, such as GDPR or CCPA, if applicable.

Testing and Optimization

Thoroughly test your social media integration on different platforms and devices. Optimize the sharing experience to be user-friendly and seamless.

Incorporating social media integration into your game can be a powerful marketing and engagement tool. When done right, it can lead to increased player retention and a thriving player community, ultimately contributing to the success of your game.

Section 13.2: Creating Shared Gaming Experiences

In the world of gaming, creating shared experiences is an effective way to engage players and build a sense of community. This section explores various methods and techniques for creating shared gaming experiences within your game.

Why Shared Gaming Experiences?

Shared gaming experiences involve allowing players to interact, collaborate, or compete with each other, enhancing their overall enjoyment of the game. Here's why it's crucial:

1. **Social Interaction**: Shared experiences encourage social interaction among players, fostering a sense of community and belonging.
2. **Increased Engagement**: When players can play together, they tend to stay engaged with the game for longer periods.
3. **Viral Growth**: Shared experiences often lead to word-of-mouth recommendations and viral growth as players invite their friends to join in.
4. **Competitive Spirit**: Competitive gaming experiences, such as leaderboards and multiplayer modes, drive players to improve their skills and compete with others.

Implementing Shared Gaming Experiences

There are several ways to implement shared gaming experiences, depending on your game's genre and platform. Here are some popular methods:

1. Multiplayer Modes:

Include multiplayer modes that allow players to team up or compete against each other. This can be done through local multiplayer, online multiplayer, or both.

2. Cooperative Gameplay:

Design levels or challenges that require cooperation between players to complete. Cooperative gameplay promotes teamwork and communication.

3. Leaderboards:

Implement global and friend-based leaderboards where players can see how they compare to others. Regularly update and reset leaderboards to keep the competition fresh.

4. In-Game Events:

Organize in-game events, tournaments, or challenges with rewards for top performers. Events create excitement and engagement.

5. Social Features:

Integrate social features such as friend lists, chat systems, and guilds or clans, allowing players to connect and collaborate.

6. User-Generated Content:

Allow players to create and share their content within the game, such as custom levels, characters, or mods. This fosters a creative and active player community.

Technical Considerations

Implementing shared gaming experiences often requires robust networking and synchronization between players' devices. Here are some technical considerations:

- **Latency**: Minimize network latency to ensure a smooth multiplayer experience.
- **Server Architecture**: Decide whether to use peer-to-peer or client-server architecture for multiplayer modes.
- **Data Security**: Implement data security measures to protect player data during online interactions.
- **Cross-Platform Play**: Consider supporting cross-platform play to broaden your player base.

Balancing Shared and Solo Play

While shared gaming experiences can be exciting, it's essential to strike a balance between solo and multiplayer gameplay. Not all players enjoy the same types of experiences, so offering a variety of gameplay options can cater to different preferences.

Incorporating shared gaming experiences into your game can lead to increased player engagement, community building, and viral growth. However, it's crucial to implement these features thoughtfully and provide a seamless and enjoyable experience for all players.

Section 13.3: Developing Asynchronous Multiplayer Games

Asynchronous multiplayer games have gained popularity because they allow players to engage with each other without needing to be online simultaneously. In this section, we'll explore the development of asynchronous multiplayer games, the benefits they offer, and how to create engaging experiences for players.

Understanding Asynchronous Multiplayer

In traditional synchronous multiplayer games, players must be online at the same time to interact, compete, or cooperate. Asynchronous multiplayer, on the other hand, allows players to take turns or perform actions independently and asynchronously, without needing real-time coordination.

Benefits of Asynchronous Multiplayer

Developing asynchronous multiplayer games can offer several advantages:

1. **Accessibility**: Asynchronous games accommodate players with varying schedules, allowing them to participate when convenient.

2. **Increased Engagement**: Players stay engaged over more extended periods, as they don't need to dedicate large blocks of time to the game.
3. **Global Player Base**: Asynchronous gameplay can attract a global audience, as players from different time zones can participate.
4. **Reduced Server Load**: Since players don't need to be online simultaneously, server loads can be lower compared to real-time multiplayer games.

Creating Asynchronous Multiplayer Experiences

To develop engaging asynchronous multiplayer experiences, consider the following:

1. **Turn-Based Gameplay**: Design gameplay mechanics that revolve around turns. Players take actions during their turn, which can be as simple as making a move or as complex as crafting a strategy.
2. **Notifications**: Implement notifications to inform players when it's their turn or when they have received a message or challenge from another player.
3. **Messaging and Communication**: Include messaging features that allow players to communicate asynchronously, discuss strategies, or engage in friendly banter.
4. **Leaderboards and Progress Tracking**: Implement leaderboards that display player rankings or achievements. Players can compare their progress with others, even if they play at different times.
5. **Challenges and Objectives**: Create challenges or objectives that players can complete asynchronously, such as daily quests or puzzles.
6. **Social Integration**: Enable social media integration, allowing players to share their achievements and invite friends to participate in the game.

Technical Considerations

Developing asynchronous multiplayer games involves specific technical considerations:

- **Server-Side Processing**: Server-side processing is essential to handle player actions, store game state, and manage notifications.
- **Data Synchronization**: Ensure that player data and game states are synchronized correctly across devices and platforms.
- **Security**: Implement robust security measures to protect player data and prevent cheating in asynchronous games.
- **Offline Play**: Consider allowing players to engage in asynchronous gameplay even when offline, with data synchronization occurring when they reconnect.
- **Cross-Platform Support**: To maximize the player base, support cross-platform play, allowing users on different devices to participate.

Examples of Asynchronous Multiplayer Games

Some popular examples of asynchronous multiplayer games include:

- **Wordament**: A word puzzle game where players compete to find as many words as possible within a time limit, with turns being taken asynchronously.
- **Chess with Friends**: A digital chess game where players can make moves at their convenience, challenging friends or random opponents.
- **Letterpress**: A word game that combines elements of Boggle and Scrabble, where players take turns forming words on a grid.

Developing asynchronous multiplayer games offers a unique and engaging gameplay experience that caters to a broader audience. By considering the technical aspects and designing captivating gameplay mechanics, you can create successful asynchronous multiplayer games that keep players coming back for more.

Section 13.4: Implementing In-Game Chat and Messaging

In-game chat and messaging systems are crucial components of modern multiplayer games, facilitating communication and interaction among players. This section explores the implementation of in-game chat and messaging features, including their significance and best practices.

The Importance of In-Game Chat and Messaging

In multiplayer games, effective communication enhances the gaming experience in several ways:

1. **Social Interaction**: In-game chat allows players to socialize, form friendships, and build communities within the game environment.
2. **Coordination**: Players can strategize, coordinate actions, and communicate important information, which is particularly valuable in team-based games.
3. **Enhanced Gameplay**: Communication contributes to a more immersive and enjoyable gameplay experience, fostering engagement and player retention.

Designing the Chat System

When implementing an in-game chat and messaging system, consider the following design aspects:

1. **User-Friendly Interface**: Design an intuitive and user-friendly chat interface that provides easy access to messages and supports features like message history and quick replies.

2. **Privacy and Moderation**: Implement privacy settings and moderation tools to ensure a safe and respectful gaming environment. Players should have control over who can message them.
3. **Message Types**: Support different types of messages, such as text, emojis, and voice messages, to accommodate various communication preferences.
4. **Group Chats**: Enable group chats for team communication or socializing with multiple players simultaneously.
5. **Notifications**: Implement real-time notifications for new messages, ensuring that players stay informed even when not actively using the chat.
6. **Emojis and Reactions**: Include a variety of emojis and reactions to allow players to express themselves and react to messages.

Technical Implementation

The technical implementation of an in-game chat system involves the following considerations:

- **Client-Server Communication**: Establish a reliable client-server communication protocol to transmit messages between players.
- **Message Storage**: Implement a message storage mechanism to preserve chat history and allow players to view previous conversations.
- **Scalability**: Design the chat system to scale with the number of players, ensuring that it performs efficiently, even in large multiplayer games.
- **Security**: Prioritize security to protect player data and prevent unauthorized access or tampering of messages.
- **Cross-Platform Compatibility**: Ensure that the chat system works seamlessly across various gaming platforms and devices.
- **Localization**: If your game has a global player base, provide support for multiple languages and character sets in the chat system.

Embracing Moderation

In multiplayer games, it's essential to maintain a positive and respectful community. Implement moderation tools to address inappropriate behavior, offensive language, and harassment. Consider providing players with the ability to report abusive messages, and establish clear rules and consequences for misconduct.

In-Game Chat as a Social Hub

In addition to functional communication, think of the in-game chat system as a social hub where players can share experiences, celebrate victories, and discuss strategies. Encourage player engagement and social interaction to foster a strong and vibrant gaming community.

```
# Example pseudocode for sending a chat message in a multiplayer game
def send_chat_message(sender, receiver, message):
    # Validate the message and sender's identity
    if validate_message(sender, message):
        # Send the message to the receiver
        receiver.receive_message(message)

# Example pseudocode for receiving and displaying a chat message
def receive_message(message):
    # Display the incoming message in the chat interface
    chat_interface.display_message(message)

# Example pseudocode for reporting an abusive message
def report_abuse(message, sender):
    # Check the message for abusive content
    if contains_abuse(message):
        # Take appropriate action, such as issuing warnings or sanctions
        sender.warn_or_sanction()
```

In conclusion, the implementation of in-game chat and messaging systems plays a vital role in enhancing the multiplayer gaming experience. A well-designed chat system not only facilitates communication but also contributes to the sense of community and engagement within your game. Balancing functionality, usability, and player safety should be at the forefront of your design and development efforts.

Section 13.5: Building a Game Community Platform

Building a game community platform is a strategic move for game developers looking to foster player engagement, enhance player retention, and create a loyal player base. This section explores the importance of game communities, the elements of a successful game community platform, and tips for building and maintaining one.

The Significance of Game Communities

Game communities play a pivotal role in the success of multiplayer and online games. They offer the following advantages:

1. **Player Retention**: A strong community can significantly increase player retention by providing social connections, shared experiences, and reasons to return to the game.

2. **Feedback and Iteration**: Communities provide a valuable source of feedback, allowing developers to understand player preferences, identify issues, and make necessary improvements.
3. **Word-of-Mouth Marketing**: Satisfied community members become advocates for the game, helping spread the word and attract new players.
4. **User-Generated Content**: Communities often contribute user-generated content, such as mods, custom maps, and fan art, which can enhance the game's content and longevity.

Elements of a Successful Game Community Platform

To create an effective game community platform, consider the following elements:

1. **Forums and Discussion Boards**: Provide a space for players to discuss the game, share tips, and ask questions. Well-moderated forums can become hubs of activity.
2. **Social Media Integration**: Integrate social media sharing and linking to allow players to easily share their in-game achievements and experiences with friends.
3. **Player Profiles**: Offer customizable player profiles where users can showcase their in-game accomplishments and stats.
4. **Leaderboards**: Implement leaderboards to encourage competition among players and highlight top performers.
5. **Events and Tournaments**: Organize in-game events, tournaments, and challenges to keep the community engaged.
6. **News and Updates**: Share regular news, patch notes, and updates to keep players informed and excited about the game's development.
7. **User-Generated Content Hub**: Create a section for user-generated content, such as mods, fan art, and player-created guides.
8. **Community Moderation Tools**: Implement robust moderation tools to ensure a safe and respectful environment within the community.
9. **Feedback Channels**: Provide channels for players to submit feedback, bug reports, and suggestions directly to the development team.
10. **Developer Interaction**: Actively engage with the community by participating in discussions, addressing concerns, and acknowledging player contributions.

Building and Maintaining a Game Community Platform

Building a game community platform requires careful planning and ongoing dedication. Here are some steps to get started:

1. **Choose the Right Platform**: Decide whether to build a custom community platform or leverage existing social media, forums, or community-building tools.
2. **Design for User-Friendliness**: Ensure that the platform is easy to navigate and encourages participation. Intuitive user interfaces and clear guidelines are essential.
3. **Moderation and Code of Conduct**: Establish a code of conduct and moderation policies to maintain a positive and respectful atmosphere. Train moderators if needed.
4. **Promotion**: Promote the community platform within the game, on the game's website, and through social media channels.
5. **Consistent Updates**: Keep the community platform up to date with new content, features, and improvements.
6. **Engage and Listen**: Actively engage with the community, respond to feedback, and incorporate player suggestions into the game when feasible.
7. **Events and Contests**: Organize regular events, contests, and challenges to encourage participation and reward community members.
8. **Analytics**: Use analytics to track community engagement, identify trends, and measure the impact of community-building efforts.

```
# Example pseudocode for organizing an in-game community event
def organize_community_event(event_details):
    # Notify the community about the upcoming event
    community_notification(event_details)
    # Set up event-specific gameplay elements and rewards
    event_gameplay_setup(event_details)
    # Monitor event participation and performance
    event_monitoring(event_details)

# Example pseudocode for community engagement analytics
def track_community_engagement():
    # Collect data on forum activity, social media mentions, and player interactions
    engagement_data = collect_engagement_data()
    # Analyze the data to identify trends and assess the impact of community-building efforts
    analyze_engagement_data(engagement_data)
```

In conclusion, building and maintaining a game community platform is a strategic investment in the long-term success of your game. By fostering a positive and engaged community, you can enhance player experiences, gather valuable feedback, and create a dedicated player base that contributes to the growth and vitality of your game.

Chapter 14: Scalable Game Architecture

Section 14.1: Design Patterns for Game Development

Design patterns are essential tools in game development that provide solutions to recurring design problems. They promote code reusability, maintainability, and scalability. In this section, we'll explore some common design patterns used in game development and understand how they can improve your game architecture.

1. Singleton Pattern

The Singleton pattern ensures that a class has only one instance and provides a global point of access to it. It's often used for managing centralized resources such as the game engine, audio manager, or input manager.

```python
class GameManager:
    _instance = None

    def __new__(cls):
        if cls._instance is None:
            cls._instance = super(GameManager, cls).__new__(cls)
            # Initialize game manager here
        return cls._instance

game_manager1 = GameManager()
game_manager2 = GameManager()
assert game_manager1 is game_manager2  # Both refer to the same instance
```

2. Observer Pattern

The Observer pattern defines a one-to-many dependency between objects. When one object (the subject) changes state, all its dependents (observers) are notified and updated automatically. It's useful for implementing event systems and handling UI updates.

```python
class EventSubject:
    _observers = []

    def attach(self, observer):
        self._observers.append(observer)

    def notify(self, event):
        for observer in self._observers:
            observer.update(event)

class EventObserver:
    def update(self, event):
        # Handle the event
```

3. Factory Method Pattern

The Factory Method pattern defines an interface for creating an object, but allows subclasses to alter the type of objects that will be created. It's useful for creating game objects like characters, enemies, or power-ups.

```python
from abc import ABC, abstractmethod

class GameObject(ABC):
    @abstractmethod
    def draw(self):
        pass

class Player(GameObject):
    def draw(self):
        # Draw the player character

class Enemy(GameObject):
    def draw(self):
        # Draw an enemy

class GameObjectFactory(ABC):
    @abstractmethod
    def create_object(self):
        pass

class PlayerFactory(GameObjectFactory):
    def create_object(self):
        return Player()

class EnemyFactory(GameObjectFactory):
    def create_object(self):
        return Enemy()

factory = PlayerFactory()
player = factory.create_object()
```

4. State Pattern

The State pattern allows an object to alter its behavior when its internal state changes. It's useful for managing game character states, AI behavior, or menu navigation.

```python
class CharacterState(ABC):
    @abstractmethod
    def handle_input(self, character):
        pass

class StandingState(CharacterState):
    def handle_input(self, character):
        # Handle input for a character in a standing state
```

```python
class JumpingState(CharacterState):
    def handle_input(self, character):
        # Handle input for a character in a jumping state

class Character:
    def __init__(self):
        self.state = StandingState()

    def set_state(self, state):
        self.state = state

    def handle_input(self):
        self.state.handle_input(self)
```

These are just a few examples of design patterns commonly used in game development. By applying these patterns effectively, you can create a scalable and maintainable game architecture that is easier to extend and debug as your project evolves. Design patterns provide a solid foundation for building complex and engaging games.

Section 14.2: Managing Large Codebases

In game development, as your project grows, so does your codebase. Managing a large codebase is crucial for maintaining a productive development environment and ensuring the stability of your game. In this section, we'll explore strategies and best practices for handling large codebases effectively.

1. Modularization

One of the fundamental principles for managing a large codebase is modularization. Break your code into smaller, self-contained modules, each responsible for a specific aspect of your game. This promotes code reusability and makes it easier to maintain and extend your project.

```python
# Example of modularization
# Separate modules for rendering, input, and game logic
import rendering
import input_handling
import game_logic

# Initialize and use modules
renderer = rendering.Renderer()
input_manager = input_handling.InputManager()
game_logic_manager = game_logic.GameLogicManager()
```

2. Code Documentation

Proper documentation is essential for large codebases. Use comments, docstrings, and inline documentation to explain the purpose and usage of functions, classes, and modules. This helps team members understand your code and accelerates the debugging process.

```
# Example of code documentation
def calculate_damage(attacker, defender):
    """
    Calculate the damage dealt by the attacker to the defender.

    Args:
        attacker: The attacking character.
        defender: The defending character.

    Returns:
        The calculated damage value.
    """
    # Calculation logic here
```

3. Version Control

Utilize version control systems like Git to track changes to your codebase, collaborate with team members, and revert to previous states if issues arise. Proper branching and merging strategies are crucial when multiple developers are working on the same project.

```
# Git commands for version control
git init
git add .
git commit -m "Initial commit"
git branch feature-branch
git checkout feature-branch
# Make changes, commit, and merge
```

4. Code Reviews

Implement a code review process within your development team. Code reviews help identify issues, enforce coding standards, and ensure that changes align with project goals. It's an effective way to maintain code quality in a large codebase.

```
# Code review process
1. Developer submits a pull request.
2. Team members review the code.
3. Issues and feedback are discussed and resolved.
4. Code is merged into the main branch.
```

5. Automated Testing

Implement automated testing to ensure that changes and additions to your codebase do not introduce new bugs. Unit tests, integration tests, and regression tests are essential components of a robust testing strategy.

```python
# Example of automated unit testing with pytest
import pytest

def test_calculate_damage():
    assert calculate_damage(attacker, defender) == expected_damage
```

6. Continuous Integration

Set up a continuous integration (CI) pipeline that automatically builds and tests your code whenever changes are pushed to the repository. CI ensures that your codebase remains stable and reliable.

```yaml
# Example configuration for a CI/CD pipeline (using GitHub Actions)
name: CI/CD

on:
  push:
    branches:
      - main

jobs:
  build:
    runs-on: ubuntu-latest

    steps:
    - name: Checkout code
      uses: actions/checkout@v2

    - name: Setup Python
      uses: actions/setup-python@v2
      with:
        python-version: 3.8

    - name: Install dependencies
      run: pip install -r requirements.txt

    - name: Run tests
      run: pytest

    # Additional steps for deployment if needed
```

By following these strategies and best practices, you can effectively manage a large codebase in your game development project. A well-organized and documented codebase ensures that your team can work efficiently and that your game remains maintainable as it evolves.

Section 14.3: Scalability in Game Design

Scalability in game design refers to the ability of a game to handle a wide range of conditions, such as different hardware specifications, screen sizes, and player experiences, without compromising performance or quality. Designing games with scalability in mind is crucial to reach a broader audience and ensure that your game performs well across various platforms and player setups.

1. Resolution Independence

One key aspect of scalability is resolution independence. Design your game's user interface (UI) and graphics assets in a way that allows them to adapt seamlessly to different screen resolutions and aspect ratios. This ensures that your game looks good on a variety of devices, from smartphones to high-resolution monitors.

```
# Example of resolution-independent UI scaling in Unity
void Update() {
    // Calculate the scaling factor based on screen resolution
    float scaleFactor = Screen.width / 1920f;  // 1920x1080 is the reference resolution
    // Apply the scale to UI elements
    uiElement.localScale = new Vector3(scaleFactor, scaleFactor, 1);
}
```

2. Performance Optimization

Scalability also relates to performance optimization. Your game should adjust its graphics and gameplay complexity based on the player's hardware capabilities. Implement settings that allow players to customize graphics quality, texture quality, and other performance-related parameters. Additionally, use level of detail (LOD) techniques to reduce the complexity of 3D models as needed.

```
# Example of LOD implementation in a 3D game engine
if (distanceToCamera > highDetailDistance) {
    renderHighDetailModel();
} else if (distanceToCamera > mediumDetailDistance) {
    renderMediumDetailModel();
} else {
    renderLowDetailModel();
}
```

3. Input and Control Options

Scalable game design also encompasses input and control options. Ensure that your game can be played with different input methods, such as keyboard and mouse, gamepad, touch screen, and even VR controllers. Provide customizable control schemes and sensitivity settings to accommodate a variety of player preferences.

```
# Example of customizable control settings in a game
def setSensitivity(value):
```

```
    playerSensitivity = value

def customizeControls(keybindings):
    # Apply custom keybindings
    playerControls.setKeybindings(keybindings)
```

4. Cross-Platform Compatibility

To achieve scalability, consider cross-platform compatibility. Design your game to run on multiple operating systems and gaming platforms, such as Windows, macOS, Linux, consoles, and mobile devices. Utilize cross-platform game engines like Unity or Unreal Engine to simplify the development process for multiple platforms.

```
# Example of cross-platform development using Unity
#if UNITY_STANDALONE || UNITY_WEBGL
    // Code for desktop and web platforms
#elif UNITY_IOS || UNITY_ANDROID
    // Code for mobile platforms
#endif
```

5. Dynamic Content Loading

Implement dynamic content loading to reduce initial loading times and memory usage. Load game assets, levels, and textures on-demand as players progress through the game. This approach minimizes the game's memory footprint and improves loading performance, especially on devices with limited resources.

```
# Example of dynamic content loading in a game engine
def loadLevel(levelName):
    # Load level assets and resources when needed
    # ...
```

6. Network Scalability

For multiplayer or online games, scalability also extends to network architecture. Design a scalable server-client architecture that can handle varying numbers of players without sacrificing performance. Implement load balancing and server scaling techniques to ensure a smooth online gaming experience.

```
# Example of a simple load balancing algorithm
if numberOfPlayers > maxPlayersPerServer:
    # Redirect new players to a less populated server
    redirectToAnotherServer()
```

By incorporating these scalability principles into your game design and development process, you can create games that can adapt to a wide range of conditions and provide a consistent and enjoyable experience for players on different devices and hardware configurations.

Section 14.4: Efficient Resource Management

Efficient resource management is a critical aspect of game development, especially when it comes to large and complex games. Properly managing resources such as textures, models, audio files, and memory usage can significantly impact your game's performance, loading times, and overall player experience. In this section, we will explore various strategies and best practices for efficient resource management in game development.

1. Resource Compression

One of the primary techniques for efficient resource management is resource compression. Compressing textures, audio files, and other assets reduces their file sizes without significantly degrading quality. This not only saves storage space but also reduces loading times since smaller files load faster from disk.

```
// Example of texture compression in a game engine
Texture myTexture = LoadTexture("my_texture.png"); // Load uncompressed texture
CompressTexture(myTexture); // Compress the texture to reduce file size
```

2. Texture Atlases

Texture atlases are another resource management technique commonly used in 2D games. Instead of loading individual textures for each game object, you can pack multiple textures into a single atlas. This reduces the number of texture switches and draw calls, which can improve rendering performance.

```
// Example of using a texture atlas in a 2D game
SpriteSheet playerSheet = LoadSpriteSheet("player_sprites.png", 64, 64); // Load a sprite sheet
Sprite playerIdle = playerSheet.GetSprite("idle"); // Retrieve a specific sprite from the sheet
```

3. Streaming and Loading Screens

For larger open-world or 3D games, consider implementing streaming techniques. This involves loading game assets, textures, and models dynamically as the player explores the game world. Loading screens or transition areas can hide the asset loading process, ensuring a smooth and uninterrupted gaming experience.

```
// Example of streaming assets in an open-world game
void LoadWorldChunk(int chunkID) {
    // Load terrain, textures, and objects for the specified chunk
    // ...
}
```

4. Memory Pools

Memory pools are used to manage frequently created and destroyed objects efficiently. Instead of allocating and deallocating memory for objects on the fly, you preallocate a pool of memory blocks and reuse them. This reduces memory fragmentation and overhead.

```
// Example of memory pool for bullets in a shooting game
Bullet[] bulletPool = new Bullet[MAX_BULLETS];
int nextAvailableBullet = 0;

Bullet GetNextAvailableBullet() {
    // Find the next available bullet in the pool and return it
    // ...
}
```

5. Resource Streaming and Unloading

In larger games with extensive content, resource streaming and unloading can help manage memory efficiently. Load only the assets needed for the current game state or level and unload assets that are no longer in use. This keeps memory usage in check and prevents memory leaks.

```
// Example of unloading unused assets in a game engine
void UnloadUnusedAssets() {
    // Unload textures, models, and audio that are no longer in use
    // ...
}
```

6. Asset Bundles

Asset bundles are a way to package game assets separately from the main game executable. This allows for post-release updates and downloadable content (DLC). Asset bundles can be streamed into the game as needed, reducing the initial download size and enabling incremental content updates.

```
// Example of asset bundles in Unity
AssetBundle myBundle = AssetBundle.LoadFromFile("my_bundle.unity3d");
GameObject prefab = myBundle.LoadAsset<GameObject>("my_prefab");
```

Efficient resource management is crucial for delivering a seamless and enjoyable gaming experience to players. By implementing these strategies and techniques, you can optimize your game's performance, reduce loading times, and ensure that your game runs smoothly even on a wide range of hardware configurations.

Section 14.5: Preparing for Future Expansion

As game development evolves, it's essential to consider how to prepare your project for future expansion and updates. While creating a successful game is a significant accomplishment, maintaining its longevity and relevance is equally important. In this section, we'll explore strategies for ensuring your game is ready for future expansion and improvements.

1. Modular Code Architecture

A modular code architecture is essential for future expansion. By organizing your code into well-defined modules or components, you can easily add new features, fix bugs, and make improvements without disrupting the entire codebase. Use design patterns such as the Entity-Component System (ECS) or Model-View-Controller (MVC) to keep your code modular and maintainable.

```python
# Example of a modular code architecture in Python using ECS
class Entity:
    def __init__(self):
        self.components = []

    def add_component(self, component):
        self.components.append(component)

class RenderComponent:
    def render(self):
        # Render the entity
        pass

class PhysicsComponent:
    def update(self):
        # Update physics simulation
        pass
```

2. Version Control

Utilize version control systems like Git to keep track of changes and collaborate with other developers. Maintaining a well-documented version history allows you to identify and revert problematic changes and ensures that you can reference previous versions of your game if needed.

```
# Example of using Git for version control
git init            # Initialize a Git repository
git add .           # Stage changes for commit
git commit -m "Initial commit"    # Commit changes with a message
git branch feature-branch         # Create a feature branch
git checkout feature-branch       # Switch to the feature branch
```

3. Extensible Game Engines and Frameworks

When choosing a game engine or framework for development, consider its extensibility. Opt for engines that allow you to create custom plugins, extensions, or scripts. This flexibility ensures that you can adapt your game to new technologies, platforms, or gameplay mechanics as they emerge.

```
// Example of extending Unity with custom C# scripts
public class CustomBehavior : MonoBehaviour {
    // Custom code and functionality
}
```

4. Regular Updates and Patches

Keep your game fresh and exciting by releasing regular updates and patches. Listen to player feedback, address bugs, and introduce new content or features. These updates can re-engage your player base and attract new players, extending the game's lifespan.

```
Version 1.1.0 Release Notes:
- Added new character skins
- Balanced gameplay mechanics
- Fixed major bug causing crashes
```

5. Community Engagement

Foster an active and engaged player community. Encourage players to share their ideas, create mods, or contribute to the game's development. Community-driven content can breathe new life into your game and extend its longevity.

```
- Player-generated mods are now supported.
- Join our official Discord server to connect with other players and modders.
```

6. Monetization and Sustainability

Consider sustainable monetization strategies. While generating revenue is important, focus on methods that provide value to players and encourage them to support your game. Avoid predatory practices and ensure that in-app purchases or advertisements are non-intrusive.

- Introducing a "Supporter Pack" with cosmetic items to fund ongoing development.
- Advertisements will be displayed only during loading screens.

7. Compatibility and Portability

Plan for compatibility and portability. Ensure that your game can adapt to new hardware, operating systems, and platforms. Consider future-proofing by developing your game using cross-platform technologies or libraries.

```
// Example of cross-platform development with SDL
#ifdef _WIN32
    // Windows-specific code
#elif __APPLE__
```

```
    // macOS-specific code
#elif __linux__
    // Linux-specific code
#endif
```

By implementing these strategies, you can future-proof your game and ensure that it remains relevant and enjoyable for years to come. Keep an eye on industry trends, player feedback, and emerging technologies to guide your decisions and maintain a successful and enduring game.

Chapter 15: Monetization and Business Strategies

Section 15.1: Monetization Models in Gaming

Monetization is a crucial aspect of game development, as it enables developers to generate revenue and sustain their projects. There are various monetization models to consider, each with its own advantages and considerations. In this section, we will explore different monetization models in gaming and discuss their implementation.

1. Free-to-Play (F2P)

The Free-to-Play model allows players to download and play the game for free. Revenue is generated through in-app purchases (IAPs), advertisements, or other microtransactions within the game. This model lowers the entry barrier for players and can attract a large user base.

```lua
-- Example of implementing in-app purchases in Lua
function onPurchaseComplete(item)
    if item == "powerup" then
        player:addPowerUp()
    elseif item == "cosmetic" then
        player:unlockCosmetic()
    end
end
```

2. Premium Games

Premium games require players to make an upfront payment to access the full game. This model guarantees revenue from the start but may limit the potential player base. Premium games often offer a complete, ad-free experience.

```csharp
// Example of defining a premium game price in C#
decimal gamePrice = 19.99m; // Set the game price in USD
```

3. Freemium

The Freemium model combines elements of both Free-to-Play and Premium models. Players can download the game for free and enjoy a basic experience. Additional content or features are available through in-app purchases. This model aims to convert free users into paying customers.

```javascript
// Example of unlocking premium features in JavaScript
function unlockPremiumContent() {
    if (player.hasPurchasedPremium()) {
        player.unlockContent();
    } else {
        promptPurchase();
    }
}
```

4. Subscription-Based

Subscription-based monetization involves offering players access to the game's content and features through a recurring subscription fee. This model provides a steady stream of income and encourages player retention.

```java
// Example of implementing a subscription model in Java
public class GameSubscription {
    private boolean isSubscribed;

    public void subscribe() {
        isSubscribed = true;
        grantAccessToPremiumContent();
    }

    public void unsubscribe() {
        isSubscribed = false;
        revokeAccessToPremiumContent();
    }
}
```

5. Advertisements

Including advertisements in your game can be a profitable monetization strategy. Ad revenue is generated based on the number of views, clicks, or interactions with ads. Consider implementing rewarded ads, where players voluntarily watch ads in exchange for in-game rewards.

```swift
// Example of integrating rewarded ads in Swift
func showRewardedAd() {
    if adService.isRewardedAdAvailable() {
        adService.showRewardedAd()
    }
}
```

6. In-App Purchases (IAPs)

In-App Purchases allow players to buy virtual goods, items, or currency within the game. This model is commonly used in Free-to-Play games and can be used to enhance gameplay or provide cosmetic upgrades.

```cpp
// Example of processing in-app purchases in C++
void purchaseItem(const std::string& itemID) {
    if (validatePurchase(itemID)) {
        player.addItemToInventory(itemID);
    }
}
```

7. Crowdfunding

Crowdfunding platforms like Kickstarter or Indiegogo can help finance game development. Developers offer various rewards or tiers to backers, such as early access, exclusive content, or physical merchandise.

- Backers who contribute $50 or more will receive a limited edition game artbook.
- The $100 tier grants early access to the game's beta testing phase.

8. Donations

Some developers rely on player donations to support their work. They may provide donation links within the game or on their website, allowing players to contribute voluntarily.

```
<!-- Example of adding a donation button in HTML -->
<button onclick="openDonationPage()">Support the Developers</button>
```

9. Sponsorships and Partnerships

Consider partnering with other companies or brands for sponsorships. This can include in-game product placements, cross-promotions, or collaborations that provide additional revenue streams.

- Featured in partnership with [Brand Name]. Unlock exclusive in-game content when you purchase their products.

10. Data Monetization

Collecting and analyzing player data can be valuable for targeted advertising and partnerships. Ensure that your data collection practices are transparent and comply with privacy regulations.

- We collect anonymized player data to improve gameplay and provide personalized experiences.

When selecting a monetization model, consider your target audience, game genre, and the value your game offers. It's also important to strike a balance between generating revenue and providing an enjoyable player experience. Successful monetization strategies align with player expectations and deliver value in return.

Section 15.2: Implementing In-App Purchases

In-App Purchases (IAPs) are a common monetization strategy in mobile games and applications. They allow developers to sell virtual goods, items, or currency within the app, enhancing the player's experience or providing cosmetic upgrades. Properly implementing

IAPs is crucial for generating revenue and retaining players. In this section, we will explore the steps to implement in-app purchases effectively.

1. Platform-Specific Integration

Each mobile platform (iOS, Android) has its own in-app purchase system and guidelines. To implement IAPs, you'll need to integrate with the platform-specific APIs and services.

iOS (Swift Example):
```swift
import StoreKit

func purchaseItem(itemID: String) {
    if SKPaymentQueue.canMakePayments() {
        let product = SKProduct(productIdentifier: itemID)
        let payment = SKPayment(product: product)
        SKPaymentQueue.default().add(payment)
    }
}
```

Android (Java Example):
```java
import com.android.billingclient.api.BillingClient;
import com.android.billingclient.api.Purchase;
import com.android.billingclient.api.BillingResult;
import com.android.billingclient.api.BillingClientStateListener;

// Initialize the BillingClient
BillingClient billingClient = BillingClient.newBuilder(context)
    .setListener(purchasesUpdatedListener)
    .enablePendingPurchases()
    .build();

// Establish a connection to the Google Play Billing service
billingClient.startConnection(new BillingClientStateListener() {
    @Override
    public void onBillingSetupFinished(BillingResult billingResult) {
        if (billingResult.getResponseCode() == BillingClient.BillingResponseCode.OK) {
            // Ready to make purchases
        }
    }

    @Override
    public void onBillingServiceDisconnected() {
        // Handle billing service disconnect
    }
});
```

2. Product Definitions

Define the products or items available for purchase within your app. Each product should have a unique identifier, a name, description, and price.

```
{
    "productID": "com.example.powerup",
    "name": "Power-Up",
    "description": "Upgrade your character's abilities",
    "price": "$1.99"
}
```

3. User Interface

Design a user-friendly interface that displays available items and their prices. Allow users to initiate purchases and provide feedback on the purchase process.

4. Handle Purchase Flow

Implement the flow for handling in-app purchases, including the purchase request, verification, and providing the purchased item to the user.

```
func handlePurchase(purchase: SKPaymentTransaction) {
    let productID = purchase.payment.productIdentifier
    if productID == "com.example.powerup" {
        // Process the purchase and unlock the power-up
        unlockPowerUp()
        // Finish the transaction
        SKPaymentQueue.default().finishTransaction(purchase)
    }
}

// Handle the purchase flow on Android
BillingResult result = billingClient.launchBillingFlow(activity, billingFlowParams);
if (result.getResponseCode() == BillingClient.BillingResponseCode.OK) {
    // Purchase initiated successfully
} else {
    // Handle errors
}
```

5. Receipt Verification

It's essential to verify purchase receipts to prevent fraud. Platforms provide APIs or tools for receipt validation.

```
func verifyReceipt(receipt: String) {
    // Send the receipt to your server for validation
    // Ensure the receipt is valid and matches the purchase
}
```

6. Restore Purchases

Provide an option for users to restore their purchases if they reinstall the app or switch devices. This enhances the user experience and builds trust.

```
func restorePurchases() {
    SKPaymentQueue.default().restoreCompletedTransactions()
}
```

7. Testing and Debugging

Thoroughly test the IAP implementation in sandbox or test environments provided by the platforms. Ensure that purchases are processed correctly and that errors are handled gracefully.

```
// Testing IAPs in the iOS simulator
// Enable the "StoreKit Testing" configuration in Xcode
// Use a test user account for purchases
```

8. Compliance with Guidelines

Adhere to the platform-specific guidelines and policies regarding in-app purchases. Violations can result in app removal from app stores.

Effective implementation of in-app purchases can lead to a successful monetization strategy for your mobile game or app. Remember to balance monetization with the overall user experience to maintain player satisfaction and retention.

Section 15.3: Advertising Strategies for Games

Advertising is a significant revenue source for many mobile games and applications. In this section, we'll explore various advertising strategies that can help you monetize your game effectively.

1. Types of Ads

a. Banner Ads

Banner ads are small, static or animated advertisements that appear at the top or bottom of the game screen. They are less intrusive but offer lower click-through rates (CTR). Consider placing them in non-gameplay screens, such as menus.

b. Interstitial Ads

Interstitial ads are full-screen ads that appear between game levels or at natural breaks in gameplay. They provide higher CTR compared to banner ads. However, they should not disrupt the player's experience.

c. Rewarded Video Ads

Rewarded video ads offer players in-game rewards, such as extra lives or virtual currency, in exchange for watching a short video ad. This strategy enhances user engagement and can increase ad revenue.

d. Native Ads

Native ads blend seamlessly with the game's content and design. They provide a non-disruptive experience and can be integrated into menus or game interfaces.

2. Ad Mediation

Ad mediation platforms allow you to manage multiple ad networks and demand sources. They optimize ad selection, ensuring that the highest-paying ads are displayed to maximize revenue. Popular ad mediation platforms include AdMob, MoPub, and IronSource.

3. Frequency and Placement

Consider the frequency and placement of ads carefully. Bombarding players with ads can lead to a negative user experience and potentially decrease retention. Balance ad frequency with player engagement.

4. Targeted Advertising

Utilize player data and analytics to deliver targeted ads. Show ads that are relevant to the player's interests and demographics. This can increase CTR and overall revenue.

5. Ad-Free Options

Offer players the option to remove ads through a one-time purchase or a subscription model. Some players are willing to pay for an ad-free experience, providing an additional revenue stream.

6. A/B Testing

Perform A/B testing to optimize ad strategies. Test different ad formats, placements, and frequencies to determine what works best for your audience. Continuously analyze ad performance and make adjustments accordingly.

7. Ad Revenue Models

Understand the various ad revenue models:

a. Cost Per Mille (CPM)

Advertisers pay a fixed amount for every thousand ad impressions. CPM is a straightforward model but may not be the most lucrative.

b. Cost Per Click (CPC)

Advertisers pay when a user clicks on their ad. CPC can provide higher revenue if you have a high CTR.

c. Cost Per Action (CPA)

Advertisers pay when a specific action is completed, such as installing an app or making an in-app purchase. CPA can be highly profitable but requires a strong user base.

8. Ad Placement Testing

Test different ad placements within your game to find the most effective spots. Monitor player feedback and adjust ad placements accordingly.

9. Ad Design and Creatives

Create compelling ad creatives that attract user attention. Well-designed ads with clear calls to action (CTAs) tend to perform better.

10. User Consent and Privacy

Ensure compliance with privacy regulations and obtain user consent for personalized ads. Failing to do so can lead to legal issues and app store removal.

11. Ad Monetization Strategy

Diversify your ad monetization strategy. Combine ads with other revenue sources, such as in-app purchases and subscriptions, to maximize earnings.

12. Ad Reporting and Analytics

Use ad reporting and analytics tools to track ad performance, revenue, and user engagement. Analyze the data to make informed decisions and optimizations.

Effective advertising strategies can generate substantial revenue for your mobile game. However, it's crucial to strike a balance between monetization and user experience to maintain player satisfaction and retention.

Section 15.4: Building and Maintaining a Player Base

Building and maintaining a dedicated player base is essential for the long-term success of your game. In this section, we'll explore strategies to attract players, engage them, and keep them coming back for more.

1. Player Acquisition

a. Marketing and Promotion

Invest in marketing and promotional efforts to make players aware of your game. Utilize social media, app store optimization (ASO), influencer marketing, and advertising to reach a broader audience.

b. App Store Optimization (ASO)

Optimize your game's app store listing with relevant keywords, attractive screenshots, and a compelling description. This increases the visibility of your game in app stores and improves discoverability.

c. Cross-Promotion

Leverage your existing player base by cross-promoting your other games within your apps. This can help attract users who are already familiar with your brand.

2. Player Engagement

a. Regular Updates

Frequent updates with new content, features, and bug fixes keep players engaged and excited about your game. Listen to player feedback and implement improvements based on their suggestions.

b. Events and Challenges

Organize in-game events and challenges that encourage player participation. Offer rewards for completing these events to incentivize continued play.

c. Social Features

Implement social features such as leaderboards, achievements, and multiplayer modes. These features foster competition and social interaction among players.

d. Community Building

Create and maintain a community around your game. Use social media, forums, and in-game chats to facilitate player interaction. Engage with your community and respond to their inquiries and feedback.

3. Monetization Strategies

a. In-App Purchases (IAP)

Offer in-app purchases that enhance gameplay, such as cosmetic items, power-ups, or additional content. Ensure that these purchases are balanced and do not create a pay-to-win environment.

b. Advertisements

Integrate advertisements strategically to monetize non-paying players. Balance ad frequency and placement to maintain a positive user experience.

c. Subscription Models

Implement subscription-based monetization, providing players with premium content, ad-free experiences, or exclusive perks for a recurring fee.

4. Player Retention

a. Personalized Experiences

Tailor the gaming experience to individual players by using data and analytics. Recommend content, challenges, or items based on their preferences and behavior.

b. Push Notifications

Use push notifications to re-engage players. Inform them about events, updates, or special offers to bring them back to the game.

c. Loyalty Programs

Reward loyal players with in-game currency, special items, or discounts. Loyalty programs encourage players to return regularly.

5. Analyze Player Data

Utilize player analytics to gain insights into player behavior. Understand where players drop off or get stuck and make improvements to those areas. Analyze metrics like player churn rate, session length, and retention to gauge the game's health.

6. Player Feedback

Listen to player feedback through app store reviews, social media, and in-game surveys. Address player concerns promptly and communicate your commitment to improving the game.

7. Community Management

Effective community management is vital. Have dedicated community managers or moderators who engage with players, enforce rules, and create a positive atmosphere within the game's community.

Building and maintaining a player base is an ongoing process that requires dedication and attention to player needs and preferences. By implementing these strategies, you can create a loyal player community that continues to enjoy and support your game.

Section 15.5: Analyzing Market Trends and Player Data

Analyzing market trends and player data is crucial for making informed decisions in game development and monetization strategies. In this section, we'll delve into the importance of data analysis and how to leverage it effectively.

1. Data Collection and Storage

a. Telemetry

Implement telemetry systems within your game to collect various data points, such as player behavior, in-game actions, and user preferences. Ensure the data collected complies with privacy regulations and user consent.

b. Data Warehousing

Set up a data warehousing solution to centralize and store the collected data securely. Cloud-based data warehouses like Amazon Redshift, Google BigQuery, or Snowflake are commonly used for scalability and ease of analysis.

2. Data Analysis Tools

a. Data Visualization

Utilize data visualization tools like Tableau, Power BI, or open-source alternatives like Matplotlib and Plotly to create visual representations of your data. Visualizations help in understanding trends and patterns more intuitively.

b. SQL and Query Languages

Learn SQL (Structured Query Language) or use query languages specific to your data warehousing solution to extract insights from your data. SQL allows you to filter, aggregate, and analyze data efficiently.

c. Machine Learning and AI

Explore machine learning and AI algorithms to discover hidden insights and predictive patterns in your player data. These technologies can help in player segmentation, churn prediction, and personalized recommendations.

3. Player Segmentation

a. Demographics

Segment players based on demographics such as age, gender, location, and language. This information can guide localization efforts and targeted marketing campaigns.

b. Behavior

Analyze player behavior to identify different playstyles, engagement levels, and spending patterns. Segmenting players by behavior helps tailor in-game experiences and monetization strategies.

c. Engagement Metrics

Segment players by engagement metrics like session frequency, session length, and player retention. Understanding player engagement segments can guide updates and content creation.

4. A/B Testing

a. Experimentation

Conduct A/B tests to evaluate the impact of changes in the game, such as user interface modifications, monetization adjustments, or feature additions. A/B testing helps in making data-driven decisions.

b. Metrics Comparison

Compare key performance metrics between control and experimental groups. Metrics may include conversion rates, revenue per user, and player retention.

5. Predictive Analytics

a. Churn Prediction

Use predictive analytics to identify players at risk of churn (discontinuing play). Implement retention strategies for these players, such as personalized offers or in-game events.

b. Revenue Forecasting

Forecast future revenue based on historical data and trends. Accurate revenue forecasts aid in budgeting, resource allocation, and business planning.

6. Privacy and Data Security

a. Compliance

Adhere to data privacy regulations, such as GDPR (General Data Protection Regulation) and CCPA (California Consumer Privacy Act), when collecting and handling player data. Implement robust security measures to protect player information.

7. Continuous Improvement

a. Iterative Analysis

Data analysis should be an iterative process. Regularly review and refine your data analysis methods to uncover new insights and adapt to changing player behavior and market dynamics.

b. Cross-Functional Collaboration

Foster collaboration between data analysts, game developers, and business stakeholders. Sharing insights and aligning strategies leads to more effective decision-making.

Analyzing market trends and player data empowers game developers to create better gaming experiences, improve monetization strategies, and build stronger player communities. By harnessing the power of data, you can stay competitive in the dynamic world of game development.

Chapter 16: Advanced User Interface Design

Section 16.1: Creating Custom UI Components

User interface (UI) design plays a critical role in shaping the overall user experience of a game. While many game engines provide built-in UI systems, there are situations where you need to create custom UI components tailored to your game's unique requirements. In this section, we will explore the process of designing and implementing custom UI components in SDL.

Understanding Custom UI Components

Custom UI components are graphical elements that allow users to interact with your game. These components can include buttons, sliders, menus, and more. Creating custom UI components gives you full control over their appearance and behavior, allowing you to match the game's visual style and functionality.

When designing custom UI components, consider the following aspects:

1. **Aesthetics**: Your UI components should align with your game's visual theme. Consider the color schemes, fonts, and overall design language to maintain consistency.

2. **Interactivity**: Determine how users will interact with the components. Will they click on buttons, drag sliders, or use keyboard shortcuts? Define the expected behaviors.

3. **Responsiveness**: Ensure that UI components respond promptly to user actions. Smooth animations and transitions can enhance the user experience.

SDL and Custom UI Components

SDL provides a foundation for creating custom UI components, but you'll need to implement the rendering, input handling, and event processing logic yourself. Here are the fundamental steps to create custom UI components in SDL:

1. **Rendering**: Use SDL's rendering functions to draw UI elements on the screen. You can use SDL's texture rendering capabilities to display custom graphics, text, and animations.

2. **Input Handling**: Detect user input, such as mouse clicks or keyboard presses, and map them to UI interactions. SDL's event system can help you capture these inputs.

3. **Event Processing**: Implement event handlers to respond to UI interactions. For example, when a button is clicked, trigger the associated action.

Creating Custom Buttons

As an example, let's create a custom button component in SDL. We'll define a button's appearance, interactivity, and event handling.

```
// Define a structure for a button
typedef struct {
    SDL_Rect rect; // Button's position and size
    SDL_Texture* normalTexture; // Texture for the normal state
    SDL_Texture* hoverTexture; // Texture for the hover state
    SDL_Texture* clickTexture; // Texture for the click state
    SDL_bool isHovered; // Flag to track hover state
    SDL_bool isClicked; // Flag to track click state
} UIButton;
```

In the above code, we've created a UIButton structure that includes properties for the button's position, size, textures for different states (normal, hover, click), and flags to track its state.

To render and handle input for the button, you'll need to write functions for drawing the button, checking mouse interactions, and responding to click events. These functions will be called from your game loop.

Creating custom UI components in SDL gives you the flexibility to design UI elements that seamlessly integrate with your game's aesthetics and functionality. Whether it's buttons, sliders, or complex menus, mastering custom UI design can greatly enhance your game's user experience.

In the next sections, we'll delve deeper into different aspects of UI design and customization, including dynamic UI adaptation, animations, accessibility, and user testing. These topics will help you refine your custom UI components and create a polished user interface for your game.

Section 16.2: Dynamic UI Adaptation and Scalability

Creating a user interface (UI) that adapts seamlessly to various screen sizes and resolutions is crucial in modern game development. Gamers play on a wide range of devices, from large monitors to small mobile screens, and ensuring your UI remains user-friendly on all of them is essential. In this section, we will explore dynamic UI adaptation and scalability techniques using SDL.

Challenges in UI Adaptation

Designing a UI that works well across different devices can be challenging due to varying screen sizes, aspect ratios, and resolutions. Here are some common challenges faced when adapting UI:

1. **Screen Size and Resolution**: Different devices have different screen dimensions and resolutions. UI elements may need to be resized and repositioned to fit each screen correctly.

2. **Aspect Ratio**: Maintaining the correct aspect ratio of UI elements is vital to avoid distortion or stretching on different screens.

3. **Touch vs. Mouse Input**: On mobile devices, users interact with touchscreens, while on PCs, they typically use a mouse and keyboard. Your UI must be responsive to both input methods.

SDL and Dynamic UI Adaptation

SDL provides tools and functions that can help you address these challenges:

1. **Window and Renderer**: SDL allows you to create a window and renderer that match the screen's resolution. This helps in rendering UI elements at the correct size.

2. **Scalable Graphics**: You can use scalable vector graphics (SVG) or high-resolution textures to ensure that UI elements remain sharp and clear on different screens.

3. **Layout Algorithms**: Implement layout algorithms that dynamically adjust the position and size of UI elements based on the screen's dimensions. Libraries like SDL_ttf for text rendering can also assist in scaling text appropriately.

Responsive UI Design

Here's an example of how to create a responsive button in SDL. We'll assume you have already created a UIButton structure as discussed in the previous section.

```
void UpdateButtonPosition(UIButton* button, int screenWidth, int screenHeight
) {
    // Calculate the new position and size of the button based on screen dime
nsions
    button->rect.x = screenWidth / 2 - button->rect.w / 2;
    button->rect.y = screenHeight / 2 - button->rect.h / 2;
}
```

In the above code, the `UpdateButtonPosition` function adjusts the button's position to center it on the screen. This ensures that the button remains centered regardless of the screen's dimensions.

Aspect Ratio Preservation

Preserving the aspect ratio of UI elements is critical to prevent distortion. To achieve this, you can calculate the scale factor for your UI elements based on the aspect ratio of the target screen and apply it uniformly.

```
void PreserveAspectRatio(UIButton* button, float targetAspectRatio) {
    float currentAspectRatio = (float)button->rect.w / (float)button->rect.h;
```

```
    float scale = targetAspectRatio / currentAspectRatio;

    button->rect.w *= scale;
    button->rect.h *= scale;
}
```

In this code, the `PreserveAspectRatio` function adjusts the button's dimensions while maintaining its original aspect ratio.

Testing on Multiple Devices

To ensure that your UI adaptation works correctly, it's essential to test your game on various devices with different screen sizes and resolutions. Emulators and device labs can help you identify and fix issues related to UI scalability.

By implementing dynamic UI adaptation and scalability in SDL, you can provide a consistent and user-friendly experience for gamers on different platforms and devices. These techniques are essential for modern game development, where reaching a broad audience is a key goal. In the next sections, we'll explore additional aspects of UI design, including enhancing user experience with animations, accessibility considerations, UI prototyping, and user testing.

Section 16.3: Enhancing User Experience with Animations

In modern game development, user experience (UX) plays a vital role in the success of a game. One powerful tool for enhancing UX is the use of animations. Animations can bring life to your game's user interface (UI) and make interactions more engaging. In this section, we'll explore how to implement animations in SDL to create a more immersive gaming experience.

Why Use Animations in UI?

Animations serve several essential purposes in UI design:

1. **Visual Feedback**: Animations provide visual cues to users, indicating that an action has occurred or that they can interact with a UI element. For example, a button changing color when hovered over.

2. **Smooth Transitions**: Animations create smooth transitions between different UI states, reducing abrupt changes that can be jarring for users.

3. **Engagement**: Animations can make your UI more engaging and enjoyable, increasing the overall user satisfaction.

4. **Storytelling**: In narrative-driven games, animations can be used to convey the story or emotions of characters.

SDL and Animation Basics

SDL provides a foundation for implementing animations in your game's UI. Here's a basic outline of how to get started:

1. **Frame Rate Control**: To create smooth animations, you should control the frame rate of your game. SDL provides timing functions to help you achieve consistent frame rates.
2. **Sprite Sheets**: If your UI includes animated sprites, use sprite sheets to manage and display frames of animation efficiently.
3. **Transition Effects**: Implement transition effects, such as fades, slides, and scaling, to create polished UI transitions.

Creating Simple UI Animations

Let's look at a simple example of how to create a fade-in animation for a UI element like a button in SDL.

```
void FadeInButton(UIButton* button, float duration) {
    Uint32 startTime = SDL_GetTicks();
    Uint32 currentTime;

    while (1) {
        currentTime = SDL_GetTicks();
        if (currentTime - startTime >= duration) {
            // Animation complete
            break;
        }

        // Calculate the alpha value based on the elapsed time
        float alpha = (currentTime - startTime) / (float)duration;
        button->alpha = alpha;

        // Redraw the UI with the updated alpha value
        RedrawUI();
    }

    // Ensure the final state is fully opaque
    button->alpha = 1.0f;
    RedrawUI();
}
```

In this code, the `FadeInButton` function gradually increases the alpha (transparency) of the button over a specified duration, creating a fade-in effect.

User-Centric Animations

When implementing animations, consider the user's experience. Ensure that animations are not overly distracting, provide clear feedback, and serve a purpose in your UI. Avoid excessive use of animations that might annoy or overwhelm players.

Animations can significantly contribute to the UX of your game when used thoughtfully and creatively. In the next section, we'll explore accessibility and inclusivity considerations in UI design, ensuring that your game is enjoyable for a diverse audience.

Section 16.4: Accessibility and Inclusivity in UI Design

Creating an inclusive user interface (UI) in your game is essential to ensure that players of all abilities and backgrounds can enjoy your game. Accessibility and inclusivity should be a fundamental part of your UI design process. In this section, we'll explore the importance of accessibility and inclusivity in game UI and how to implement them using SDL.

Why Accessibility Matters

Accessibility refers to designing products and services that are usable by people with disabilities. In the context of game UI, it means making sure that players with disabilities can access and enjoy your game on equal terms. Here are some key reasons why accessibility matters:

1. **Equal Access**: Everyone, regardless of their abilities, should have equal access to your game. Accessibility ensures that no one is left out.
2. **Legal Requirements**: In many regions, there are legal requirements for software accessibility. Complying with these regulations is not only ethical but also a legal obligation.
3. **Expanded Player Base**: By making your game accessible, you can attract a more diverse player base and potentially increase your game's popularity.

Implementing Accessibility in SDL UI

Here are some guidelines and techniques for implementing accessibility in your SDL-based game UI:

1. **Keyboard Navigation**: Ensure that all UI elements can be navigated and interacted with using a keyboard. This is crucial for players who cannot use a mouse.
2. **Text-to-Speech (TTS)**: Implement TTS support for in-game text. This helps visually impaired players by reading out text content.

3. **High Contrast Mode**: Provide a high-contrast mode that enhances visibility for players with visual impairments.
4. **Resizable Fonts**: Allow players to resize fonts to suit their preferences, making text more readable for those with vision impairments.
5. **Alternative Text**: Provide alternative text descriptions for images, icons, and other visual elements. Screen readers can use this information to describe the UI to visually impaired players.
6. **Colorblind-Friendly Palettes**: Avoid relying solely on color to convey information. Use patterns, shapes, and labels to help colorblind players understand UI elements.
7. **Customizable Controls**: Allow players to customize controls to accommodate various input devices and preferences.

SDL and Accessibility

SDL provides a solid foundation for implementing accessible UI features in your game. You can use SDL functions to capture keyboard input, manage text rendering, and handle screen reader compatibility.

```
// Example SDL code for keyboard input handling
SDL_Event event;
while (SDL_PollEvent(&event)) {
    switch (event.type) {
        case SDL_KEYDOWN:
            // Handle key presses here
            break;
        case SDL_KEYUP:
            // Handle key releases here
            break;
        // Handle other events as needed
    }
}
```

By capturing keyboard input and providing customizable controls, you can ensure that players with mobility impairments can play your game comfortably.

Remember that accessibility is an ongoing process. Regularly test your game with players who have disabilities and gather feedback to make continuous improvements to your UI design.

In the next section, we'll explore the process of prototyping and user testing in UI design to ensure that your game's UI is user-friendly and effective.

Section 16.5: UI Prototyping and User Testing

User Interface (UI) prototyping and user testing are crucial steps in the game development process, ensuring that your game's UI is user-friendly and effective. In this section, we'll delve into the importance of UI prototyping and user testing and how to apply these concepts to your SDL-based game.

The Significance of UI Prototyping

UI prototyping involves creating preliminary designs or mockups of your game's user interface before implementing the final version. This step allows you to:

1. **Visualize the Design**: Prototypes provide a visual representation of your UI, helping you assess its layout, aesthetics, and usability.

2. **Gather Early Feedback**: By sharing prototypes with your team or potential users, you can collect feedback and make necessary adjustments before investing time in development.

3. **Identify Issues**: Prototyping helps identify design flaws, usability issues, or missing features early in the process, saving time and resources in the long run.

Steps in UI Prototyping

Here's a simplified process for creating UI prototypes:

1. **Define Objectives**: Clearly define the objectives and goals of your UI design. Understand what you want to achieve with the interface.

2. **Sketch Ideas**: Begin with rough sketches of your UI layout and features. These sketches can be done on paper or digitally.

3. **Wireframing**: Create wireframes that outline the structure of your UI. Wireframes focus on layout and content placement without concerning themselves with visual details.

4. **Interactive Prototypes**: Develop interactive prototypes using tools like Adobe XD, Sketch, or Figma. These tools allow you to create clickable prototypes that simulate user interactions.

5. **User Testing**: Conduct user testing with your interactive prototype. Invite testers to use the prototype and gather feedback on usability, navigation, and overall user experience.

6. **Iterate and Refine**: Based on user feedback, make necessary changes and refinements to your prototype. Iterate this process until you achieve a satisfactory design.

Implementing UI Prototyping in SDL

SDL can be used to create simple prototypes of your game's UI elements. While it won't replace specialized UI prototyping tools, it can help you quickly test basic interactions and concepts. For example, you can create a simple SDL application that simulates button clicks and menu navigation.

```
// Example SDL code for simulating button clicks
#include <SDL.h>

// Initialize SDL
SDL_Init(SDL_INIT_VIDEO);

// Create a window and renderer
SDL_Window* window = SDL_CreateWindow("UI Prototype", SDL_WINDOWPOS_CENTERED,
SDL_WINDOWPOS_CENTERED, 800, 600, SDL_WINDOW_SHOWN);
SDL_Renderer* renderer = SDL_CreateRenderer(window, -1, SDL_RENDERER_ACCELERA
TED);

// Main loop
bool quit = false;
SDL_Event event;
while (!quit) {
    while (SDL_PollEvent(&event)) {
        if (event.type == SDL_QUIT) {
            quit = true;
        }
        // Handle button clicks or other UI interactions here
    }

    // Clear and render UI elements
    SDL_SetRenderDrawColor(renderer, 255, 255, 255, 255);
    SDL_RenderClear(renderer);

    // Render UI elements (buttons, menus, etc.)

    SDL_RenderPresent(renderer);
}

// Cleanup and exit
SDL_DestroyRenderer(renderer);
SDL_DestroyWindow(window);
SDL_Quit();
```

This code snippet demonstrates a basic SDL application with an event loop. You can use SDL's rendering capabilities to display UI elements and simulate user interactions during prototyping.

User Testing in SDL

User testing with SDL prototypes can be done by providing testers with a standalone executable of your prototype. Gather feedback on the usability and intuitiveness of your UI elements and use this feedback to refine your design.

In the next chapter, we'll explore the challenges and strategies involved in localizing your game for international audiences, ensuring that your game can be enjoyed by players from diverse cultural backgrounds.

Chapter 17: Localization and Internationalization

Localization and internationalization are essential aspects of game development, especially if you aim to reach a global audience. In this chapter, we'll explore the importance of adapting your game to different languages and cultures and provide guidance on how to implement localization and internationalization in your SDL-based games.

Section 17.1: Preparing Your Game for Global Audiences

Expanding your game's reach to international markets requires careful planning and execution. Here's how to prepare your game for global audiences:

1. Cultural Sensitivity
   - **Research**: Understand the cultural norms, values, and taboos of the target regions. Avoid content that could be considered offensive or inappropriate.
   - **Localization Team**: Hire or collaborate with experts in the target culture or region to ensure accurate translations and cultural adaptations.

2. Multilingual Support
   - **Unicode**: Ensure that your game's codebase and text rendering support Unicode, which allows the display of characters from various languages.
   - **Fonts**: Select fonts that support a wide range of characters and diacritics to accommodate different languages.

3. Text Handling
   - **Dynamic Text Layout**: Implement a dynamic text layout system that can handle text expansion and contraction in different languages.
   - **Text Concatenation**: Avoid concatenating strings for in-game text, as word order varies between languages.

4. Audio Localization
   - **Voice Acting**: If your game includes voiceovers, provide options for multiple languages or subtitles to cater to players who don't speak the game's original language.
   - **Localized Sound Effects**: Consider localizing sound effects, such as character reactions or environment sounds.

5. Time and Date Formats
   - **Date and Time Display**: Use appropriate date and time formats based on the player's region.
   - **Time Zones**: Account for time zone differences when implementing real-time events or daily rewards.

6. User Interface (UI) Localization
- **Translate UI Elements**: Translate all in-game menus, buttons, tooltips, and HUD elements.
- **Resizable UI**: Design a resizable UI to accommodate longer text in translations.

7. Testing and Feedback
- **Localization Testing**: Test your game with native speakers of the target languages to identify and fix any linguistic or cultural issues.
- **Feedback Channels**: Establish channels for players to report localization issues and provide feedback.

8. Legal and Compliance
- **Regulations**: Ensure that your game complies with regional regulations and content rating requirements.
- **Privacy**: Address privacy and data protection laws that vary by region.

By following these guidelines and considering the cultural context of your target audience, you can create a more inclusive and enjoyable gaming experience for players worldwide.

In the next sections, we'll delve deeper into best practices for localization, including managing multilingual content, conducting testing, and addressing potential issues that may arise during the process.

Section 17.2: Localization Best Practices

Localizing a game involves more than just translating text; it requires a comprehensive approach to ensure a seamless and culturally relevant experience for players in different regions. In this section, we'll explore best practices for effective game localization:

1. Contextual Translation
- **Maintain Context**: Provide translators with the context of the text within the game, including the character's emotions, the scene, and any cultural references. This helps ensure accurate translations.
- **In-Game Preview**: Implement a feature that allows translators to see how their translations appear in the game to make context-based decisions.

2. Consistency
- **Glossary**: Create a glossary of terms and phrases used consistently throughout the game. This ensures that key terminology remains the same across all translations.
- **Translation Memory**: Use translation memory tools that remember previously translated phrases and suggest them for reuse.

3. Expandable User Interface (UI)
   - **Text Expansion**: Design your UI elements to accommodate text expansion. Some languages may require more space than others, and a flexible UI prevents text from overflowing or being truncated.
   - **Whitespace Handling**: Pay attention to whitespace handling, as the space required for words and sentences can vary between languages.

4. Pluralization and Gender Neutrality
   - **Plural Forms**: Account for pluralization differences in languages that have multiple plural forms, such as English, Arabic, or Russian.
   - **Gender-Neutral Language**: Use gender-neutral language whenever possible to ensure inclusivity and avoid unintended biases.

5. Date and Time Formatting
   - **Localized Formats**: Implement date and time formatting based on the player's region. For example, use "dd/mm/yyyy" for some regions and "mm/dd/yyyy" for others.
   - **Time Zones**: Display time zone information when necessary, especially in games with real-time events.

6. Keyboard and Input Method Support
   - **Input Methods**: Ensure that your game can handle various keyboard layouts and input methods, such as different alphabets or characters.
   - **Key Mapping**: Provide customizable key mapping options for players to adapt the controls to their preferred layout.

7. Quality Assurance (QA) Testing
   - **Localization QA**: Conduct thorough testing with native speakers to identify and correct translation issues, text overflows, or UI alignment problems.
   - **Functional Testing**: Ensure that the localized version functions correctly and that gameplay remains consistent across all languages.

8. Updates and Post-Launch Support
   - **Ongoing Localization**: Plan for ongoing updates and maintenance to address localization issues and provide new content in multiple languages.
   - **Community Feedback**: Encourage player feedback regarding localization issues and respond promptly with fixes.

By adhering to these best practices, you can create a localized version of your game that feels natural and engaging to players in different regions. Effective localization enhances the accessibility and appeal of your game, contributing to its success in international markets. In the following section, we'll delve into the importance of cultural sensitivity in game design and how to navigate cultural nuances effectively.

Section 17.3: Cultural Sensitivity in Game Design

Cultural sensitivity is a critical aspect of game design, especially when creating content for a global audience. Failing to consider cultural differences can lead to misunderstandings, misinterpretations, and even controversies. In this section, we'll explore the importance of cultural sensitivity and how to navigate cultural nuances effectively in game design.

1. Research and Understand Cultures

To create culturally sensitive content, start by researching and understanding the cultures you are representing in your game. This includes:

- **Language**: Learn about the languages spoken in the target region, including common phrases, idioms, and dialects.

- **History and Traditions**: Familiarize yourself with historical events, traditions, festivals, and cultural practices that are significant to the culture.

- **Stereotypes**: Avoid relying on stereotypes, as they can perpetuate negative biases and offend players. Instead, focus on portraying diverse and authentic characters and settings.

2. Consult Cultural Experts

Consider collaborating with cultural experts, consultants, or advisors from the target culture. They can provide valuable insights and ensure that your game accurately represents their culture.

3. Avoid Cultural Appropriation

Cultural appropriation occurs when elements of one culture are used inappropriately or without permission. It's essential to respect intellectual property and cultural symbols. Seek permission and collaboration when necessary.

4. Localization with Cultural Context

When localizing your game, go beyond mere translation. Adapt content to suit the cultural context, including adjusting visuals, references, and scenarios to resonate with the target audience.

5. Avoid Religious and Political Controversy

Steer clear of religious and political content that can lead to controversies. These topics can be sensitive and divisive, potentially alienating players or causing offense.

6. Diverse Character Representation

Ensure that your game includes diverse character representations, both in terms of ethnicity and backgrounds. Representation matters, and players from various backgrounds should see themselves reflected in your game.

7. Testing and Feedback

Conduct cultural sensitivity testing with players from different cultures to gather feedback. Listen to their concerns and make necessary adjustments to the game content.

8. Inclusivity and Accessibility

Consider accessibility features that cater to diverse players, including those with disabilities. Ensure that all players can enjoy your game without barriers.

9. Post-Launch Responsiveness

Be prepared to address cultural sensitivity concerns post-launch. Monitor player feedback and make necessary updates or clarifications to address issues as they arise.

10. Promote Positive Cultural Exchange

Use your game as a platform for positive cultural exchange and education. Showcase the richness and diversity of cultures in a respectful and enlightening manner.

By prioritizing cultural sensitivity in your game design, you not only create a more inclusive and respectful gaming experience but also expand your game's appeal to a broader and more diverse audience. Cultural sensitivity is not only ethical but also a strategic consideration for the success of your game in the global market. In the following section, we'll delve into managing multilingual content and testing for localization issues.

Section 17.4: Managing Multilingual Content

Multilingual content management is a critical aspect of game development when targeting global audiences. It involves adapting your game to different languages and cultures, ensuring that players from various regions can enjoy your game in their native language. In this section, we'll explore the key considerations and best practices for managing multilingual content effectively.

1. Plan for Localization Early

Localization should be considered from the early stages of game development. Ensure that your game's architecture and code are designed to accommodate different languages and text lengths.

2. Unicode and Character Encoding

Use Unicode (UTF-8) for text encoding to support a wide range of languages and special characters. Ensure that your game engine and text rendering systems fully support Unicode.

3. Separate Text from Code

Keep all in-game text separate from the source code. Use localization files or databases to store text strings, making it easier to update translations without modifying the game's code.

4. Translation Tools and Services

Consider using professional translation tools and services. These tools can help manage translations efficiently and maintain consistency across different languages.

5. Cultural Sensitivity in Translation

When translating content, be mindful of cultural differences. Phrases, idioms, and jokes may not translate directly and can lose their meaning or even cause offense if not adapted properly.

6. Test with Native Speakers

Involve native speakers of the target language in the testing and proofreading of translations. They can identify linguistic nuances and ensure accuracy.

7. Expandable User Interfaces

Design user interfaces (UI) to be expandable, allowing for text expansion or contraction in different languages. Ensure that UI elements can accommodate longer text strings.

8. Text Overflow Handling

Implement text overflow handling to prevent text from spilling outside UI elements. Consider truncation, ellipsis, or dynamic resizing of text boxes.

9. RTL Languages

Support right-to-left (RTL) languages, such as Arabic and Hebrew, if your game targets regions where these languages are prevalent. Ensure that UI elements adapt correctly.

10. Font Considerations

Choose fonts that support a wide range of languages and characters. Avoid fonts that may not display correctly for certain languages.

11. Localized Assets

In addition to text, consider localizing other game assets, such as images, audio, and videos, to better resonate with the target audience.

12. Localized Marketing

Extend localization efforts to your marketing materials, store descriptions, and community engagement. A consistent message in the player's language can boost interest.

13. Update and Maintenance

Be prepared for ongoing localization updates. As your game evolves with patches and expansions, ensure that new content is also translated and localized.

14. Localization Testing

Thoroughly test your game in each target language to identify any text-related issues, including layout problems, text truncation, or encoding errors.

15. Legal Considerations

Understand legal requirements and regulations related to localization and multilingual content, such as age ratings and content restrictions in different regions.

Effective management of multilingual content is essential for creating an inclusive and accessible gaming experience for players around the world. It not only expands your game's global reach but also demonstrates a commitment to diversity and cultural inclusivity. In the next section, we'll explore the importance of testing for localization issues and ensuring that your game is culturally sensitive.

Section 17.5: Testing for Localization Issues

Testing for localization issues is a crucial step in the game development process, ensuring that your game is ready for global audiences and that the localization process has been implemented correctly. In this section, we'll explore the importance of localization testing and provide guidelines for conducting effective tests.

1. Localization Test Plan

Start by creating a detailed test plan specifically for localization. This plan should outline the languages you're targeting, the areas of the game to be tested, and the test scenarios to be executed.

2. Functional Testing

Begin with functional testing to ensure that the game functions correctly in each localized version. Verify that menus, dialogs, and in-game systems work as expected with different languages.

3. Text Verification

Check all text elements in the game, including UI text, subtitles, dialogues, and in-game messages. Verify that text is displayed correctly, without issues like truncation or text overlapping.

4. Language Selection

Test the language selection feature thoroughly. Ensure that changing the language setting properly updates all in-game text and UI elements.

5. Special Characters and Fonts

Pay special attention to languages with unique characters or scripts. Test the display of special characters, diacritics, and fonts specific to each language.

6. Text Expansion and Contraction

Test how text responds to language differences in terms of expansion (languages with longer words) and contraction (languages with shorter words). Ensure that UI elements adapt accordingly.

7. Right-to-Left (RTL) Languages

If your game supports RTL languages, verify that UI elements, text alignment, and reading order are correct. Test the game's overall layout for RTL languages.

8. Numerical and Date Formats

Test numerical formats, date formats, and other region-specific data presentation to ensure they match the expectations of players in each region.

9. Voiceovers and Subtitles

For games with voiceovers and subtitles, ensure that audio and text are synchronized correctly in all languages. Verify that subtitles do not overlap or obscure important visuals.

10. Cultural Sensitivity

Assess the game's cultural sensitivity in each localized version. Ensure that content, jokes, and cultural references are appropriate and well-adapted to each culture.

11. Consistency

Check for consistency in terminology and phrasing across all localized versions. Inconsistencies can lead to confusion and affect the player's experience.

12. Testing with Native Speakers

Involve native speakers of the target languages in the testing process. They can provide valuable feedback on linguistic nuances and cultural appropriateness.

13. Compatibility and Platform Testing

Test your game on various platforms and devices to ensure that localization works correctly across all supported configurations.

14. Bug Tracking and Reporting

Use bug tracking tools to report and prioritize localization issues. Ensure that developers have clear information to fix reported problems.

15. Regression Testing

After localization-related issues have been fixed, conduct regression testing to verify that new updates or changes haven't introduced new problems in localized versions.

16. Post-Launch Monitoring

Continue monitoring and addressing localization issues post-launch. Player feedback and ongoing testing can help identify and resolve issues that may surface after release.

17. Accessibility Testing

Consider accessibility testing to ensure that localized versions are equally accessible to players with disabilities, including those who use screen readers or alternative input methods.

Effective localization testing is essential for providing a seamless and enjoyable experience for players from different regions. It demonstrates a commitment to quality and cultural inclusivity, helping your game reach a broader global audience. In the next chapter, we'll delve into ethical considerations in game development, addressing social issues through games and promoting responsible representation and diversity.

Chapter 18: Ethics and Responsibility in Game Development

Section 18.1: Addressing Social Issues through Games

Addressing social issues through games is a powerful and increasingly common approach in the game development industry. Games have the potential to engage players on important social and cultural topics, raise awareness, and promote positive change. In this section, we'll explore the role of games in addressing social issues and provide insights into effective strategies for incorporating these themes into your game development projects.

1. Choosing Social Issues

Start by selecting the social issue or topic you want to address in your game. Consider issues such as environmental conservation, mental health, social justice, diversity, and more. The chosen issue should align with your game's theme and narrative.

2. Research and Understanding

Thoroughly research and gain a deep understanding of the chosen social issue. Engage with experts, read books, articles, and engage in discussions to ensure your representation of the issue is accurate and respectful.

3. Storytelling and Narrative

Craft a compelling narrative that weaves the social issue into the game's storyline. Develop relatable characters and situations that resonate with players and convey the issue's significance.

4. Game Mechanics and Interactivity

Use game mechanics and interactivity to immerse players in the issue. Create gameplay elements that make players directly engage with the issue, making it an integral part of their gaming experience.

5. Awareness and Education

Consider your game as a tool for raising awareness and educating players about the social issue. Provide in-game information, facts, and resources related to the topic to inform players.

6. Emotional Impact

Aim to evoke emotions and empathy in players. Well-crafted storytelling and gameplay can lead to a deeper emotional connection, making players more receptive to the issue's message.

7. Avoiding Stereotypes and Sensationalism

Be cautious not to perpetuate stereotypes or exploit sensitive issues for shock value. Represent characters and situations authentically and sensitively.

8. Community Engagement

Encourage players to discuss the social issue within the game's community. Create spaces for dialogue and reflection, fostering a sense of community around the topic.

9. Measuring Impact

Define metrics to measure the impact of your game in addressing the social issue. Monitor player feedback, track engagement with educational materials, and gather data to assess the game's effectiveness.

10. Collaboration and Partnerships

Consider collaborating with non-profit organizations, experts, or activists working on the social issue. Partnerships can provide valuable insights and resources to enhance your game's impact.

11. Responsibility and Ethical Considerations

Be aware of the ethical responsibilities associated with addressing social issues. Ensure that your game's message aligns with ethical principles and does not harm or trivialize the issue.

12. Positive Outcomes

Celebrate and share positive outcomes and stories resulting from your game's impact on players and communities. Showcase how games can be a force for positive change.

13. Player Feedback and Iteration

Continuously gather player feedback and be open to iteration. Use feedback to refine your game's message and impact on addressing the social issue.

14. Promoting Diversity and Inclusion

Promote diversity and inclusion both in your game development team and within the game itself. Ensure that voices from diverse backgrounds are heard and represented.

15. Long-Term Commitment

Understand that addressing social issues through games is a long-term commitment. Continue to support and update your game to maintain its relevance and impact.

Games have the potential to be a powerful medium for addressing social issues, creating awareness, and inspiring positive change. By responsibly and thoughtfully incorporating these themes into your game development projects, you can make a meaningful contribution to society while creating engaging and impactful gaming experiences. In the next section, we'll delve into the importance of responsible representation and diversity in game development.

Section 18.2: Responsible Representation and Diversity in Games

Responsible representation and diversity in games have become increasingly important topics in the game development industry. As games continue to reach diverse global audiences, it's crucial to create experiences that respect and reflect the richness of human experiences and identities. In this section, we'll explore the significance of responsible representation and diversity in games and provide guidelines for incorporating these principles into your game development process.

1. Why Representation Matters

Representation in games matters because it impacts players' experiences and perceptions. When players see characters, stories, and cultures that resonate with their own backgrounds, it enhances their connection with the game. Conversely, the absence or misrepresentation of certain groups can lead to feelings of exclusion and perpetuate stereotypes.

2. Diverse Characters and Identities

Diversify your game's characters to reflect a wide range of identities, including gender, race, ethnicity, sexual orientation, and abilities. Avoid tokenism by creating well-developed characters with their own stories and motivations.

3. Authentic Storytelling

When incorporating diversity into your game, prioritize authenticity. Consult with individuals from diverse backgrounds to ensure accurate and respectful representation. Avoid stereotypes, cultural appropriation, and harmful clichés.

4. Inclusive Game Worlds

Design game worlds that are inclusive and welcoming to all players. Consider the accessibility of your game for players with disabilities and provide options for customization to accommodate different preferences and needs.

5. Diversity Behind the Scenes

Foster diversity within your game development team. Embrace a variety of perspectives and voices, as this can lead to richer and more inclusive game experiences. Encourage diverse talent in hiring, leadership roles, and decision-making processes.

6. Avoiding Cultural Insensitivity

Be cautious when incorporating elements from cultures that are not your own. Respect cultural norms, symbols, and practices, and seek guidance or collaboration with experts to ensure cultural sensitivity.

7. Addressing Controversial Topics

If your game addresses controversial topics, do so with care and consideration. Provide context, trigger warnings, or resources for players who may be affected by sensitive content.

8. User-Generated Content

If your game allows user-generated content, implement moderation systems to prevent hate speech, harassment, and inappropriate content. Encourage a positive and inclusive community.

9. Community Engagement

Foster a positive and inclusive community around your game. Set clear guidelines for behavior and actively address toxic behavior or hate speech. Create spaces for constructive dialogue and feedback.

10. Accessibility and Inclusivity

Prioritize accessibility in your game design. Ensure that players with disabilities can enjoy your game by providing options for customizable controls, text-to-speech, subtitles, and other accessibility features.

11. Representation in Marketing

Extend responsible representation to your game's marketing materials. Represent the diverse identities and experiences present in your game in promotional materials and advertisements.

12. Player Feedback and Iteration

Listen to player feedback regarding representation and diversity. Be open to making improvements and updates based on constructive feedback.

13. Commitment to Continuous Improvement

Understand that responsible representation and diversity are ongoing commitments. Continue to educate yourself and your team on these topics and adapt your practices accordingly.

14. Industry Collaboration

Collaborate with industry organizations and initiatives that promote responsible representation and diversity in games. Share knowledge and best practices with the broader game development community.

15. Setting an Example

By prioritizing responsible representation and diversity in your games, you set an example for the industry and inspire positive change. Your efforts contribute to making the gaming world a more inclusive and welcoming place for all.

Incorporating responsible representation and diversity into your game development process is not only ethically sound but also enhances the quality of your games and expands your audience. By creating games that authentically reflect the diverse world we live in, you contribute to a more inclusive and vibrant gaming industry. In the next section, we'll discuss gaming addiction and player health, addressing another important aspect of game development ethics.

Section 18.3: Gaming Addiction and Player Health

Gaming addiction and its impact on player health have garnered increasing attention in recent years. As video games continue to gain popularity, it's essential for game developers to consider the potential risks associated with excessive gaming and take steps to promote player well-being. In this section, we will explore the concept of gaming addiction, its effects on player health, and strategies for responsible game development.

1. Understanding Gaming Addiction

Gaming addiction, often referred to as "Internet Gaming Disorder" or "Gaming Disorder," is characterized by a persistent and compulsive engagement with video games to the detriment of other life activities. It can lead to significant negative consequences in various aspects of a person's life, including physical and mental health, relationships, and work or education.

2. Recognizing the Signs

Game developers should be aware of the signs of gaming addiction, which can include:

- Preoccupation with gaming and constant thoughts about games.
- Neglecting responsibilities or neglecting personal hygiene and well-being due to gaming.
- Loss of interest in other hobbies or activities.
- Irritability, restlessness, or mood swings when not gaming.
- Lying about the amount of time spent playing games.
- Failed attempts to cut down or control gaming.
- Continued gaming despite negative consequences.

3. Health Impacts

Excessive gaming can have various negative health impacts, including:

- **Physical Health:** Prolonged gaming sessions can lead to physical issues such as eye strain, sleep disturbances, musculoskeletal problems, and a sedentary lifestyle, which may contribute to obesity and related health conditions.
- **Mental Health:** Gaming addiction has been associated with mental health issues like depression, anxiety, social withdrawal, and reduced self-esteem. Players may also experience increased stress and irritability.
- **Social Relationships:** Excessive gaming can strain personal relationships, leading to isolation and conflict with family and friends. Players may prioritize gaming over social interactions.
- **Academic and Occupational Problems:** Neglecting school, work, or other responsibilities can result in academic underachievement, job loss, or career stagnation.

4. Responsible Game Design

Game developers have a responsibility to create games that are engaging and enjoyable without encouraging addiction. Here are some strategies for responsible game design:

- **Balanced Gameplay:** Design games with balanced gameplay mechanics that encourage breaks and diversification of activities. Avoid mechanics that incentivize endless grinding or long uninterrupted sessions.
- **Time Management Features:** Implement features that allow players to set limits on their gaming time or receive reminders to take breaks. Respect players' time and real-life commitments.
- **Meaningful Progression:** Reward players for skill and strategic thinking rather than time investment. Make sure that achievements and rewards are attainable through skill and not just by spending excessive time in the game.
- **Community and Social Features:** Encourage social interaction within the game, such as multiplayer modes and in-game communities, to foster healthy social connections.
- **Transparency:** Provide information about the potential risks of excessive gaming in your game's documentation or loading screens. Encourage players to take regular breaks and prioritize other life activities.

5. Player Education and Support

Game developers can also contribute to player education and support:

- Create resources within the game that provide information on responsible gaming, the signs of addiction, and where to seek help.
- Collaborate with mental health organizations to provide resources and support for players struggling with gaming addiction.

6. Industry Initiatives

The game development industry as a whole can take steps to address gaming addiction:

- Support and participate in research on gaming addiction and its effects.
- Share best practices for responsible game design and player education.
- Advocate for policies and regulations that promote responsible gaming practices.

7. Balancing Engagement and Well-being

Ultimately, game developers can create engaging and enjoyable games while also promoting player well-being. Responsible game design and a commitment to addressing gaming addiction contribute to a healthier gaming community and help ensure that players can enjoy games in moderation without compromising their health and life responsibilities. In the next section, we will delve into the topic of privacy and data protection in games, another critical aspect of ethical game development.

Section 18.4: Privacy and Data Protection in Games

Privacy and data protection are essential considerations in modern game development. As games become increasingly connected and collect more user data, it's crucial for developers to prioritize the security and privacy of player information. In this section, we will explore the importance of privacy in games, legal and ethical obligations, and best practices for safeguarding player data.

1. The Importance of Privacy

Privacy is a fundamental human right, and players expect their personal information to be handled with care and respect when they engage with online games. Game developers must understand the value of player data and the potential consequences of mishandling it.

2. Legal Obligations

Many countries have enacted data protection laws to safeguard individuals' personal information. Game developers are subject to these laws and must comply with regulations such as the General Data Protection Regulation (GDPR) in the European Union or the California Consumer Privacy Act (CCPA) in the United States. Compliance involves obtaining informed consent from players before collecting their data, providing mechanisms for data access and deletion, and ensuring the security of stored data.

3. Ethical Considerations

Beyond legal obligations, ethical considerations play a significant role in how game developers handle player data. Developers should be transparent about the types of data collected, the purposes for which it will be used, and how long it will be retained. Respecting player privacy builds trust and enhances the player experience.

4. Data Collection in Games

Games often collect various types of data, including:

- **Account Information:** Usernames, email addresses, and account credentials are common data collected during registration.
- **Gameplay Data:** Developers may track player behavior, in-game purchases, and progress to improve gameplay experiences.
- **Device Information:** Data about the player's device, such as hardware specifications and operating system, may be collected for optimization purposes.
- **Location Data:** Some games request access to a player's location for features like geolocation-based gameplay.
- **Social Data:** Games with social features may access a player's friend list or social media connections.

5. Best Practices for Data Protection

To protect player privacy and ensure compliance with data protection laws, developers can follow these best practices:

- **Data Minimization:** Collect only the data necessary for the intended purpose. Avoid collecting excessive or irrelevant information.
- **Informed Consent:** Clearly communicate data collection practices to players and obtain their explicit consent. Allow players to opt out of data collection if possible.
- **Data Security:** Implement robust security measures to protect stored data from breaches. Encryption, access controls, and regular security audits are essential.
- **Data Access and Deletion:** Provide players with mechanisms to access their data, correct inaccuracies, and request data deletion.
- **Data Retention Policies:** Define clear data retention periods and delete data when it is no longer needed for its original purpose.
- **Third-Party Services:** Be cautious when integrating third-party services that collect data. Ensure that these services also comply with privacy regulations.

6. Transparency and Communication

Open and honest communication with players regarding data practices is key to building trust. Developers should have a privacy policy easily accessible to players and offer support channels for privacy-related inquiries or concerns.

7. Regular Audits and Updates

Privacy practices in games should evolve with changing regulations and technology. Regularly audit data handling processes and update policies to stay compliant and responsive to player needs.

8. Conclusion

Privacy and data protection are integral to responsible game development. By respecting player privacy, complying with legal requirements, and following ethical principles, developers can create a safer and more enjoyable gaming environment. In the next section, we will delve into the topic of promoting positive gaming communities, emphasizing the importance of fostering inclusive and respectful interactions among players.

Section 18.5: Promoting Positive Gaming Communities

Creating and maintaining a positive gaming community is essential for the long-term success and sustainability of an online game. In this section, we will explore strategies for promoting positive interactions among players, fostering inclusivity, and ensuring a welcoming environment within the gaming community.

1. The Importance of Positive Communities

A positive gaming community enhances the player experience, encourages player retention, and can lead to increased player engagement. On the other hand, a toxic or unwelcoming community can drive players away and harm the reputation of a game.

2. Inclusivity and Diversity

Inclusivity is a core principle of positive gaming communities. Developers should strive to create games and communities that are welcoming to players of all backgrounds, regardless of gender, race, ethnicity, age, or other characteristics. Representation in games and community leadership is essential to achieving inclusivity.

3. Community Guidelines and Codes of Conduct

Games should have clear and enforced community guidelines or codes of conduct that outline expected behavior and consequences for violations. These guidelines should promote respect, fair play, and positive interactions.

4. Moderation and Reporting Tools

Implement robust moderation tools within the game to allow players to report abusive or inappropriate behavior. Ensure that reports are reviewed promptly, and appropriate actions are taken, such as warnings, suspensions, or bans.

5. Education and Awareness

Raise awareness about the importance of positive community behavior through in-game messages, social media, and community events. Educate players about the impact of their words and actions on others.

6. Community Events and Engagement

Organize community events, tournaments, and activities that encourage positive interactions among players. These events can foster a sense of belonging and camaraderie.

7. Community Management

Invest in community management teams or personnel who can actively engage with the community, address concerns, and promote positive behavior. Community managers should serve as role models for desired conduct.

8. Zero Tolerance for Harassment and Hate Speech

Enforce a zero-tolerance policy for harassment, hate speech, and discriminatory behavior. Players should feel safe and respected, and those who violate these principles should face consequences.

9. Feedback Channels

Provide channels for players to offer feedback and suggestions for improving the game and community. Act on constructive feedback to demonstrate that player input is valued.

10. Regular Check-Ins

Periodically check in with the community to assess its health and sentiment. Conduct surveys, focus groups, or community meetings to gather insights and make adjustments as needed.

11. Incentivize Positive Behavior

Consider rewarding positive behavior, such as sportsmanship, helping new players, or contributing to the community. Positive reinforcement can encourage players to be more respectful.

12. Transparency and Communication

Maintain transparent communication with the community. Be open about changes to the game, the enforcement of rules, and efforts to improve the community.

13. Lead by Example

Game developers and community leaders should lead by example and adhere to the same standards of behavior expected from players. This sets a positive tone for the entire community.

14. Conclusion

Promoting a positive gaming community is an ongoing effort that requires dedication and vigilance. By creating an inclusive, respectful, and enjoyable environment, developers can foster a sense of belonging among players and contribute to the long-term success of their games. In the following section, we will explore strategies for post-launch support and updates, including managing patches, gathering player feedback, and planning for game expansions and sequels.

Chapter 19: Post-Launch Support and Updates

In the ever-evolving landscape of game development, post-launch support and updates are crucial to maintaining a successful and engaged player base. This chapter delves into the strategies and best practices for managing game patches, community management post-launch, gathering and implementing player feedback, and planning for long-term game maintenance, expansions, and sequels.

Section 19.1: Managing Game Patches and Updates

Game patches and updates are essential for addressing bugs, adding new content, improving game balance, and enhancing the overall player experience. However, managing these updates effectively requires careful planning and execution.

1. Patch Frequency

Determine a patch frequency that strikes a balance between addressing issues promptly and avoiding excessive disruptions to players. Frequent patches can be annoying, while infrequent ones might lead to unresolved issues.

2. Patch Notes

Always provide detailed patch notes to inform players about what changes and fixes are included in each update. Transparency builds trust and keeps players informed.

3. Bug Tracking System

Implement a bug tracking system to collect and prioritize bug reports from players. This helps ensure that critical issues are addressed promptly.

4. Testing and Quality Assurance

Thoroughly test patches and updates to avoid introducing new bugs or balance issues. Consider establishing a public test server where players can help identify and report problems before a wider release.

5. Hotfixes

For critical issues that require immediate attention, be prepared to release hotfixes outside the regular patch schedule. Communicate the necessity of these hotfixes clearly to players.

6. Version Compatibility

Ensure that updates are backward compatible whenever possible to avoid fragmenting the player base. In cases where incompatibility is unavoidable, communicate this in advance.

7. Player Feedback Integration

Actively gather and consider player feedback when planning patches and updates. Prioritize addressing issues that matter most to the player community.

8. Balancing Updates

Regularly assess game balance and make adjustments as needed. Avoid making drastic changes that disrupt the core gameplay experience.

9. New Content

Balance bug fixes and quality-of-life improvements with the addition of new content. New features and content can reinvigorate the player base and attract new players.

10. Communication

Maintain transparent and timely communication with the player community. Announce upcoming patches, their content, and expected release dates in advance.

11. Player Involvement

Involve the player community in the update process when appropriate. Gather ideas, suggestions, and feedback through surveys, forums, or dedicated feedback channels.

12. Backups and Rollback Plans

Prepare for unexpected issues by having backups and rollback plans in place. This ensures that, in case of a critical problem, you can revert to a stable state quickly.

13. Community Support

Provide support resources and a dedicated community manager to address player concerns and questions related to patches and updates.

14. Monitoring and Analytics

Implement monitoring tools and gather analytics data to track the impact of updates on player behavior, engagement, and satisfaction. Use this data to inform future updates.

15. Conclusion

Managing game patches and updates is an ongoing process that requires agility, responsiveness, and a deep understanding of player needs and expectations. In the next section, we will explore community management post-launch, including strategies for fostering a positive gaming community and addressing player concerns and feedback.

Section 19.2: Community Management Post-Launch

Community management plays a pivotal role in the post-launch success of a game. It involves fostering a positive and engaged player community, addressing concerns, and maintaining open lines of communication. Here are essential strategies for effective community management:

1. Community Engagement

Actively engage with your player community on various platforms such as forums, social media, and official game channels. Participate in discussions, respond to questions, and acknowledge feedback.

2. Clear Communication

Maintain clear and transparent communication with the player base. Share development updates, news about upcoming content, and responses to player feedback. Ensure that communication is timely and consistent.

3. Community Guidelines

Establish and enforce community guidelines to maintain a friendly and respectful environment. Clearly define what is considered acceptable behavior and the consequences for violating these guidelines.

4. Community Managers

Assign dedicated community managers who can interact with players, address concerns, and serve as a bridge between the player community and the development team.

5. Feedback Channels

Provide dedicated channels for players to submit feedback, bug reports, and suggestions. Actively listen to and consider player input when making decisions about the game's future.

6. Events and Contests

Organize in-game events, contests, or challenges to keep the player community engaged and excited. Offer rewards and recognition to active and loyal players.

7. Support Resources

Ensure that players have access to support resources, such as FAQs, troubleshooting guides, and a customer support system. Promptly address technical issues and concerns.

8. Developer Blogs

Create developer blogs or behind-the-scenes content that gives players insights into the game's development process. This can help players feel more connected to the development team.

9. Player Ambassadors

Identify dedicated and passionate players who can serve as ambassadors for your game. These players can help answer questions, guide newcomers, and promote a positive atmosphere.

10. Moderation Tools

Equip your community managers with effective moderation tools to handle inappropriate behavior and content promptly. Implement a fair reporting system for players to report misconduct.

11. Feedback Implementation

Regularly update players on how their feedback has been implemented in the game. Show appreciation for their contributions, and explain how their input has shaped the game's development.

12. Listening and Adaptation

Be receptive to changing player needs and adapt your community management strategies accordingly. Flexibility and responsiveness are key to maintaining a healthy player community.

13. Conflict Resolution

Address conflicts and disputes among players promptly and fairly. Encourage constructive communication and provide resources for conflict resolution.

14. Event and Update Teasers

Build excitement and anticipation for upcoming events or updates by teasing new content or features in advance. Generate buzz and discussions among the player community.

15. Surveys and Feedback Loops

Conduct player surveys to gather detailed feedback on specific aspects of the game. Use this information to make informed decisions about future updates and improvements.

16. Positive Reinforcement

Celebrate milestones, achievements, and positive contributions within the community. Recognize and reward outstanding players for their dedication and positive impact.

17. Consistency

Maintain consistency in your community management efforts. Regular engagement and communication help build trust and a sense of community.

18. Conclusion

Effective community management is an ongoing process that requires dedication and a genuine commitment to fostering a positive and engaged player community. In the next section, we will explore the process of gathering and implementing player feedback to improve the game further.

Section 19.3: Gathering and Implementing Player Feedback

Collecting and implementing player feedback is a crucial aspect of post-launch support for your game. It allows you to address issues, improve gameplay, and enhance the overall player experience. In this section, we'll explore strategies for gathering, analyzing, and effectively implementing player feedback.

1. Feedback Channels

Create dedicated channels for players to submit feedback, bug reports, and suggestions. These channels can include forums, in-game feedback forms, or even external platforms like social media and email. Make sure players know where and how to provide feedback easily.

2. Feedback Tags and Categorization

Implement a system to categorize and tag incoming feedback. This makes it easier to identify common issues or suggestions and prioritize them accordingly. Tags like "bugs," "balance," and "feature request" can be helpful.

3. Feedback Triaging

Assign a team or individual responsible for triaging incoming feedback. They should assess the severity and impact of reported issues and prioritize them based on criticality and frequency.

4. Player Surveys

Conduct regular player surveys to gather structured feedback on specific aspects of the game, such as gameplay mechanics, user interface, or overall satisfaction. Surveys provide valuable quantitative data.

5. Player Behavior Analysis

Analyze player behavior data, including gameplay analytics, to identify trends and pain points. Data-driven insights can help pinpoint areas that require improvement.

6. Community Input

Engage with the player community and actively listen to their discussions and suggestions. Community forums and social media platforms can provide valuable qualitative feedback.

7. Feedback Aggregation

Aggregate similar feedback and issues to avoid duplication. A clear record of reported problems ensures that nothing is overlooked.

8. Feedback Acknowledgment

Acknowledge players who provide feedback, whether it's a bug report or a suggestion. Let them know that their input is valuable and appreciated. This encourages continued participation.

9. Roadmap and Prioritization

Develop a roadmap for addressing feedback and implementing changes. Prioritize items based on their impact on the player experience and your development resources.

10. Transparency

Keep players informed about the status of reported issues and the progress of suggested improvements. Transparency builds trust and keeps players engaged.

11. Testing and Validation

Before implementing changes based on feedback, thoroughly test them to ensure they don't introduce new issues or negatively impact other aspects of the game. Beta testing and QA processes are essential.

12. Iterative Approach

Don't try to address all feedback at once. Implement changes incrementally, gathering more feedback at each stage. This iterative approach helps maintain game stability.

13. Feedback Implementation Timeline

Communicate a timeline for when players can expect to see their feedback implemented. Keep them informed about development milestones and updates.

14. Patch Notes and Change Logs

Clearly document changes, bug fixes, and improvements in patch notes and change logs. This allows players to see the direct impact of their feedback.

15. Feedback Closure

When issues are resolved or suggestions are implemented, close the feedback loop by notifying players who initially reported them. This demonstrates that their feedback led to tangible improvements.

16. Feedback Analytics

Use analytics tools to track the impact of implemented changes. Measure how these changes affect player behavior, retention, and overall satisfaction.

17. Player Appreciation

Show appreciation for your player community by occasionally rewarding those who contribute significantly to improving the game through their feedback and suggestions.

18. Conclusion

Gathering and implementing player feedback is an ongoing process that demonstrates your commitment to delivering a great gaming experience. It fosters player loyalty and helps your game evolve and thrive in the competitive market. In the next section, we'll delve into long-term game maintenance strategies.

Implementing these strategies will not only enhance your game's quality but also build a strong and loyal player base, ensuring the long-term success of your game.

Section 19.4: Long-Term Game Maintenance Strategies

Long-term game maintenance is a critical aspect of post-launch support that involves keeping your game up to date, relevant, and enjoyable for players. In this section, we'll explore strategies for effectively maintaining your game over an extended period.

1. Version Control and Code Documentation

Maintain a version control system for your game's source code, assets, and configurations. Document code and development processes comprehensively, making it easier for your team to understand and modify the game in the future.

2. Bug Tracking and Issue Management

Continue to track and manage bugs and issues post-launch. Implement a robust bug tracking system to prioritize and address issues promptly.

3. Regular Updates and Patches

Release regular updates and patches to address bugs, improve gameplay, and add new content. This keeps players engaged and demonstrates your commitment to the game.

4. Content Expansion

Consider expanding your game's content with downloadable content (DLC) or expansions. New levels, characters, storylines, or features can reinvigorate player interest.

5. Balancing and Tuning

Continuously balance and tune your game based on player feedback and data analytics. Adjust difficulty levels, character abilities, and in-game economies to ensure a satisfying experience.

6. Security Updates

Stay vigilant against security threats and vulnerabilities. Regularly update third-party libraries and frameworks to protect player data and ensure the game's security.

7. Performance Optimization

Keep optimizing your game's performance as hardware and technology evolve. Performance improvements can extend the game's lifespan and reach a broader audience.

8. Community Engagement

Maintain an active presence in the player community. Respond to player feedback, engage in discussions, and organize events or contests to keep players connected.

9. Player Support

Continue providing player support through customer service channels. Address technical issues, answer questions, and offer guidance to players experiencing difficulties.

10. Compatibility Updates

Ensure your game remains compatible with the latest hardware, operating systems, and platforms. Regularly test and update compatibility to prevent player frustrations.

11. Analytics and Data-Driven Decisions

Leverage analytics tools to monitor player behavior and engagement. Use this data to inform decisions about updates, content, and monetization strategies.

12. Monetization Strategy

Review and adapt your monetization strategy as player preferences and industry trends change. Explore new revenue streams while maintaining player satisfaction.

13. Content Retirement

Consider retiring outdated or less popular content to streamline game maintenance and focus on enhancing the core experience.

14. Roadmap and Vision

Maintain a clear development roadmap and long-term vision for your game. Share this with the community to keep players excited about the game's future.

15. Player Feedback Integration

Continue integrating player feedback into your development process. Players appreciate seeing their suggestions and concerns addressed.

16. Community Content and Mods

Encourage and support community-generated content and mods. This extends the game's longevity and fosters a dedicated player community.

17. Testing and Quality Assurance

Maintain a robust testing and quality assurance process to catch and fix issues before updates are released. Test across various platforms and configurations.

18. Legal and Compliance Updates

Stay informed about changes in legal and compliance requirements, such as privacy regulations and accessibility standards, and ensure your game remains compliant.

19. Player Appreciation Events

Host special in-game events or rewards to show appreciation for your player community. Celebrate milestones, anniversaries, or holidays together.

20. Conclusion

Long-term game maintenance requires dedication, adaptability, and a strong connection with your player base. By implementing these strategies, you can ensure your game remains enjoyable and successful for years to come.

Maintaining your game post-launch is an ongoing commitment that can lead to a thriving and loyal player community, making your game a memorable and enduring experience. In the next chapter, we'll explore planning for game sequels and expansions.

Section 19.5: Planning for Game Sequels and Expansions

Planning for game sequels and expansions is a crucial aspect of long-term game development and business strategy. These follow-up projects can extend the life of your game franchise and continue to engage your player base. In this section, we'll explore key considerations and strategies for planning and executing game sequels and expansions.

1. Player Feedback and Data Analysis

Before embarking on a sequel or expansion, gather and analyze player feedback and data from the current game. Understand what players enjoyed, what they didn't, and where there is room for improvement.

2. Story Continuation

For story-driven games, plan a compelling continuation of the narrative that builds upon the events of the previous game. Maintain consistency in the storyline and character development.

3. New Gameplay Elements

Introduce new gameplay elements, mechanics, or features that differentiate the sequel or expansion from the original. This keeps the experience fresh and exciting for returning players.

4. Improved Graphics and Audio

Enhance the game's graphics and audio to take advantage of advancements in technology and to create a visually and aurally stunning experience.

5. Compatibility and Save Data Transfer

Ensure that players can easily transfer their progress and achievements from the original game to the sequel or expansion. This encourages player loyalty.

6. Content Expansion

Consider offering substantial additional content, such as new levels, characters, weapons, or modes, to justify the purchase of the sequel or expansion.

7. Release Timing

Plan the release timing carefully to coincide with market demand and player anticipation. Announce the sequel or expansion well in advance to build excitement.

8. Marketing and Promotion

Invest in marketing and promotional efforts to create awareness and generate interest in the upcoming sequel or expansion. Teasers, trailers, and social media campaigns can be effective tools.

9. Community Involvement

Involve the player community in the development process by seeking their input and feedback. This can help shape the direction of the sequel or expansion and create a sense of ownership among players.

10. Monetization Strategy

Decide on the monetization strategy for the sequel or expansion. It could involve selling the expansion as a standalone product, offering it as part of a season pass, or using a free-to-play model with in-app purchases.

11. Platform Considerations

Determine which platforms the sequel or expansion will be available on. Ensure that it reaches a wide audience by considering various gaming platforms and devices.

12. Quality Assurance

Maintain a rigorous quality assurance process to ensure a smooth launch without major bugs or issues. Test the sequel or expansion extensively on different platforms and configurations.

13. Post-Launch Support

Plan for post-launch support, including regular updates and patches to address any issues that may arise after release.

14. Player Engagement

Implement features that encourage player engagement, such as leaderboards, challenges, and community events. Keep players invested in the long-term success of the game.

15. Loyalty Rewards

Reward loyal players who have been with the franchise from the beginning. Offer exclusive content, discounts, or bonuses to incentivize their continued support.

16. Feedback Loop

Maintain an open feedback loop with the player community during and after the sequel or expansion's release. Address concerns and make necessary adjustments based on player input.

17. Ethical Considerations

Ensure that the sequel or expansion adheres to ethical guidelines, respects player privacy, and avoids exploitative monetization practices.

18. Long-Term Vision

Maintain a long-term vision for your game franchise. Consider how the sequel or expansion fits into the larger narrative and where the franchise may go in the future.

19. Conclusion

Planning for game sequels and expansions requires a strategic approach that balances player expectations, business goals, and creative vision. By carefully considering these factors, you can create a successful and enduring game franchise that captivates players for years to come.

In the final chapter, we'll explore the future of SDL and game technology, discussing emerging trends and the role of SDL in shaping the future of gaming.

Chapter 20: The Future of SDL and Game Technology

Section 20.1: Emerging Trends in Game Development

The world of game development is constantly evolving, driven by advancements in technology, changes in player preferences, and emerging trends. In this section, we'll explore some of the most notable emerging trends in game development that are shaping the future of the industry.

1. Immersive Realism with Ray Tracing

Ray tracing technology is becoming increasingly accessible, allowing developers to create highly realistic and immersive visuals. Real-time ray tracing is expected to play a significant role in next-generation games, delivering lifelike lighting, reflections, and shadows.

2. Cloud Gaming and Streaming

Cloud gaming platforms are gaining momentum, offering players the ability to stream games to various devices without the need for powerful hardware. This trend is expected to continue, potentially changing how games are distributed and played.

3. AI-Driven Content Generation

Artificial intelligence (AI) is being used to generate game content dynamically. This includes procedural level design, AI-generated characters and dialogues, and adaptive gameplay experiences that respond to the player's actions.

4. Virtual Reality (VR) and Augmented Reality (AR)

VR and AR technologies continue to evolve, opening up new possibilities for immersive gaming experiences. As hardware becomes more affordable and accessible, VR and AR games are likely to become more prevalent.

5. Blockchain and NFTs in Gaming

Blockchain technology is being explored for its potential to enable ownership of in-game assets as non-fungible tokens (NFTs). This can lead to player-driven economies and unique digital item ownership.

6. Cross-Platform Play and Progression

Cross-platform gaming, where players can play together across different devices and platforms, is becoming increasingly common. Games are also adopting cross-platform progression, allowing players to carry their progress across platforms seamlessly.

7. Accessibility and Inclusivity

Game developers are placing a stronger emphasis on accessibility features, making games more inclusive for players with disabilities. This trend is expected to grow, ensuring that games are enjoyable for a wider audience.

8. Live Services and Game as a Service (GaaS)

Many games are shifting towards a GaaS model, offering ongoing content updates, events, and monetization options. Live services keep players engaged and generate long-term revenue.

9. Sustainability and Green Game Development

Game developers are increasingly conscious of environmental impact. Sustainable practices, energy-efficient game design, and eco-friendly packaging are becoming more prevalent in the industry.

10. Social Impact and Meaningful Games

Games are being used to address social issues, educate players, and raise awareness. Meaningful games that tackle important topics are gaining recognition.

11. Data Privacy and Security

With growing concerns about data privacy, game developers must prioritize user data protection and cybersecurity to maintain player trust.

12. Retro Revival and Nostalgia

Nostalgia-driven games that pay homage to retro classics are seeing a resurgence. This trend appeals to both older players and newcomers.

13. Indie Game Innovation

Indie game development continues to thrive, with indie studios pushing the boundaries of innovation and creativity. These smaller teams often lead in experimenting with new ideas.

14. User-Generated Content

Games are increasingly incorporating tools for user-generated content, empowering players to create and share their own levels, mods, and experiences within the game.

15. Virtual Economies and Microtransactions

Virtual economies within games are expanding, and microtransactions are becoming more prevalent. Game developers are exploring new ways to offer in-game purchases without compromising player experience.

16. Conclusion

The future of game development holds exciting possibilities and challenges. Staying informed about emerging trends and technologies is essential for developers and businesses to remain competitive in this dynamic industry. As SDL c ontinues to evolve and adapt, it will play a vital role in shaping the future of gaming.

In this book, we've covered a wide range of advanced topics in game development using SDL. We hope this knowledge equips you with the tools and insights needed to create exceptional games and contribute to the ever-evolving world of game development.

Section 20.2: SDL's Role in Future Gaming Technologies

As we look ahead to the future of game development, it's important to consider the role that SDL (Simple DirectMedia Layer) will play in shaping gaming technologies. SDL has been a reliable and versatile library for game developers for many years, and its adaptability positions it well for the evolving landscape of game development. In this section, we'll explore how SDL can continue to be relevant in future gaming technologies.

1. Cross-Platform Compatibility

SDL's core strength has always been its ability to provide cross-platform support. As gaming platforms diversify and new technologies emerge, SDL's commitment to cross-platform compatibility will remain invaluable. Game developers will continue to rely on SDL to write code once and deploy it across multiple platforms seamlessly.

2. Hardware Acceleration and Performance

The demand for high-performance games will persist, and SDL's support for hardware acceleration will continue to be vital. As new graphics cards and hardware technologies are developed, SDL will adapt to harness their power efficiently, enabling developers to create visually stunning and fast-paced games.

3. Integration with Emerging Technologies

SDL has a history of integrating with emerging technologies. Whether it's supporting VR/AR devices, new audio hardware, or the latest input methods, SDL's versatility ensures that game developers can adopt these technologies without major overhauls to their codebases.

4. Community and Open Source Development

SDL's open-source nature fosters a thriving community of developers who contribute to its growth. This collaborative environment ensures that SDL will remain up-to-date with the latest technologies and trends. Community-driven updates and optimizations will be crucial in keeping SDL relevant.

5. Education and Learning

SDL has long been used as an educational tool for aspiring game developers. Its simplicity and wide adoption make it an ideal choice for teaching game development concepts. As more individuals enter the field, SDL will continue to serve as a valuable learning platform.

6. Indie Game Development

The indie game development scene is expected to remain vibrant. SDL's ease of use and low barrier to entry make it a preferred choice for indie developers. As more indie studios emerge, SDL will support their innovative and creative projects.

7. Localization and Global Reach

With games reaching global audiences, SDL's support for localization and internationalization will remain relevant. Games will continue to be translated into multiple languages, and SDL's features for handling diverse cultural content will be essential.

8. Retro Gaming and Emulation

Retro gaming and emulation of older games are likely to persist. SDL's ability to work with legacy technologies and its support for older hardware and platforms will remain valuable in preserving and enjoying classic games.

9. Security and Data Privacy

As data privacy concerns grow, SDL will need to adapt by providing secure ways to handle player data. Keeping player information safe will be a priority for game developers, and SDL's role in ensuring security will be crucial.

10. Conclusion

SDL has been a cornerstone of game development for years, and its adaptability ensures it will continue to be relevant in the ever-changing landscape of game technologies. Developers and enthusiasts can look forward to SDL playing a pivotal role in the creation of innovative and cross-platform games in the future.

As we conclude this section and the book, it's clear that SDL's legacy is far from over. The future of SDL and game technology holds exciting opportunities and challenges, and SDL will remain a key player in shaping the gaming experiences of tomorrow.

Section 20.3: Preparing for Next-Generation Game Development

As the game development industry continues to evolve, it's essential to prepare for the next generation of gaming technologies and platforms. This section will discuss some key considerations and strategies for developers and studios looking to stay at the forefront of the industry.

1. Adopting New Technologies

To stay competitive, game developers must keep an eye on emerging technologies. This includes hardware innovations like faster CPUs and GPUs, new input methods (gesture recognition, haptic feedback), and advancements in AI and machine learning. Being early adopters of these technologies can provide a significant advantage in creating cutting-edge gaming experiences.

2. Optimizing for Performance

With the expectation of more immersive and graphically intensive games, optimizing performance becomes crucial. Developers should focus on efficient code, resource management, and leveraging the capabilities of modern hardware to ensure smooth gameplay experiences.

3. Cross-Platform Development

The diversity of gaming platforms is expected to grow, including consoles, PC, mobile, and emerging platforms like cloud gaming services. Adopting tools and frameworks that support cross-platform development, such as SDL, will be essential to reach a broader audience.

4. Enhanced Realism

Realism in games will continue to improve, driven by advancements in graphics rendering, physics simulations, and AI. Developers should explore techniques for realistic character animations, dynamic environments, and lifelike simulations to deliver immersive experiences.

5. VR and AR Integration

Virtual Reality (VR) and Augmented Reality (AR) are likely to become more prominent in the gaming industry. Preparing for VR and AR integration will require understanding the unique challenges and opportunities these technologies present.

6. Player-Centric Design

The focus should always be on creating enjoyable player experiences. Understanding player behavior through data analytics and feedback will be crucial for designing games that resonate with audiences.

7. Storytelling and Narrative

Storytelling remains a key aspect of game development. Advancements in narrative design, including branching storylines, player choices, and interactive storytelling, will shape the future of game narratives.

8. Community Engagement

Building and maintaining a strong player community is essential for long-term success. Developers should invest in tools for player interaction, feedback, and community events.

9. Ethical Considerations

As games become more influential and reach wider audiences, ethical considerations become more critical. Developers should consider inclusivity, diversity, representation, and the potential impact of their games on players' mental and emotional well-being.

10. Open Source and Collaboration

The open-source community continues to contribute to the growth of game development. Collaborative efforts, shared resources, and open-source tools can help accelerate the adoption of new technologies and best practices.

11. Accessibility and Inclusivity

Ensuring that games are accessible to a wide range of players, including those with disabilities, is essential. Developers should follow accessibility guidelines and prioritize inclusivity in design.

12. Sustainability and Responsibility

Game development studios should adopt sustainable practices, reduce their carbon footprint, and consider the environmental impact of their operations. Additionally, responsible monetization practices should be a priority to avoid predatory tactics.

13. Conclusion

The future of game development promises exciting opportunities and challenges. Staying at the forefront of the industry requires a commitment to innovation, adaptability, and a player-centric approach. By embracing new technologies, optimizing performance, and prioritizing ethical and inclusive game design, developers can shape the next generation of gaming experiences.

As we conclude this section and the book, it's evident that the future of game development is bright, with endless possibilities for creativity and innovation. Developers, studios, and enthusiasts alike can look forward to being part of a dynamic and ever-evolving industry.

Section 20.4: SDL Contributions and Open Source Development

One of the strengths of the game development community is its collaborative nature, often seen in the form of open-source contributions. SDL (Simple DirectMedia Layer) itself is an open-source project that has benefited greatly from the collective efforts of developers worldwide. In this section, we'll delve into the significance of SDL contributions and the broader context of open source in game development.

1. The Power of Open Source

Open-source software plays a vital role in the game development ecosystem. It enables developers to access and modify code freely, fostering innovation and collaboration. SDL, as an open-source library, has empowered countless game developers to create cross-platform games efficiently.

2. Community-Driven Development

SDL's development is community-driven, with a global network of contributors continually improving the library. This collaborative effort ensures that SDL remains up-to-date, reliable, and capable of adapting to the evolving landscape of game development.

3. Benefits of Contributing to SDL

Contributing to SDL offers several advantages. Developers can influence the library's direction, fix bugs, add new features, and gain valuable experience by working with a large codebase. It's also an opportunity to give back to the community and enhance SDL for everyone's benefit.

4. How to Contribute

Those interested in contributing to SDL can start by visiting the official SDL website or repository. There, they can find information on the development process, coding guidelines, and documentation. SDL welcomes contributions in various forms, including code, bug reports, documentation improvements, and community support.

5. Licensing and Collaboration

SDL's open-source nature means that developers can use it in their projects without worrying about licensing costs. It promotes collaboration and knowledge sharing among game developers and serves as a foundation for many successful games and game engines.

6. The Future of SDL Development

The future of SDL development depends on the continued support and contributions from the community. As new technologies and platforms emerge, SDL must adapt to meet the demands of modern game development. This ongoing collaboration ensures that SDL remains a valuable tool for game developers worldwide.

7. Conclusion

In the ever-evolving world of game development, open source, and collaborative efforts like SDL are essential. They empower developers, promote innovation, and democratize access to game development tools. Whether you're an experienced developer or someone just starting in the field, the open-source spirit exemplified by SDL provides an inclusive and dynamic environment for creating games that captivate players worldwide.

As we conclude this section, it's worth emphasizing the role of open source in shaping the future of game development. By contributing to projects like SDL and embracing the principles of open source, developers can make a significant impact on the industry and create a more accessible and vibrant gaming landscape for all.

Section 20.5: Vision for the Future of SDL Gaming

As we reach the final section of this book, it's essential to look forward to the future of SDL (Simple DirectMedia Layer) and its role in game development. SDL has been a cornerstone for game developers for many years, but what lies ahead for this versatile library?

1. Continued Cross-Platform Excellence

SDL's core strength lies in its ability to provide a consistent interface across various platforms. In the future, SDL will continue to adapt to emerging platforms, ensuring that game developers can target new and diverse audiences effortlessly.

2. Enhanced Performance and Optimization

With advancements in hardware and software, SDL will evolve to take full advantage of the available resources. Expect improvements in performance and optimization, allowing developers to create more resource-intensive and visually stunning games.

3. Expanded Multimedia Capabilities

SDL's multimedia capabilities will likely expand further. Support for new audio and video codecs, 3D audio spatialization, and advanced graphics features will enable developers to create immersive gaming experiences that push the boundaries of technology.

4. Incorporating Emerging Technologies

As new technologies like virtual reality (VR), augmented reality (AR), and mixed reality (MR) gain traction, SDL will likely incorporate support for these technologies. This will open up exciting possibilities for creating immersive and innovative gaming experiences.

5. Community-Driven Development

The strength of SDL lies in its community. Future development will continue to be driven by passionate contributors from around the world. This ensures that SDL remains up-to-date, secure, and aligned with the evolving needs of game developers.

6. Accessibility and Inclusivity

The future of SDL gaming will prioritize accessibility and inclusivity. Expect tools and features that make it easier to create games that can be enjoyed by players of all abilities and backgrounds.

7. Integration with Emerging Trends

SDL will integrate seamlessly with emerging trends in the gaming industry, such as cloud gaming, game streaming, and cross-play capabilities. This will enable developers to create games that are more accessible and connected than ever before.

8. Enhanced Documentation and Resources

SDL's documentation and educational resources will continue to grow. Developers can expect comprehensive guides, tutorials, and examples that make it easier to harness the full power of SDL.

9. Support for New Programming Languages

SDL will likely expand its support for new programming languages, making it accessible to a broader range of developers. This could include bindings for languages that are gaining popularity in the game development community.

10. Embracing Sustainability and Responsibility

As the gaming industry matures, SDL will play a role in promoting sustainable practices and ethical game development. Expect SDL to provide resources and guidelines for responsible game development that considers social and environmental impact.

11. Conclusion

The future of SDL gaming is bright and full of possibilities. As technology advances and the gaming industry evolves, SDL will remain a trusted and adaptable tool for developers. Its commitment to openness, accessibility, and community-driven development ensures that it will continue to be a cornerstone of the game development world.

In closing, we encourage you to explore SDL's ongoing development, contribute to its growth, and embark on your journey in the ever-evolving landscape of game development. The future of SDL gaming is not just about technology; it's about the creative, passionate, and innovative developers who use it to craft memorable gaming experiences for players worldwide.

Printed in Dunstable, United Kingdom